URBAN POLICE

in the

UNITED STATES

Other Books by James F. Richardson

The New York Police: Colonial Times to 1901 (1970)

The American City: Historical Studies (1972)

The Urban Experience (1973)
(with Raymond A. Mohl)

James F. Richardson

URBAN POLICE

in the

UNITED STATES

National University Publications
Kennikat Press • 1974
Port Washington, N. Y. • London

Kennikat Press
National University Publications
Interdisciplinary Urban Studies

General Editor

Raymond A. Mohl
Florida Atlantic University

HV
8138
.R52

Library of Congress Catalog Card No. 74-77648
ISBN: 0-8046-9083-9

Manufactured in the United States of America

Published by
Kennikat Press Corp.
Port Washington, N.Y./London

To my children

Moira, Pierce, Kieran, Margaret, and John

Contents

Preface

In the past ten years, academic and popular interest in the police has reached flood tide. Books and articles abound, written by journalists, policemen, attorneys, sociologists, political scientists, and historians. This literature assesses the police role in society, the difficulties facing departments in an age of rapid social change and conflicts of values and life styles, and the problems involved in reconciling concerns for law and justice with demands for order, police efficiency, and fear of crime in the streets.

Scholarly and popular attention to the police is justified because they have an important role in making possible a civilized urban life. In this context "civilized" does not refer to the "high culture," the theaters, museums, art galleries, and concert halls, but rather to the level of civility people exhibit in their dealings with one another. The question this book sets out to answer is how well police history has prepared urban police departments to perform as civilizing agencies.

As an historian, it is my conviction that the only way we can understand the present is through study of the past; only if we see how things came to be can we hope to know what they are. This is especially true of the police, where tradition is such an important determinant of contemporary behavior. Conversely, study of the present illuminates the past. Contemporary social scientists have developed ideas and techniques which can be used by historians in their work. Often historians choose the questions they will ask of the past on the basis of current interests and concerns. When citizens and scholars took police for granted there was little written on police history; in contrast, the current scholarly and public interest on contemporary police practices and problems has generated a corresponding increase in historical investigation. Several books on police history have already appeared and more are on the way as younger scholars have chosen topics in the field for their doctoral dissertations.

Historians, whether they like to admit it or not, must have overarching concepts or ideas in mind when they come to study and evaluate the past. One concept that has guided this book is that Americans have rarely if ever agreed on the proper scope and function of the police and that such conflicts have molded police performance in a variety of ways. Most police administrators have responded to whichever group was making most noise at the moment rather than following a consistent and thought-out line of policy. Commanders have dealt with many thorny policy questions involving the exercise of police discretion by ignoring them, thus leaving it up to the individual man on the beat or in the radio car to make the key decision. No department can enforce the law one hundred percent—we would all be in jail in short order—or apply resources equally to all the varied tasks assigned to police officials. Administrators often leave subordinates without clear guidelines on the exercise of discretion because any policy set forth would alienate some group in the community. There have been instances, such as toleration of vice activities and police performance in labor disputes, where policy is well understood throughout a department, although minorities, whether moral reformers or strikers, have questioned the legitimacy of these policies.

A second general premise of this book is that the primary function of the police is to preserve order and render service to people in need, *not* to fight crime and enforce the law or regulate public morals. Police have had these multiple responsibilities since the beginning of their history as salaried public officials in the nineteenth century; my contention, however, is that both the public and police departments themselves have not devoted sufficient attention to their peace keeping and service tasks, which engage the majority of most policemen's active duty time. Thanks to scholars who have classified the calls coming into a police department on a typical day or who have clocked the amounts of time patrolmen on duty devote to various assignments, we have substantial evidence about contemporary police allocation of resources. We do not have this kind of evidence for the nineteenth century, although it seems safe to say that the nineteenth century patrolman spent more of his time dealing with family squabbles, troublesome drunks, lost children, and stray horses than he did on safe cracking and bank robberies.

We have more evidence on past police organizational and administrative patterns which are important both for what they tell us about past cities and for their influence upon subsequent police developments. Political parties contested vigorously to control police patronage and power, which meant sometimes rapid shifts in the structure of police administration. These contests precluded American departments from following exactly their supposed model, the London Metropolitan Police. In the pages that follow, I have devoted considerable attention to the origins of the London model and the American deviations.

Much of the book deals with the most recent developments, those of the last twenty years. I have allocated space in this fashion because most readers would be more concerned with their own time; also for this period I have been able to draw upon the rich scholarship on contemporary police.

No sane person would undertake the task of producing a book without the assurance of being able to call for support and help when needed. A number of graduate assistants, especially Charles Waechter and Charles Undrisky, searched the literature with energy and intelligence. Arlene Lane and the secretarial staff of the Urban Studies Department of the University of Akron typed the manuscript with speed and accuracy. My colleague, H. Roger Grant, read an earlier draft and saved me from several bloopers; of course I bear responsibility for those that remain. My children knew enough to stay away when their father was working, and my son, Pierce, helped with the index. My wife, Marie, in addition to pursuing her own career and running a house, puts up with me on those occasions— the majority—when the words do not come easily and shares the exhilaration on those rare days when they do.

URBAN POLICE

in the

UNITED STATES

Chapter 1

The English Background of American Police

Colonial America represented an extension of European culture across the Atlantic. The American environment modified this European inheritance to some extent so that a full understanding of American developments requires study of the interaction between the European background and American conditions. Europe continued important after the first generation of colonists, indeed after American independence. Until at least the middle of the nineteenth century, Americans looked to London and Paris and later to German cities for leadership in municipal affairs. The transmission of European culture to America at first took place in a rural and village setting. The characteristic form of settlement in the seventeenth century was the agricultural village or the self-contained small farm. Only gradually did America develop urban communities paralleling the provincial cities of England. Even after Boston, New York, and Philadelphia developed into important trading centers, London remained *the* metropolis of eighteenth-century America. When in the nineteenth century, American cities grew to reach tens and hundreds of thousands of people, the tide of innovation continued to flow from east to west. Eastern cities copied European cities and western urbanites borrowed from eastern.

The Atlantic was a highway as well as a barrier; indeed in the period before the introduction of steam railroads, water travel was cheaper, faster, and more reliable than land. People, books, and ideas could move between Europe and America, so that Americans, faced with new and complex problems of municipal government, could look for help to larger, older cities. London provided models of police protection as well as fashions in clothes, books, and plays well into the nineteenth century.

3

America's borrowing from England was selective. The impulse and general form of innovation in police came from England, although Americans modified and transformed English patterns to fit their political culture. Examination of the English original and the American variations illumines the complex process of adoption and adaptation that produced characteristic American police institutions by the second half of the nineteenth century.

Thus in the seventeenth century, colonists struggled to establish European civilization in a wilderness environment, in the eighteenth century the urban component of a mature colonial society moved closer culturally to the metropolis, and in the nineteenth century English innovations led to similar but not identical American developments.

When Europeans came to America in the seventeenth century, they brought with them ideas and patterns of government as well as clothes and pots and pans. In the small villages and towns established along the Atlantic seaboard to conduct trade with the mother country, the instruments of government for keeping the peace paralleled those to be found in England and Holland. Since these societies had not created organized, uniformed police, it is not surprising that the colonial towns also lacked such forces. Following English precedent, New York (controlled by the Dutch and known as New Amsterdam until 1664), Philadelphia, and Boston relied on the institution of the night watch and a number of constables to maintain order and apprehend offenders.

As in England, the colonial constable had a number of difficult duties, low prestige, and occasionally ran the risk of verbal and physical abuse from citizens. In both England and the American colonies, the constables, elected for a term of one year, had to preserve order, bring criminals to justice, prevent violations of the Sabbath, keep paupers from becoming public charges if at all possible by not letting them gain a settlement in village or town, and make sure that public officials and citizens lived up to their civic responsibilities. English dramatists constantly made fun of constables as ignorant, self-important little men who deserved to be the butt of coarse humor. Certainly the constable had less prestige than his responsibilities warranted. In 1722 the mayor of Philadelphia instructed Constable Thomas Todd as follows: "Thou art principally to weigh and consider anything which may conduce to the glory of God, honour of the King, and benefit of the inhabitants in having a well-governed city, wherein all just endeavors are used to suppress all manner of vice and debauchery, . . . [and] to exert thyself in a punctual performance and discharge of thy duty." If this is what Todd was expected to do "principally," one wonders what he was supposed to do secondarily.

The authorities often had great difficulty in getting men to accept appointment or election as constables; of seventeen chosen in Boston in 1743, only five agreed to serve, ten men paid fines for refusing, and two were excused without fine. An English judge once said that considering the low caliber of many constables, it was just as well that most did not know the extent of their legal powers. The same point could be made about many of the colonial constables.[1]

The watch varied in number and effectiveness between different cities, and in the cases of London and New York, within the same city. In London the watch was organized on a parochial basis; some parishes raised the money for an adequate number of watchmen, while others limited their watch to a few old or infirm men who thus would not have to be supported by the parish poor rate. In New York the watch varied in size and effectiveness at different periods, depending upon whether the citizens' fear of disorder or dislike of paying taxes was greater at any given time.[2]

As cities grew in size and complexity, their problems of maintaining order and coping with crime and vice also intensified; but political leaders never agreed completely on the establishment, or the proper organization and role, of the police. In both England and the American colonies and later the United States, many citizens strongly objected to the creation of organized police forces, which might be as much or more instruments of government repression as protectors of the public. An organized police too closely resembled a standing army, which gave government potentially despotic control over citizens and subjects. The English distrust of a standing army derived first from the rule of Oliver Cromwell's major generals, who in the seventeenth century attempted to close England's theaters and alehouses. The reigns of Charles II (1660-1685), and especially James II (1685-1688), heightened fears of despotic power. Protestant Englishmen believed that James, a Catholic, would use the army to subvert Protestantism. The English, with the help of William of Orange, deposed James to solve the immediate problem; but the antipathy to a standing army remained.

Above all else, Englishmen wanted to prevent tyranny and absolute power in the hands of central government. The principles developed by the aristocracy to limit the power of the king could later be appealed to by those who were not aristocrats but who had even better reason to fear and distrust unlimited governmental power. John Locke provided a rationale for a people resisting their government if it acted in a manner contrary to their natural rights. Men who came after Locke developed a tradition of resistance to arbitrary government, which could be applied against the parliamentary aristocracy just as easily as it could against the monarch. Those Englishmen who opposed the thrust of the English government in the eighteenth century later found a receptive audience among those Americans who rebelled against English rule.[3]

The American revolutionaries built upon the English dissenting tradition in fashioning a political theory which stressed the contrast and the contest between liberty and power as the essential problem of politics. In this view active and dynamic power always threatened static and passive liberty. Power tended to corrupt, and no man or group of men was so pure as to be allowed to exercise power without being carefully watched and checked. The safest way to deal with power was to keep it limited and divided and to prevent the possession of unrestrained power by any one man or agency. In this context, a standing army or an organized, uniformed police which resembled a standing army seemed to be more an instrument of potentially despotic power than a guarantor of liberty.[4] Thus both English and American communities left the job of keeping the peace and dealing with crime and vice to a patchwork of weak instruments, aided by the military at periods of peak tension, until well into the nineteenth century.

England took the lead in fashioning new police institutions, with the United States following. Subsequent American changes did not exactly duplicate the English model; still, examination of English police reorganization provides necessary background for understanding American developments.

In England in the eighteenth century the fear of crime resulted in a savage penal code in which hundreds of crimes, some very minor by present standards, carried the death penalty. Yet the English considered the prevention and detection of crime more of a private than a public responsibility. English police officers were not public servants in the way we now think of policemen; they were members of a liberal profession who operated on the principle of fee for service. If a man had been robbed, he could go to a magistrate's court like that at Bow Street and hire a police officer to try to get his property back. The officers worked independently of each other, each keeping his own sources of information and his own lines to the underworld. An officer's reputation and income depended upon his ability to develop these sources and satisfy his clients by recovering stolen property.[5]

Officers also received rewards from the government for arresting criminals. Authorities considered the reward system the best method of getting prompt and vigilant action from officers; it would be to their interest to work hard on major crimes if they received forty pound rewards for their perpetrators. Edwin Chadwick, a utilitarian reformer who remained interested in police reform throughout his long life, argued that "All testimony, all experience proves that in the government of a body of men like the police, whatever individual exceptions may occur among them, their naked pecuniary interests can alone be relied upon as motives of constant and sure operation."[6] In 1821, an experienced magistrate charged that "the manner in which hordes of thieves are suffered to prowl about the Metropolis and its neighborhood and rob and maltreat passengers when a crowd is assembled, is a disgrace to our police system. Yet while these things are going on, officers in abundance are loitering about the police offices, in waiting for hire. Protection is reserved for individuals who will individually pay for it."[7]

When police officers did leave the office they sought the company and confidence of young criminals who frequented "flash houses," combination bars, brothels, and transfer points for stolen goods. When he had evidence of a serious crime, the officer dropped his mantle of friendship and protection for the criminal responsible and made an arrest. A parliamentary report of 1816 asserted that "The officers will never meddle with a thief until he weighs his weight; the thief catchers will not take him until they are sure of getting 40 pounds by him." Despite the endless possibilities for corruption in such an arrangement, the reward system and the view of the detective as a private entrepreneur survived into the middle of the nineteenth century.[8]

The most potent argument for an organized police in England derived from the fear of riots and disorders and the inability of the civilian authorities to cope with them. Riots were not always outbreaks of mindless violence by the riffraff of society; rather, rioters had quite definite grievances and targets of attack and viewed the riot as a form of social protest. The occasion of riots could be food shortages, high prices, the introduction of machinery, or religious prejudice, such as the Gordon Riots in London in 1780 when the government proposed to end Catholic political disabilities. The crowds usually destroyed property, although it was rare for them to take human life.

To some extent the riot served as a vehicle for expressing grievances in a society where political power was concentrated in a small segment of the population, primarily those who owned substantial amounts of property. In the eyes of the aristocracy and well-to-do merchants, government existed for the protection of property. Those who rioted looked to other values, the maintenance of tradition or of their own status, which could be threatened by making prices the result of the "natural" laws of supply and demand or by introducing labor-saving machinery.[9]

The English upper and middle classes wanted to protect their property and preserve order; they also wished to prevent tyranny and despotism and to preserve liberty. In absolute terms, these goals were contradictory. The prevention of riots might involve constant government surveillance and the systematic use of spies and informers. Such a system would be incompatible with liberty. To suppress riots quickly, the authorities would have to be able to mass large numbers of trained and possibly armed men on short notice. What would prevent such a force from being used to impose a hateful despotism on England? These contrary concerns of social upheaval from below and despotism from above made quick and decisive action impossible. Dealing with one threat increased the possibility of danger from the other. If government had the resources to deal with riots, it could just as easily use them to suppress all dissent. If government lacked instruments of oppression, it would also lack means to cope with disorder.

Before the establishment of an organized, uniformed police for London in 1829, the authorities had a number of possible steps they could take in controlling disorder, none of them very satisfactory. They could swear in as special constables law-abiding citizens who had a stake in the existing order and could be counted on to defend the status quo. Such men lacked any special skill or training in dealing with disorder and might well do more harm than good. However, the government relied on them as late as the Chartist demonstrations of 1848, after the London Metropolitan Police had been in operation for almost twenty years.[10]

The militia, which dated from the reign of Charles II in the second half of the seventeenth century, constituted a more organized force of antirioters. The officers of this body were local landowners whose rank depended upon the size of their estates. William Wilberforce, a leading reformer of the early nineteenth century, said of the militia that it was a force "officered by country gentlemen, men of property, of family, of domestic connections, of personal influence, whose arms were in no conjunction likely to be turned against their country." While the officers of the militia might be men of substance whose sympathies would be with the protection of property and the suppression of riotous protest, the rank and file often identified with the rioters and so could not be relied on by the authorities. If a disorder grew out of a dispute between employer and employees, a force led by the employer would hardly be regarded as impartial and disinterested.[11]

The "yeomanry," organizations of cavalry volunteers, were better disciplined than the militia but even more open to attack as men who could pursue their private interest under the guise of public service. These cavalry units consisted of small farmers under the leadership of leading local landowners. Naturally, they would have little sympathy with urban working-class crowds protesting the high price of food. In 1819 the yeomanry charged a crowd assembled at St. Peter's field in Manchester in an incident long bitterly remembered as the "Peterloo massacre." Eleven people were killed and hundreds of men, women, and childen injured in this unjustified assault by the yeomanry. As employers and farmers the cavalrymen wanted cheap labor and expensive food, the very conditions the rioters were protesting; and even moderates came to question the propriety of using such forces to quell riots. In urban areas there were some volunteer groups which wanted to be supplied with arms, to be allowed to exercise and drill, and sometimes to intervene in disorders without having been called upon by the authorities.[12]

In view of the weaknesses of the police and the objections to the various volunteer groups, the army provided the most reliable and the most disciplined force available in riot situations. Yet even here there were problems. English legal philosophers such as William Blackstone regarded the very existence of a standing army in time of peace as a menace to liberty. Parliament as part of its struggle for power against the monarch had insisted that the Mutiny Act be limited to one year in duration. This meant that the crown had to receive annual authorization for the existence of the army, and, theoretically at least, this authorization could be withheld if the government were using the army in a despotic manner. Until 1870 officers had to pay for their commissions. This provision limited army commands to men of substantial property and social position who supposedly would not be likely to use the army to advance their own interests. If they were already privileged and propertied, their interest would be the maintenance of the existing order rather than its overthrow. Also the enlisted men of the army were much more likely to follow the orders and directions of the officers than were the volunteers of the militia and yeomanry.[13]

Army commanders as well as libertarians worried about the use of the army to control civil disorders. Few professional officers liked the prospect of troops firing on civilians whose arms might be limited to clubs and pitchforks, and there was always the possibility that using the army in riots might undermine morale and discipline. After the widespread protests of 1819 the army was increased by 11,000 men as politicians such as Lord Palmerston pictured a society on the verge of civil war. Yet the Duke of Wellington, England's great military hero in the Napoleonic Wars, thought that an effective alternative to the army must be provided "to preserve the lives and properties of His Majesty's subjects against domestic insurrection and disturbance, which is more properly the business of the civil government and of the police." His support was vital for the passage of the London Metropolitan Police Act in 1829. A sensible military man like General Sir Charles James Napier found that the magistrates were too prone to bring in the army to deal with protestors, that the more often the troops were called out the less effective they became as the people held them less in awe, and that good humor was often more effective than force in handling crowds.[14]

Any proposal for a stronger police still encountered the old cries of despotism. In 1812 one writer argued for the necessity of a stronger night watch but opposed a centralized police as "a system of tyranny; an organised army of spies and informers, for the destruction of all public liberty, and the disturbance of all private happiness. Every other system of police is the curse of despotism. . . ." In 1818 a parliamentary committee feared that a proposed police plan "would make every servant of every house a spy on the actions of his master, and all classes of society spies on each other." By the late 1820s the fear of crime and disorder overshadowed the potential threats to liberty inherent in an organized police, at least for the politically dominant upper classes.[15]

In the aftermath of the French Revolution, moralists grew increasingly concerned about the depraved state of society. Men such as Wilberforce, who devoted much of his energies to the abolition of the slave trade, also wished to reform manners and suppress vice. A number of societies were formed to advance these ends. In 1804 Richard Watson, the Bishop of Llandaff, said to the Society for the Suppression of Vice: "The Laws are good; but they are eluded by the Lower Classes, and set at nought by the Higher. The Laws are good; but they are fallen into contempt, and require the Zeal, the activity, the Discretion of such a Society as this to Renovate their Vigour." In addition to moral persuasion, the societies also initiated prosecutions against offenders.[16]

The London Metropolitan Police Act of 1829 grew out of these fears of riot and crime and desire for moral reformation. The police was designed as an organized and uniformed force for the prevention and detection of crime and the suppression of civil disorder. In addition, it would be an instrument to improve the morals of the people by acting against public drunkenness and other popular pastimes which offended the upper and middle classes. The *General Instructions* of the new force stressed its preventive nature:

It should be understood, at the outset, that the principal object to be attained is *"the prevention of crime."* To this great end every effort of the Police is to be directed. The security of person and property, all the other objects of a Police Establishment, will thus be better effected, than by the detection and punishment of the offender after he has succeeded in committing the crime. . . . When in any Division offences are frequently committed, there must be reason to suspect that the Police is not in that Division properly conducted. The absence of crime will be considered the best proof of the complete efficiency of the Police.[17]

Patrick Colquhoun and the noted utilitarian philosopher Jeremy Bentham, among others, had been advocating creation of such a force for years. Colquhoun, born in Scotland in 1745, had spent some time in Virginia before moving to London in 1770. He became a magistrate in 1792 and remained in office until 1818, two years before his death. He had no sympathy with the French Revolution and worried about the possibility of riots, the extent of crime in London, and the low state of public morals. He proposed a centrally controlled "police for the prevention of crimes" which would be united to a "police of the Poor."[18] Colquhoun received considerable support from Bentham, who tried to build a science of politics and ethics based upon the pleasure-pain calculus.[19] Edwin Chadwick, a disciple of Bentham's, applied the principle to the police. "A preventive police would act . . . by placing difficulties in the way of obtaining the objects of temptation. If to obtain a given object of desire, as much mental or physical exertion be requisite as would suffice to obtain it honestly, the honest course will undoubtedly be preferred." In this view, all men, criminals included, acted according to rational, quantitative judgments of the balance of effort and rewards.[20]

Bentham was the great exponent of rationalized administration based on the principles of efficiency and centralization and opposed to tradition and local control. For Bentham unless an institution, a law, or a practice could meet the test of utilitarian value—the greatest happiness of the greatest number—it should be scrapped no matter how ancient or hallowed by tradition. What if Englishmen clung to local independence as the best way of preserving their traditional rights and liberties? If the objects of a police—the prevention of crime and disorder and the control of the behavior of the poor—could be achieved by a centralized agency, then create such an agency no matter what the local feelings. Sir Robert Peel apparently intended that the London Metropolitan Police would be only the first step in the establishment of a nationwide police system. Because the forces of local control and resistance to anything that smacked of administrative tyranny proved stronger than the utilitarian philosophy had bargained for, it was not until the following generation that there was any substantial extension of the principles of the Metropolitan Police to the rest of England.

Provincial towns and rural areas were less than eager for the spread of a rationalized, centralized administrative apparatus which would be controlled from London and which would be more concerned with predictability and regularity than the interests and traditions of local elites. Yet cities like Birmingham and Manchester had grown so rapidly with the spread of the industrial revolution that their problems of crime and disorder outdistanced traditional methods for preserving the peace. After the passage of the London Police Act, other cities could call upon that force for help in the suppression of riots; and in the 1830s policemen often left London for this purpose. However, the presence of the "Peelers" did not always have the intended effect. In Birmingham the presence of London police enraged rather than quieted the crowd, and such incidents increased the degree of support for an extension of the organized, uniformed police to the provinces. In 1856 parliament established a mixed system, which provided for financial assistance for localities establishing police forces subject to inspection by the Home Office.[21]

Even in London the long-standing reservations about the role of an organized police did not die out immediately upon passage of the London Metropolitan Police Act. In 1831 *Blackwood's Magazine* referred to the Metropolitans as "general spies" and "finished tools of corruption." The police did infiltrate the National Political Union by having one of their men become a member to keep the government informed of this group's activities. A parliamentary committee accepted the government's need to keep informed about the activities of radical agitators but opposed the use of spies in general as "a practice most abhorrent to the feelings of the people and most alien to the spirit of the Constitution." Obviously the committee was torn between the traditional hostility to the trappings of tyranny and its desire to repress radical political groups.[22]

Within a few years, however, the politically dominant upper and middle classes came to support the police with great enthusiasm. A parliamentary committee of 1834 noted the possibility of abuses of power; still it found the Metropolitan Police "well calculated to maintain the peace and order...both effectively and constitutionally." The police had not imposed any restraints upon the people which were not "entirely consistent with the fullest practical exercise of every civil privilege and with the most unrestrained intercourse of private society." The committee considered the force to be "one of the most valuable of modern institutions." The police had shown itself to be a worthwhile instrument for an establishment under attack.[23]

The working classes and those who wanted to democratize the political structure of England had a different view. The poor and the alienated considered the police more as an element of control than as a group of protectors. In a sense the police monitored the behavior of the dangerous classes so that the comfortable and satisfied could sleep more soundly at night or not be annoyed by the sight of public drunkenness.

Yet the long English heritage of negative liberty, that there were certain things that government must not be permitted to do, did moderate police behavior. Englishmen had too strong a sense of freedom and resistance to tyranny to tolerate an excessively interfering police. Moreover, the first commissioners of the Metropolitans, Charles Rowan and Richard Mayne, realized that the effectiveness of the police would depend upon their winning public support, that ultimately their authority was a moral one, and that lawless behavior on their part would erode public confidence. The commissioners discouraged policemen from bringing actions against civilians for assault and admonished their men to treat civilians civilly no matter what the provocation. In 1830 the commissioners ordered that "no Constable is justified in depriving a man of his liberty for words only, the language however violent against the Police Constable himself is not to be noticed . . . a Constable who allows himself to be irritated by any language whatsoever shows that he has not that command of his temper which is absolutely necessary in an Officer invested with such extensive powers by the law." The fact that such orders were issued repeatedly is an indication that they were widely disobeyed. Salaries were very low, and too many of the men appointed policemen turned out to be drunks.[24] Yet by the 1850s the English police were thought of as a body of respected public servants who operated under the law, not outside or above it.

English law provided the police with a large amount of discretionary legal authority, but commissioners and judges carefully supervised its exercise to preserve public support for the police. By the middle of the nineteenth century, the middle and upper classes in England no longer looked upon the working class as an undifferentiated mob. Now when they used the term the "dangerous classes" they referred to professional criminals, not workers in general. The slang term "crusher" which workers used to refer to a policeman in the early years of the force's existence gives some idea as to their opinion of the police. In the early 1830s physical assaults on policemen were not uncommon; later in the century music-hall jokes provided sufficient outlets for working class resentment of police power. London policemen were more restrained in their use of the power to arrest on suspicion and in their interrogation of suspects and made fewer arrests for drunkenness and disorderly conduct than their New York counterparts. English police officials worked effectively to prevent the passage of general Sabbatarian legislation which would set the police against popular behavior and charge them with enforcing virtually unenforceable laws. The English police, operating in a less violent society, never considered arming their members and thereby increasing the potentiality for violence.[25]

The traditions of extensive legal discretion for the police but careful administrative control of the exercise of that discretion have continued into the twentieth century. Until recent years England has been blessed by a high standard of police performance. The record is not unblemished, from the occasional fabrication of evidence to win convictions to undue use of force against unpopular groups. Still, English society and its police have usually maintained peace and civility without arms and with more good humor than hostile confrontations. Geoffrey Gorer, an English anthropologist, has argued that one reason for the stability of English society for the last century is that the policeman has formed a model of the ideal adult male character, marked by strength, reserve, even-temperedness, and integrity.[26]

By the middle of the nineteenth century England had become a policed society. It was by no means a police state in the modern totalitarian sense, but the dominant groups in society now had an instrument to impose their values and conception of morality upon the people as a whole. In the words of sociologist Allan Silver, "The policed society is unique in that central power exercises potentially violent supervision over the population by bureaucratic means widely diffused throughout civil society in small and discretionary operations that are capable of rapid concentration." Far from being a recent phenomenon, this conception of their role was present from the very beginning of organized police in England. Theorists and administrators of that day recognized that for the police to be effective over the long run, they had to have public support. Only with moral cooperation could the police hope to create moral conformity.[27]

These English developments had great impact upon the United States, although the differences between the American and British political and social structures meant important differences in police arrangements. As a more self-consciously class-based society than the United States, England could more readily assume the legitimacy of the upper and later the middle classes' legislating the control of workers' activities. From the beginning of the Metropolitan force the English conceived of the police as a bureaucratic and professional group with a broad legal mandate to regulate popular behavior. To prevent an arbitrary imposition of governmental authority, the English relied on a cautious exercise of the police's legal powers and stressed both the importance of the rule of law and police restraint. As previously noted, England did not arm her policemen, considering them citizens in uniform and relying on a moral consensus between police and people to maintain order. American society, with its tradition of frontier and urban violence, put its faith in the tough, well-armed cop to curb the disorderly and criminal.

Americans also put more emphasis on control of the police by the popular will than by the law or administrative direction. Americans assumed that democracy, the will of the people, public opinion, was the best regulator of governmental behavior. Keeping the police under popular control, either by electing police heads or making them directly responsible to locally elected officials, would prevent the development of police tyranny. However, Americans later decided that the police could not be both democratic and efficient at the same time, that control by the popular will meant control by local politicians who perverted the police function to serve their own ends. Increasingly the cry became to "take the police out of politics," to reduce the power of wardheelers over the force. The removal of direct popular control over the police was not replaced by the kind of careful legal and administrative supervision present in England.

In effect, American police were left without any guidelines in the use of their broad authority other than tradition and the possibility of court reversal in individual cases. Court review has had little effect on general policy with the exception of those rare instances where higher courts have invalidated specific police practices relating to interrogation and the admissibility of confessions. American police administrators have not set forth policy statements for the exercise of police discretion as have English commissioners. The result has been considerably wider variation in discretionary situations between precincts and individual policemen in the United States than in England. Moreover, in the nineteenth century the courts in New York City at least tolerated illegal and irregular police practices to a much greater extent than their English counterparts. American public opinion has traditionally supported arbitrary police behavior against unpopular minorities.[28]

This extensive catalog of differences may make the relationship between English and American police seem tenuous indeed; yet the linkages and similarities are significant. For all practical purposes, American towns and cities in the eighteenth century were self-policing communities. When the elites of these communities later decided that they needed more formal police arrangements, they borrowed the concept of a salaried, bureaucratic, uniformed police from England. The early rule book of the New York police copied heavily from that of the London Metropolitan Police, and some American departments used the same ranks and titles as English forces. More important than these trappings is the very idea of a policed society in which the community creates an agency responsible for imposing order and discipline upon deviant members. Englishmen and Americans who feared threats to the social order, the institution of property, and proper morality chose similar solutions. Americans established police agencies akin to those currently in existence in England. Despite common motivations in their formation, police agencies in England and the United States soon followed different paths. Explaining that deviation requires an examination of American cities in the first half of the nineteenth century.

Chapter 2

The Establishment of Organized Police in the United States

American cities and towns of the eighteenth and early nineteenth centuries had their problems of crime, vice, and disorder, and some men complained strongly about the extent of prostitution, brawling, and robbery. Yet few cities felt impelled to make substantial changes in the traditional pattern of night watch and unsalaried police officers before the 1830s. One reason for this is that serious crimes, by the standards of subsequent decades at any rate, were infrequent. On the occasion of a homicide in New York City in 1819, one knowledgeable observer noted, "For the honour of our city, I believe this to be the first fatal assault that has ever occurred in it." Boston had only one reported murder for the years 1822 to 1834.[1]

The cities that did have more elaborate police arrangements were those with large slave populations where white masters lived in dread of possible black uprisings. Charleston, Savannah, and Richmond provided for combined foot and mounted patrols to prevent slaves from congregating and to repress any attacks upon the racial and social status quo. In Charleston, for example, police costs constituted the largest item in the municipal budget.[2]

By the 1830s, larger northern cities found their problems of crime and disorder outstripping traditional instruments for dealing with them. New York, Boston, and Philadelphia underwent rapid social and economic change during these years, change that so intensified group conflict that new instruments for maintaining order seemed imperative. Immigration jumped substantially after 1830. The total number of arrivals at New York port was more than four times greater in the 1830s than it had been in the previous decade. Boston had almost twice as many people in 1840 as twenty years before;

in the next two decades penniless Irish immigrants helped increase the population even more. Philadelphia in these years was well on the way to becoming one of the major industrial cities of the world. Not only were there more people, many of whom came from an impoverished rural background to a strange, hostile urban environment, but men and women found themselves in new spatial and social arrangements.

From the outset of mass immigration into the United States in the 1830s and 1840s, major American cities have been socially and ethnically mixed. Benjamin Disraeli considered England in the 1840s to be two nations, the well-to-do and the poor, but the United States had divisions not only between classes, but also between whites and blacks, Irish and native born, Protestant and Catholic, and beer drinkers and prohibitionists. These political and social cleavages profoundly affected the 'development of urban police in the United States.

In burgeoning port cities the population grew faster than the available stock of housing, and newcomers had to crowd into cellars, attics, old breweries, and any other structure that might provide some shelter. Established urban residents saw their pleasant neighborhoods overrun and invaded by the Irish and reacted with fear and trembling. Many newcomers were poor, unwashed, whiskey drinking, and Catholic, a devastating combination in a society that tended to judge a man's worth by his wealth and regarded decency and respectability as synonymous with Protestantism.

These social strains coincided with important economic changes. Growing national population, migration westward, and improvements in transportation increased the potential market for producers of manufactured goods. As Adam Smith noted in his famous *Wealth of Nations* of 1776, the size of the market determined the potential division of labor, and the larger the market the greater the possibilities and rewards for specialization. Entrepreneurs capitalized on this principle by enlarging the size of their labor forces and introducing a division of labor. So even without mechanization as such, productivity could be increased by organizing men, women, and children into larger work groups and dividing their tasks into simple, repetitive assignments that did not involve a high level of skill and could be quickly learned. This enlargement of the work group and the concomitant impact on the worker's autonomy and status had profound social implications. Some men, the fortunate entrepreneurs, might reap great rewards, while others would find their status and security both declining.[3]

A third source of tension was racial. In 1830 and 1831, two perceptive Frenchman, Alexis de Tocqueville and Gustave de Beaumont, toured the United States to study prison reform. They were surprised to learn that there was more overt hostility and hatred toward blacks in the North, where slavery did not exist, than in the South, where it did. Those who challenged the status quo by demanding the abolition of slavery suffered verbal and physical abuse in northern cities. There was no Mason-Dixon line as far as racial prejudice was concerned, and conservatives looked upon the abolitionists as dangerous radicals whose goals and tactics threatened social stability.[4]

In the mid-1830s these sources of cleavage and tension led to repeated riots and outbursts of violence in a number of American cities. New York City had so many upheavals in 1834 that it was long remembered as the year of riots. Disorders arose from the mayoralty election of that year, and the antiabolitionist sentiment precipitated the burning and looting of churches and the houses of abolitionists and blacks. The authorities called out the militia when it seemed that the destruction might affect whites. In 1835 the militia again had to be called out to contain widespread looting accompanying the great fire of that year which destroyed much of the Pearl Street textile area.[5]

Boston suffered three major riots in the years 1834 to 1837. In 1834 a mob burned the Charlestown Convent. The long-lasting and intense anti-Catholicism of New England had not yet been gentled into social exclusiveness and electoral contests between Irish and Yankees. The following year, William Lloyd Garrison, the famous abolitionist editor, was assaulted by a mob that contained some of Boston's more prominent citizens. In 1837 volunteer firemen and other anti-Irish workingmen turned out perhaps 15,000 strong to attack the Irish residents of Broad Street. As a result of this riot, the militia was called out for the first time in the city's history.[6]

Philadelphia, the city of brotherly love, was a very disorderly community in the 1830s and 1840s. In 1838 and 1842 the city underwent severe anti-Negro riots which resulted in the burning of Pennsylvania Hall and many deaths. In May and July of 1844 conflicts between nativists—those who hated immigrants—and the foreign born caused widespread death and injury and the destruction of churches and public buildings.[7] Baltimore and other cities had similar disorders.

These events, plus the existence of a model in the London Metropolitan Police, encouraged the formation of organized police forces whose primary job would be to control riot and disorder. The old opposition to a police as an instrument of despotism did not give way easily, and the organization of police forces proceeded hesitantly and fitfully. In New York City, for example, Mayor Cornelius Lawrence proposed the establishment of a London-style police as early as 1836. However, it was not until 1845 that the New York Police Department came into being. In the interim, opponents stressed the incompatibility of the United States's republican institutions and a formal police; they argued "that more reliance may be placed upon the people for aid, in case of any emergency, than in despotic governments," and that in this country, "the police is but a part of the citizen."

Before 1845, New York City's police arrangements consisted of two constables elected in each of the city's wards, a high constable chosen by the Common Council, one hundred marshals appointed by the mayor, and a part-time night watch which contained 1,096 men just before its abolition in 1845. The constables and marshals were not salaried but compensated by fees and rewards. Accordingly they spent their time in the service of civil processes to earn fees or pursuing stolen property whose return would bring substantial rewards. They did not engage in any patrol activity or other preventive measures to curb crime and disorder, although they could be called on by the mayor to keep order at fires or quell riots. They functioned in much the same way as the police officers attached to the Bow Street court in London; both groups were more private entrepreneurs than public servants. The night watch consisted of men who had other occupations during the day and literally moonlighted as watchmen, or ne'er-do-wells who had no other means of earning a living. The Common Council kept control of the watch, and any change in the party composition of the council meant substantial turnover among the watch. The watch kept an eye for fire and riot and hoped to deter burglars. As the city grew in geographical area, population, and social complexity, the watch proved unequal to the challenge. Its prestige, never high to begin with, declined further as the scope of its responsibilities widened. Increasingly, the idea that New York could be a self-policing community with minimal formal police arrangements lost its credibility.

The movement for a London-style police received stronger support after the unsolved murder of Mary Cecilia Rogers in 1841. (Poe used this case as the basis for his *The Murder of Marie Roget.*) What disturbed newspapers like the *Herald* and the *Star* was that the existing police officers would not work on a homicide unless they had been promised substantial rewards. Because their incomes came from fees and rewards, they spent their time on the recovery of stolen property. The *Star* believed that "All parties, however much they differ in other matters, are determined on the reorganization of the police." In 1842 Governor William Seward cited the Rogers case in calling for a stronger police for New York City.

In the next three years, various politicians proposed plans for police reform. The man most responsible for the proposal finally adopted was Robert H. Morris, a Democrat who was elected to his first term as mayor in 1841. Morris pressed the case for action in his messages to the Council, and the press attributed his reelection as mayor in 1843 to his identification with the cause of police reform. In the summer of 1843 Morris presented a sweeping proposal designed not only to establish a formal police but also to make basic changes in the pattern of municipal government by creating ward legislative councils. These councils would handle governmental matters of immediate interest to the locality, while the city's Common Council would act only on those questions which concerned the city as a whole.

The state legislature severely modified this nineteenth-century version of community control. The legislature had basic authority in this matter because American cities are legally creatures of their respective legislatures. In the nineteenth century there was no constitutional provision guaranteeing "Home Rule" to cities, and the New York legislature could enact minute regulations for the city's government. It could even adopt major changes in the city's charter, the basic grant of power and the prescribed form of government for the municipal corporation, by a simple legislative act, which did not require the approval or even the consultation of municipal authorities.

In 1844 the legislature adopted the police portion of Morris's proposals. The act abolished all existing agencies of police, except the constables, in favor of a "Day and Night Police" of not more than 800 men. Marshals remained in existence to serve civil processes. Each ward constituted a separate patrol district and policemen had to live in the ward in which they served. All members of the force were appointed for terms of only one year by the mayor on nomination of the council members of the particular ward. The act did create a chief of police whose supervisory powers over the police were limited. Finally, the act stipulated that it would not go into effect until it had been approved by the municipal authorities.

The legislature inserted this last provision at the insistence of the Native American party, which had captured control of New York City's government in the spring elections of 1844. The Native Americans opposed Governor Seward's concessions to the Catholics in the school aid question and wanted to limit the political power and participation of foreign-born Catholics. Members of this group attributed the city's problems to its foreign-born population and the unscrupulous politicians, Democrats, who used them. James Harper of the publishing family served as mayor under this party's aegis, and the nativists had majorities in both boards of the city's Common Council. Harper submitted the legislative act to the council, which rejected it. It was not until after the Democrats had recaptured control of the municipal government in 1845 that the state law received the approval of the municipal government and went into effect. In the interval the Native Americans had created a police force of their own, usually known as "Harper's Police," which supplemented rather than replaced such bodies as the night watch. Harper's Police wore uniforms, and citizens sometimes attacked them as "liveried lackeys" and a standing army. This body went out of existence when the Democrats recaptured control of the city's government in 1845 and adopted the state law of the previous year. The new force did not wear uniforms between 1845 and 1853, although officers were supposed to wear a small star-shaped badge they could use to identify themselves when necessary. For this reason they were sometimes referred to as the "star police."[8]

Philadelphia also experienced substantial transformation of its social fabric and police institutions from the 1830s on. During the 1830s and 1840s the city greatly expanded in size and complexity under the impetus of major transportation innovations, the impact of immigration, and the restructuring of the city's economic life to take advantage of new opportunities for profit. Other members of the community found the changes to be more threats than benefits. The riots that rocked Philadelphia in these decades were the most spectacular manifestation of the resulting breakdown of social cohesion and control in the city. Men who feared a loss of security and status in the new and uncertain economic and social climate found available scapegoats in blacks, abolitionists, and the Catholic Irish.[9]

As early as 1831 the will of Stephan Girard, a wealthy merchant and banker, stimulated interest in improved police protection. Girard provided a substantial sum of money for the city to establish "a competent police." The authorities responded with an ordinance in 1833 for a day police of 24 men in addition to the night watch of 120 men, both groups to be appointed by the mayor and under the centralized control of the "captain." In 1835 the ordinance was repealed and Philadelphia returned to a system of district autonomy. In 1848 the city established an independent day police of 34 men, while the night watch retained its old form.[10]

The police created by this legislation could not cope with the repeated disorders of the 1830s and 1840s. From 1834 on, the authorities had to call out the militia on numerous occasions to curb rioting. However, the militia, recruited from the same social group as the rioters, did not employ any substantial force until July, 1844, when clashes between rioters and militia resulted in fourteen deaths.

The shock of the May and July riots of that year vastly increased public sentiment for a professional police force that would encompass the entire Philadelphia area. It was obvious that the multiplicity of jurisdictions prevented effective control of potentially dangerous situations. This was especially true in border areas, such as the edges of the city and adjoining suburbs. Proponents of consolidation had to overcome the opposition of office holders of the small political units, and politicians warily calculated the probable political effects of enlarging the city. Another race riot in 1849 helped convince many waverers, and in 1854 the legislature granted Philadelphia a new charter enlarging the boundaries of the city to include all of Philadelphia County. By this action the area of the city grew from about two to almost one hundred and thirty square miles. The proponents of consolidation quickly implemented their plans for a professional police force to restore order and social control. No longer would criminals and rioters be able to escape the city's police by fleeing to a nearby suburb.

At first the new police force appointed only native-born Americans, and Irish spokesmen opposed it as maliciously intent on imposing prohibition on an unwilling populace. However, Richard Vaux, a shrewd and ambitious politician, soon captured the mayoralty by making an alliance with Irish politicians and began appointing Irishmen as well as natives to the police force. Philadelphia still had its red-light districts and its gangs, such as the notorious Schuylkill Rangers, but the city escaped much of the street violence that marked New York throughout the 1850s and which culminated in the Draft Riots of 1863.[11]

Boston had long had a reputation as a comparatively orderly and well-governed community. Until 1822 it continued to be governed as a town—that is, the town meeting had final authority in local matters and chose the various officials. Boston's growth made the system increasingly unworkable, and in 1822 Boston became a city to effect, as one contemporary put it, "alterations in the present government of the police." In this context, police did not refer exclusively to criminal matters; rather it had a broader meaning encompassing such concerns as health and municipal housekeeping as well as maintaining order.

Josiah Quincy, the first mayor of the city of Boston, deliberately set out to improve the police of the city without adding an army of constables and watchmen. In 1823 the aldermen adopted an ordinance creating the office of Marshal of the City. Benjamin Pollard, a lawyer and Harvard graduate, served as the first marshal from 1823 to 1836. The marshal had only one or two deputies so he had to set priorities in carrying out his manifold responsibilities encompassing the police of the city broadly considered. Pollard wrote only one formal report during his long tenure, a report which made no mention of crime or criminals. He conceived of his task as enforcing the corporation ordinances, those municipal regulations designed to protect the city's public health; he did not concern himself with the state's criminal law.

During the 1830s, however, the level of crime and disorder surpassed permissible limits. A certain amount of disorder had been traditional and both expected and accepted. The riots of the mid-1830s raised disturbing issues in that they involved political and social conflicts, going far beyond the traditional rampages of rowdy juveniles. After the third serious riot in four years, the city council announced its intention "to initiate, as far as may be, the system of London, were [sic] a similar patrol is established and is found to be of advantage in various ways besides the enforcement of laws."

Roger Lane, the historian of police in nineteenth-century Boston, points out that the authorities were not too sure just what the system of London was; but they did want a full-time salaried group who would be on the lookout for trouble to prevent its reaching crisis proportions. Therefore, in 1838 the Massachusetts General Court allowed Boston to appoint a number of policemen, under the command of the marshal, to deal with the immediate problem of riot. The night watch, a small group of underpaid casual laborers, remained in existence under this law. The police and watch departments were combined in 1854, and the more than two-centuries-old night watch went out of existence.[12]

Newer and smaller cities found in the 1840s and 1850s that they had need of some sort of organized police protection. Milwaukee was first settled by white men in the 1830s, and by 1845 the city required a watch. In 1855 the city established a formal police department, consisting of twelve men, eight of whom were foreign born. William Beck, a German who served as the first chief, believed that it was necessary "to whip a man in a fair fight before you could arrest him."[13]

While it would be impossible to formulate a set of generalizations that would apply to all urban police departments in the 1840s and 1850s, there are some common themes. For one thing, policing was not considered an independent professional service which demanded physical fitness, special training and skill, and security of tenure. In March 1847 a New York police surgeon found fifty men chronically unfit for duty, all of whom were drawing full pay. Some of these men were marked as "old and feeble" in the records of the department. In the early 1850s an English visitor noted that New York's police were "of all ages and sizes, including little withered old men, five feet nothing high. . . ."[14]

In most cities, policemen were appointed for limited terms by political officeholders and could be and were turned out of office with each change in the wheel of party fortune. If a Democrat's term expired when the Whigs or later the Republicans were in power, he could be reasonably sure of having to find a new job. Whigs and Republicans suffered the same fate under Democratic politicians. Police forces served as patronage vehicles for local party organizations, and initial appointment and subsequent reappointment depended more upon a man's political connections than his qualifications.[15]

The police, then, were not neutral in local campaigns and elections but exerted themselves for the right candidates and party. The Baltimore police in 1857 worked for the Know-Nothings at the polls. Their political opponents charged the police with "ruffianism" and "bloody tyranny." In New York, Mayor Fernando Wood's control of the police proved one of his strongest political assets in the mid-1850s. In a number of cities, chiefs, captains, and sometimes policemen themselves were elected by the voters. Cincinnati elected all members of the force. Philadelphia, San Francisco, Chicago, Cleveland, and other cities selected their heads of police for a few years at least. Brooklyn, New York, an independent city until the 1890s, elected captains as well as the chief. Similar proposals were made at various times in New York City, although never adopted. These provisions exemplified the American faith in popular control of the police.

Most of the early police forces were not uniformed. Other occupational groups, such as servants—many of whom insisted on being called "help"—and railroad conductors also refused to wear uniforms in the 1830s. Many Americans thought of uniforms as signs of degradation more fitting to the class consciousness of Europe than to the egalitarian democracy of the United States. However, as the number of the unskilled and propertyless rose with immigration and farm-to-city movement, people who believed in the values of efficiency and authority succeeded in imposing uniforms upon policemen, servants, and railroad conductors. New York's police became uniformed in 1853, Philadelphia's in 1860, and Chicago's in 1861.[16]

Nor were the police highly centralized, at least in the larger cities. Several other cities followed the New York pattern of having each ward constitute a separate patrol district with little administrative supervision by the chief. The technology of the age, or rather the lack of it, encouraged such decentralization. Before the spread of the telegraph in the late 1840s and 1850s, a chief could communicate with his precincts only by messenger; nor was there any way of getting word to and from the man on the beat and his station house without the physical movement of a human being.

At the same time some groups wanted the police to expand their functions to control public drunkenness and other offenses to a heightened conception of public order. The temperance movement increasingly looked to the police and the criminal law as mechanisms for achieving desirable goals. Massachusetts enacted a fifteen-gallon law in 1838 which forbade the sale of alcohol in any amount smaller than fifteen gallons. The obvious purpose of the law was to keep the poor from buying and using liquor.[17] In New York the legislature adopted a prohibitory law in 1855 which outlawed the sale and use of alcohol except for medicinal or sacramental purposes. Moralists wanted the police to suppress public prostitution and gambling and to enforce Sunday laws which decreed that saloons and other businesses remain closed on the Sabbath.[18]

These laws did not enjoy universal support. Thirsty urbanites resented attempts to close the saloons on any day, especially Sunday, which was the one day workingmen could call their own. Port cities with an unattached floating and transient population provided customers for commercialized recreation and vice. Saloonkeepers and sporting men had a common interest in controlling police behavior; their interests, whether as suppliers or consumers, required at least the tacit consent of the police.

The police had the impossible task of being required to enforce laws which a large segment of the community did not want enforced. The state legislatures which enacted these laws had majorities who lacked both knowledge of and sympathy for urban conditions. Conversely, in the cities themselves, opponents of the vice laws often held the effective political power. In New York from the 1850s on, many public offices were held by men either formerly or currently in the liquor business. The saying was that if anyone wanted to clear out a political meeting in a hurry, he put his head in the door and shouted, "Your saloon is on fire."

Yet New York's police and courts made more arrests and noted more convictions for drunkenness than London's. Statistics such as this are troublesome in that there are several possible explanations.

One is that New York adopted a more punitive attitude toward alcohol abuse as part of a general campaign to impose social control. It may also be that there was more drunkenness among New Yorkers than Londoners. Variations in arrest records for a variety of offenses can result either from more criminal or increased police activity or some combination of the two. In this case, however, the American desire to use the police and criminal law in a punitive manner seems primary. English police officials fought hard and successfully to limit sabbatarian legislation which would make popular actions violations of law. There could hardly be a moral consensus between police and people if the police tried to suppress popular pastimes. In New York the police enforced the law to the point where the number of arrests encompassed more than ten percent of the population, and the majority of arrests were either for simple intoxication or drunk and disorderly, but never to the point demanded by moralists.[19]

In Boston the law, which had formerly condemned only habitual drunkenness, in 1835 made public intoxication a crime. Now policemen could arrest for a single incident, and the number of arrests for intoxication went up sharply from a few hundred a year in the 1830s to several thousand a year in the 1840s and 1850s. Men such as Theodore Parker, a leading scholar and minister, regarded arrest and imprisonment as an opportunity for moral regeneration and thought that the police could serve as "moral missionaries." However, with the coming of the Irish in the late 1840s and 1850s, the policy broke down. There were too many drunks to be rehabilitated. Even before this, only some policemen cooperated with the reform program.[20]

Prostitution existed in American cities from the beginning of settlement. As cities grew and as a sensational press came into being in the 1830s and 1840s, prostitution came to be considered a "problem" in ways that it had not been twenty or thirty years before. Moralists wanted the police either to suppress prostitution completely or at least make it less visible. In Boston the police had rough compassion for many of the prostitutes, especially the young girls just off the farm. In New York the police sometimes arrested individual streetwalkers, but for the most part they ignored the houses in the red-light districts. Prostitution was too embedded in urban life for the moralists' goals ever to be achieved, and overly energetic attempts to eliminate it might raise tensions to a dangerous level.

In many instances it would be impossible to "enforce the law" and "maintain order" at the same time. Attempts to enforce unpopular laws could lead to serious breaches of the peace, and the police had to make a trade-off between the two. In New York's *Kleindeutschland,* "Little Germany," closing the saloons on Sunday once led to three days of rioting. Moreover, policemen were little disposed to enforce those laws which forbade behavior they themselves engaged in. Officers who liked to gamble could hardly get exercised about the existence of policy betting shops or faro parlors. Indeed, in New York policemen themselves often acted as "steerers" or "ropers" for the gambling houses. Thus the vice laws constantly formed the subject of a political tug of war between those who wanted to use the law and the police to control other people's behavior—to impose their moral codes on all members of the community—and those who wanted the police simply to leave them alone. These themes of conflict over morals legislation and police characterized smaller cities and towns as well as the nation's urban giants.[21]

The Kansas cattle town, which from the late 1860s to the mid-1880s flourished as the meeting place of Texas cattle drives and rail connections for shipment to market, formed a special type of urban settlement. Yet despite the legends perpetuated in such TV shows as *Gunsmoke* and innumerable films, the law enforcement problems and instruments of such towns as Abilene, Wichita, and Dodge City were surprisingly similar to those of New York and Chicago. The cattle towns supplied a market for the cattle and provided the paid-off cowboys with new clothes, liquor, gambling, and women. The leaders of these towns wanted to attract the cowboys' business without having an undue amount of violence and disorder. Therefore liquor, girls, and gambling would be available, but the authorities would also exercise effective police control to prevent excesses. Toward this end the towns established police forces—the largest item in their budgets —consisting of a marshal, an assistant marshal, and a number of policemen. These officers were chosen annually by the city councils and closely supervised.

Although at a higher level of intensity during the trading season, their tasks paralleled those of policemen elsewhere. They had to cope with unruly drunks and the disorders arising from whoring and gambling. They did not have to deal with an unusually high level of homicide. The average number of killings per cattle-town trading season came to only 1.5; and policemen were responsible for more of these deaths than any other group. Most homicides between civilians arose over disputes connected with women, not with gambling.[22]

As the towns matured, their population profile showed less of a preponderance of adult males and more women and children. Reform elements sprang up which wanted to suppress at least the visible signs of prostitution and gambling. As long as the cattle trade remained the basis of a particular town's economy, these groups were doomed to frustration. The cattle trade shifted from one town to another with railroad extension and the movement of a quarantine line by which local cattlemen kept out Texas herds because of the danger of disease. By the mid-1880s, the Texas cattle trade was virtually at an end, and local moralists had more success. There was also an increasing sentiment for prohibition, and the police became the battleground between those who wanted liquor suppression and the wets. The demise of the cattle trade did more to advance the reformers' ends than anything else. Saloonkeepers, gamblers, and prostitutes faded out as their customers disappeared; they were not driven out by the police as long as there was a substantial market for their services.[23]

In addition to enforcing the law and maintaining order, police departments had the responsibility of preventing and detecting crime. In the period between the establishment of the London Metropolitan Police and the creation of organized forces in American cities, the term "preventive police" was used frequently and loosely. Preventive seemed to mean that by their presence the police would inhibit the commission of crime and that they would deal with potentially serious situations before they reached the crisis stage. Detection of crime in both England and America had long been considered a private rather than a public matter. Police officers sold their services to the victims of crime who wished to recover their stolen property. The private interest of recovering the property took precedence over any public interest of apprehending and punishing the criminal. Even after the formation of organized police departments, detectives continued to function according to established patterns. In New York veteran police officers, those who had functioned on the old fee basis, continued as members of the new department created in 1845. No matter what their official titles, they continued to act as professional returners of stolen property, for which they often received handsome rewards. Robert Bowyer, who had been a police officer before the establishment of the department in 1845, used the contacts and the knowledge he had built up in his years of experience to earn $4,700 in rewards between January 1, 1855, and April 30, 1857, a sum more than twice his salary for the same period.[24]

To be effective, detectives needed wide knowledge of professional criminals who alone could provide them with the stolen property they sought to return. Compounding with the thief was the easiest way to recover property. The detective gave the thief either money or immunity in return for the stolen goods, and the rightful owner received his property less whatever he had agreed upon as a reward with the detective. Some victims found it cheaper to advertise in the newspaper and deal directly with the thieves, thus eliminating the detective as a middleman. As late as the 1890s witnesses before the Lexow Committee in New York, a legislative group investigating the Police Department, charged that detectives would not work on cases unless promised money beforehand. In a number of cities professional criminals had reached an understanding with the detectives and would not work without such protection. One of the points of these agreements was that if anyone of sufficient power and prestige had been robbed, the thief had to return his property.[25]

The establishment of police forces did not solve all of the social problems of American cities. Competing social groups and conflicting life styles continued to coexist uneasily in crowded urban space. While the police might arrest drunks, they could not stop alcohol abuse. Nor could they eliminate thievery. Expectations that the police would be disinterested public servants, dedicated to the moral imperatives of middle-class Protestantism, ran afoul of the realities of urban social and political life. A homogeneous community could be largely self-policing because deviancy was rare, easily recognized, and subject to strong social sanctions. But mid-nineteenth-century cities were anything but homogeneous. Heterogeneity made it more difficult to determine what was acceptable and what was deviant behavior. Moreover, urban diversity encouraged a political life based upon ethnic and racial cleavages as well as clashes of economic interests. Democratic control of police assured that heterogeneous cities would have constant conflicts over police organization and shifts of emphasis depending upon which groups controlled the political machinery at any one time. In addition policemen developed interests of their own which molded their behavior more than did the formal dictates of the law.

The combination of political control and police self-interest thus led to partisan involvement of the police, limited enforcement of vice laws, and a permissive attitude toward certain crimes and criminals. In turn these developments helped bring about major changes in patterns of police administration in the second half of the nineteenth century.

Chapter 3

Patterns of Police Administration

By the 1850s American urban police departments had three major responsibilities: maintaining order, preventing and detecting crime, and regulating public morality. In addition the police had a number of other functions, such as dealing with citizens who threw their garbage into the streets or with builders and merchants who obstructed the sidewalks. If the number and severity of public complaints are an accurate index, the police performed few of these tasks satisfactorily.

Despite the existence of an organized police, mobs and gangs often controlled the streets of New York, Philadelphia, and Baltimore. Groups such as Baltimore's Blood Tubs and Rip Raps, Philadelphia's Schuykill Rangers, and New York's Bowery Boys and Dead Rabbits could sometimes muster more men and more force than the city police. Election days in several cities were tumultuous and bloody affairs as rival gangs struggled for control of ballot boxes and polling places. Competing groups of volunteer firemen fought each other for the privilege of fighting fires; by the time the issues were decided, buildings had burned. Fire companies used fists, feet, and sometimes knives and revolvers in their combat. Residents and visitors alike complained about the insecurity of life and property in New York. Editors spoke of a "carnival of murder" and asserted that the streets of the city were more dangerous than the plains of Kansas during the height of the free-soil/proslavery conflict there. Saloons rarely closed on Sundays, and no one who had eyes could fail to find girls and gambling.[1]

Respectable observers attacked "our system of party and government" for the rampant vice and crime. One writer argued in 1871 that "the better classes of society need that the ultimate control of the police should be out of reach of municipal politics, as much as if not more than they need that the city budget should be safe from the same influences."[2] It was easy to blame the evil politician for the dislocations arising from rapid urbanization and the complications caused by the increased scale of municipal governmental responsibilities. The response was to change the structure of police administration.

In the first half of the nineteenth century, basic power in urban government rested with the city councils, which combined legislative, executive, and even some judicial functions. Councils decided how many policemen should be assigned to each precinct, who the commanding officer should be, and appointed and often removed the members of the department. In the late 1840s and early 1850s, councils in various cities found their functions being reduced. The mayor became a stronger executive and councilmen no longer served as judges. In New York individual aldermen had used their magistrate's power to hold court in police stations and release arrested followers. Police commanders had long complained about this kind of interference.

More important, at least as far as the police were concerned, was the emergence of the independent administrative board. City after city created such a board to oversee its police department. The board arrangement had several advantages. It weakened the control of the council which had neither the time nor the expertise to administer a department. Moreover, some members of council came from the very groups, saloonkeepers and such, that respectable people wanted suppressed. The board also prevented the concentration of power in the hands of one man. If social conditions required a police, at least that police could be administered by a number of men rather than one. In those cities where policemen or commanders previously had been elected by the voters, an elected board which appointed members of the force provided a means of introducing greater stability and a degree of professionalism while retaining some popular and democratic control.[3]

The New York law of 1853 became the model for boards all over the country, although there were many variations to the basic plan. The impetus for the New York law lay with a group known as the

City Reform party. Organized by such public-spirited citizens as the noted philanthropist Peter Cooper, the reformers wanted to curb corruption and improve the efficiency of municipal government. They prevailed upon the state legislature to invest administrative control of New York City's police department in a board of commissioners consisting of three elected officials, the mayor, the recorder (a judicial officer), and the city judge. This board had the power to appoint, discipline, transfer, and remove policemen from the department. However, the board had to show cause why a policeman should be removed; in effect, therefore, policemen now served for terms of good behavior rather than the limited terms for which they were appointed before 1853. The board tightened discipline and, over the strenuous objections of some members, made a uniform mandatory for the force. In the next two decades, New Orleans, Cincinnati, San Francisco, Detroit, St. Louis, Kansas City, Buffalo, Cleveland, Richmond, and Atlanta established police boards. The composition and authority of these boards varied widely, but all reflected the concern to keep power limited and divided.[4]

However, ambitious politicians like Fernando Wood, whose first term as mayor of New York began in 1855, found ways of circumventing these limitations. Wood impressed everyone at the beginning of his term as an energetic and dedicated reformer. He promised that he would make the police more disciplined and military in character, that he would suppress gambling houses and brothels, and that he would maintain a complaint book so that every citizen who felt aggrieved could register and have the matter attended to personally by the mayor. When some members of the state legislature in March 1855 proposed to transfer the control of the city's police to state officials, Wood received widespread support from the city's mercantile, political, and editorial elite to frustrate the attempt.

His conduct in office and especially his dealings with the police department cost him much of this respectable support over the next several months. It soon became apparent that Wood's campaign against purveyors of vice was both selective and shortlived; his supporters in these businesses were left alone. His opponents charged that policemen of a different political persuasion than the mayor faced removal from the department for any offense no matter how trivial, while fellow Democrats suffered lightly or not at all for major

breaches of discipline. Wood in effect told policemen not to enforce
the prohibition law passed by the legislature in 1855. In 1856, when
he was a candidate for reelection, he forced members of the department to contribute to his campaign fund, and some men were fur-
loughed to canvass for him. On Election Day, the police did not
interfere with the numerous bands of repeaters who roamed the city
casting multiple ballots for the mayor. He was able to use these
tactics because one of the other members of the board usually supported him.

Wood succeeded in his quest to maintain power in the city, but
his opponents captured both the governor's office and a majority in
the state legislature. They used their power to enact the Metropolitan
Police Law in 1857, which transferred control of the New York
Police Department to state officials. Originally this proposal applied
only to New York City. Opponents objected that the New York State
Constitution of 1846 required that officeholders of cities, towns, or
villages be either elected by the voters or chosen by the officials of
the local government in question. The legislature, therefore, created
a special police district consisting of the cities of New York and
Brooklyn plus some suburban areas. Because this district transcended
the boundaries of any established unit of local government, the spon-
sors argued, and the courts later agreed, that the members of the
board of commissioners for the metropolitan police were state officials
and that the legislature could determine their mode of appointment.
The board consisted of five members chosen by the governor plus
the mayors of New York and Brooklyn. All members of the New
York and Brooklyn police forces before the passage of the law auto-
matically became members of the metropolitan department.

Wood and his New York City supporters fought this innovation
bitterly. One newspaper charged that he had spent $100,000 to pre-
vent passage in the state legislature, and after the governor signed
the bill, Wood continued to deny its validity. He had the Council
adopt an ordinance for a municipal police; at the same time he contested the constitutionality of the metropolitan police in the courts.
The proponents of the metropolitans cited the precedent of the London Metropolitan Police as justification for taking the control of the
police out of the hands of municipal authorities; Wood responded
that the old city of London, a small area within the metropolis,

retained a separate police and that New York City could do the same. The mayor told policemen that if they obeyed the new commissioners and the courts later declared the law unconstitutional, they would not be taken back into the municipal department. About 800 of the 1,100 members of the New York Police Department prior to the passage of the metropolitan law refused to recognize the new commissioners. The metropolitans then had only a minority of the old force and had to fill their ranks by a variety of expedients.

For several weeks the citizens of New York found themselves in the anomalous position of having two police forces, each of which claimed to be the sole legitimate protector of life and property in the city. Members of the rival forces sometimes fought on the streets and in the station houses. Prisoners arrested by one force might be rescued by another. On June 17, 1857, a brawl between elements of the two groups broke out on the steps of City Hall, where a large number of Wood's municipals routed a small group of metropolitans. It was not until the Court of Appeals, the state's highest tribunal, decided in favor of the Metropolitan Police Law that Wood disbanded the municipal police and took his seat as a member of the metropolitan board.

The 1857 legislature also changed the charter of the city in other ways designed to increase Republican power in the normally Democratic city's government. By these enactments Republicans would have a share in the city's patronage and an almost equal voice in the municipal government. Changing the structure of police administration had partisan implications and was not simply an attempt to give the city better police protection. In 1860 the political motives became clearer when the legislature removed the mayors of New York and Brooklyn from the police board and reduced the number of appointed commissioners to three. All the men selected were Republicans. The three-man board remained until 1864, when the legislature enlarged the board to four members by naming two men from each of the major parties. There was no stipulation in the law that future appointments to the board had to be equally divided between the parties.[5]

The 1864 legislation resulted from a crisis caused by the antagonism between Governor Horatio Seymour, a Democrat, and the Republican police commissioners. Governor Seymour opposed the draft law passed by Congress during the Civil War and especially its application. He thought that the state of New York had been assigned an excessive number of men and that the cities of New York and Brooklyn had been discriminated against within the state. His critics thought that his utterances had encouraged the outbreak of the Draft Riots of July 1863 and that he had been too conciliatory by far to the rioters during the disorders.

The governor opposed Republican control of New York City's police. Seymour threatened to remove the police commissioners from office as his first official act in January 1863, and he repeated his charges against them in June of that year. In both instances he failed to carry out his threat. However, in January 1864 he did act after he read their report on the Draft Riots, which he took to be an unwarranted attack upon himself. He removed the commissioners and appointed replacements more to his liking. The commissioners refused to vacate their offices and a stalemate threatened. The legislature resolved the impasse by enlarging the board from three members to four, including two of the existing Republican commissioners and two of Seymour's Democratic appointees. This four-member board remained until the metropolitan police came to an end in 1870, although it was not always equally divided between the parties.[6]

The political and administrative history of police in other cities duplicated some of the elements of the New York situation. The Maryland and Missouri legislatures took control of the Baltimore, St. Louis, and Kansas City police departments in the early 1860s. The boards for these departments were chosen either by the governor of the state or by the legislature, and state control lasted into the twentieth century. During these same years, the procedures by which the commissioners of the Chicago police were chosen varied according to which party controlled the legislature. The party in power saw to it that the Chicago police would protect its interests and give the police patronage to its members. Detroit had its force controlled by state-appointed officials for twenty-six years beginning in 1865. In Cleveland, on the other hand, state control lasted only two years, from 1866 to 1868. Other cities to have state boards for some years at least included New Orleans, Cincinnati, Indianapolis, Omaha, and San Francisco.[7]

One of the last departments to come under state control, and ironically where such control proved especially long lasting, was Boston. The Boston police remained under the administrative direction of a committee of the board of aldermen until the 1870s. In that decade two major questions arose in regard to the political status of the force. The first problem involved the role of the police in providing lodging and soup for vagrants, and the second issue concerned the perennial problem of liquor control. The debates over these issues heightened dissatisfaction with part-time, unpaid administration such as that provided by the aldermen. Proponents of "scientific charity" protested that the indiscriminate serving of soup promoted pauperism and prevented the moral regeneration of the poor. The issuance of liquor licenses and the supervision of the licensees was vitally important to anyone interested in building and maintaining a political power base in the city. The controversies surrounding police treatment of vagrants and liquor licenses led the Massachusetts legislature in 1878 to create a three-member board of commissioners for the department. The commissioners were chosen by the mayor with the consent of the city council. The law also gave these commissioners the power, which had formerly belonged to the council, to issue liquor licenses. For the next eight years mayors consciously sought to make the board reflect their own political party's interests and views on the liquor question.[8]

In the late 1870s and early 1880s increased partisan and ethnic rivalry characterized Boston politics. As the Irish came to dominate the Democratic party, Republicans in city and state responded with fear and trembling. In 1884 Boston elected its first Irish Catholic mayor in Hugh O'Brien, and O'Brien saw to it that the police board had a majority of Irishmen. The following year Republicans in the legislature introduced a bill transferring control of the Boston police to state appointees. The Democrats of Boston fought the bill long and hard, resorting to a filibuster. The Republican majority, however, pressed on, and in June 1885 the Boston police force came under state control, where it remained until 1962. Until 1906 it was governed by a board, after that date by a single commissioner appointed by the governor.[9]

State control in New York, Chicago, Boston, and other cities thus grew out of the social and political differences between city and state. The cities had cosmopolitan populations with a large number of first-

and second-generation Americans who had little sympathy for the temperance forces. Alcohol was an integral part of life for many of the immigrants and their children, and they resisted any attempts to close the saloons on Sunday, the one day workingmen had for recreation and pleasure. Cities with a large number of unattached males and transients, whether they be visiting businessmen or sailors on shore leave, generated demands for girls and gambling, demands that entrepreneurs were more than willing to meet. Respectable citizens of small towns and rural areas, as well as the home-owning portion of the urban population itself, half condemningly, half enviously deplored this aspect of metropolitan life. If the city's police refused to do anything about prostitution and saloons that did business as usual or better than usual on Sunday, perhaps the state should step in to enforce compliance with the law. The hopes of the moralists that state control of urban police forces would ensure "proper" police performance were often doomed to frustration; the pressures for a tolerant attitude toward illegal but popular businesses proved too strong.

Those politicians who sought state control of urban police departments as a way of getting a share of the patronage pie and having more influence in urban elections did rather better. Most of the senior officers of the New York metropolitan police, the superintendent, inspectors, and captains, were Republicans. Despite the advantages state control gave New York Republicans, they were unable to maintain it beyond 1870. In the late 1860s, as the Republicans increased the amount of state interference in New York City's government by creating metropolitan commissions for fire protection, public health, and the regulation of the liquor trade, William M. Tweed rose to an unprecedented but unstable position of power in New York City's dominant Democratic organization, Tammany Hall. By 1869 Tweed had succeeded in capturing the state as well by electing a Democratic majority in the legislature and a Democratic governor, John A. Hoffman. Hoffman, former mayor of New York City, condemned the pattern of state commissions administering municipal functions. Tweed introduced a new charter for New York City in the legislature which abolished the metropolitan commissions and returned municipal government to city officials. He received the support not only of organization Democrats but also of reformers such as Peter

Cooper who believed in the principle of home rule—that is, that cities should be free to govern themselves and not be subject to constant state interference. Tweed later also admitted that he spent $600,000 to ensure the passage of this new charter through the legislature.[10]

The Tweed charter maintained the administrative board, although henceforth the four members were to be chosen by the mayor with the consent of the board of aldermen rather than by the governor or the legislature. Police commissioners served for terms of six years, and the custom continued of having bipartisan representation, which meant that each of the major parties had representation on the board and therefore a significant voice in patronage matters. The four members of the board acted in turn on appointments and promotions so that each member had an equal chance at naming patrolmen or captains. Occasionally, one party had a three-to-one majority on the board.[11]

The police board also controlled the board of elections and selected poll inspectors and clerks. The police themselves supervised the balloting and later the counting of ballots. Repeating, a practice by which a single person cast multiple votes, and colonizing voters by registering transients and derelicts out of flophouses could take place on a large scale only with police approval. In 1894, the Lexow Committee, a special investigating group of the state legislature dominated by upstate Republicans, made the case that whenever Tammany secured a majority of the board vote, frauds by Democrats increased tremendously.

The Republican legislature's solution was to make a bipartisan board, equally divided between the major parties, legally mandatory; what had been only a custom and not a universally observed one, now became a legal necessity. Theodore Roosevelt, who served as a member of the board from 1895 to 1897, thought that "a more foolish or vicious law was never enacted by any legislative body. It modeled the government of the police force somewhat on the lines of the Polish parliament, and it was avowedly designed to make it difficult to get effective action." The law, however, satisfied the needs of the party organizations, and the bipartisan pattern remained when the charter for Greater New York was adopted in 1897. By this act New York City was expanded to include its present five boroughs, and Brooklyn lost its status as an independent city.[12]

At the very end of the century, the Republican state boss, Thomas Collier Platt, proposed to revive the metropolitan idea or to create some other device which would increase even further Republican power and influence in the New York Police Department. These proposals were objected to as unwarranted interference with the city's home rule and never became law. In 1901 the legislature replaced the board with a single police commissioner appointed by the mayor. However, the possibility of state interference remained because the act gave the governor power to remove the police commissioner. All over the country cities intensified their opposition to state interference and demanded that they be left free to govern themselves. Getting the respective state legislatures to agree with this principle was not always easy.[13]

One of the interesting case studies of the conflict between city and state took place in Ohio. Ohio's nineteenth-century constitution provided that the legislature had to pass general laws for municipal government—that is, that laws had to apply to classes of cities and would be invalid if meant for a single city. However, the courts allowed a very large loophole by permitting minute classifications. A law would apply to all cities which at the last census had a population of between 5,500 and 5,540, or the law would be so worded that only one city in one county could qualify. Cincinnati, Cleveland, Columbus, Toledo, and Dayton were the only cities in their respective classes.

Patterns of municipal government varied widely. Akron and Youngstown had an absurd form in which the mayor had little real executive power; his primary function was to hold the police court. The executive responsibility lay with a bipartisan board of commissioners appointed by the mayor and the probate judge of the county. These commissioners were not really responsible to anybody, and as often happened in these bipartisan arrangements, Republicans and Democrats collaborated to maintain the stability of their respective party organizations as their first priority.

Until 1891 Cleveland had a charter calling for independent boards and commissions with little coordination between them. A structure of such diffused power and responsibility encouraged the formation of political machines to provide the coordinating role that the formal governmental system discouraged. In 1891 Cleveland secured a new charter which centralized executive responsibility in the mayor; this form was usually referred to as the federal plan of municipal government, and most of the political scientists of the period endorsed it as the best way to bring about good government.[14]

The courts created a crisis by invalidating these special arrangements and insisting that the legislature adopt a uniform municipal code in line with the state constitution. In the resulting special session, Republicans in the legislature were especially anxious to limit the power of Democratic reform mayors like Tom Johnson of Cleveland and Samuel "Golden Rule" Jones of Toledo. In the case of Toledo the Republicans had previously tried to take the police force away from the mayor and give it over to a bipartisan board appointed by the governor. Jones refused to recognize the validity of the act and brought the court case which invalidated the special laws.[15] Johnson seemed like a dangerous radical to many Republicans with his call for reduced streetcar fares on private lines and his support for public ownership of quasi-public corporations. Johnson also was a devotee of the theories of Henry George, the author of *Progress and Poverty,* a book published in 1879 which condemned all forms of urban real-estate speculation.[16]

Conservative Republicans preferred an arrangement whereby the police forces of all Ohio cities would be under bipartisan boards appointed by the governor, thereby seriously limiting the power of Jones and Johnson. In the intense bargaining surrounding the drafting of a uniform municipal code, advocates of home rule for cities blocked complete state control. The code as adopted provided for departments of public safety in all cities. These departments would include police, fire, and certain other functions under bipartisan boards appointed by the mayor with the consent of two-thirds of the city council. If the council did not ratify the mayor's appointments, the governor then named the board.[17] In 1908 Cleveland's board gave way to a single safety director. It was not until 1912 that the cities succeeded in overturning the bulk of the 1902 code and pushing through a home rule amendment to the Ohio constitution, which allowed cities to draft their own charters.[18]

The structure of police administration in the second half of the nineteenth century and the early years of the twentieth was thus notoriously unstable as a variety of groups hoped they could find a way to ensure that the police would advance their interests. The scope and sensitivity of the police mandate made administration of the department a prize worth contending for. Whoever governed the police had a major source of patronage, could control entry into and operation of illegal businesses and those legitimate businesses subject to public regulation, such as saloons, and had a major advantage in elections. No matter how one conceived of one's goals, whether simply making money or acquiring personal power or struggling to advance good government and the cause of morality, control of the police was a fundamental asset toward achieving them.

The struggle for domination of the police took place within city governments and between the urban majorities and the state legislature. Those groups outvoted in a city could look to the state capital for relief, relief which was often granted because the interests of the urban and the state majority conflicted. The concept of state sovereignty and municipal dependence allowed state legislatures to intervene at will in municipal government, a power they exercised frequently. Only at the very end of the nineteenth century and in the opening decades of the twentieth did cities secure constitutional protection against legislative manipulation of their governing structure.[19]

These conflicts and resulting changes in administrative format were one of the targets for those men who wanted to "take the police out of politics." How could the police become an agency devoted to the public interest if politicians constantly tinkered with its administrative structure? If top leadership could be changed almost capriciously, how could the police develop into a stable, disinterested group of public servants? What would be policemen's view of their own organization if their "bosses" were replaced arbitrarily? Each change in governance was another lesson to policemen that they had to tread warily, that their occupation placed them in a dense political thicket where the bold or unaware could easily be hurt.

Chapter 4

Policemen and Policing in the Nineteenth Century

The late nineteenth-century policeman had a difficult job. He had to maintain order, cope with vice and crime, provide service to people in trouble, and keep his nose clean politically. In becoming a policeman he found that he had embarked upon a way of life as well as taking a job. He would soon be separated from his old associates and looked upon with suspicion by most citizens. The advantages were steady work with no layoffs, if the political climate permitted (in Kansas City, Missouri, politically inspired dismissals lasted until the 1920s), and the prospect of a pension after twenty or twenty-five years of service. The nature of his work and expectations of a pension tied him closely to his organization and his colleagues. Even though policemen might be strenuous competitors internally for good assignments and promotions, they banded together to protect themselves against hostile outside forces. They were reluctant to endanger their positions, and so solidarity and the avoidance of error became key principles. A number of studies in recent decades show the desire for economic security to be the most common motivation for embarking upon a police career. It seems safe to say that similar impulses prevailed in the nineteenth century, although under quite different conditions, given the political environment in which police departments and their individual members had to operate.

By the 1850s the major eastern cities had a surplus of unskilled labor. For those recently arrived from Europe or the American countryside, jobs were hard to come by, there was a great degree of instability of employment, and many men had a difficult time supporting their families. Securing a position on the police force solved many of these economic problems. New York policemen were paid about twice as much as unskilled labor, they did not have to worry about layoffs, and they could look forward to holding the job for as long as they wanted it.

Police departments then had more applicants than they had positions, and the problem was one of selection. In most cities the basis of selection rested on political influence and money, even after civil service laws supposedly introduced the merit system of choosing policemen. In New York the Lexow inquiry showed that a young man had to have the support of a party district leader and usually had to pay $300 for an appointment as a patrolman. A few cities had wholesale turnovers in the department whenever party control changed.[1]

Most cities required that men be residents of the city for a year before they could be eligible for the department. In Cleveland residents of other areas in Ohio could become members of the Cleveland Police Department in the early twentieth century, but such appointees would have to take up residence in the city. In New York the reform board headed by Theodore Roosevelt sought applications for the department from residents of upstate areas and did, in fact, appoint a considerable number of what disgruntled Tammanyites called "bushwackers" who, when appointed, "could not find their way to a single station house."[2]

The Roosevelt action contravened the American tradition of local boys for local jobs. In England, on the other hand, police commanders consciously sought out recruits from outside their own localities. The London police preferred to get its new men from areas outside London. This would eliminate any possibility of "familiarity begets contempt" between a policeman and those he worked among. City boys might be too wise to the ways of the metropolis and too involved with local people to maintain the separation and detachment that police authorities wanted.[3]

Even though American policemen had to be residents, and many were natives, of their cities, they also became separated and detached to some degree from the civilians among whom they worked. Partly, this was a result of the policeman's work schedule. He was on duty when other men had quit for the day, and he spent a good many lonely hours on the street when most men were sleeping. The nature of the policeman's work also kept him apart from civilians. He had the power to deprive citizens, in some circumstances at least, of life and liberty, and therefore he could be a cause of fear to many people. Children were kept in line with threats of "I'll have the cops after you." Boys and men saw policemen as killjoys who tried to keep them from playing ball in the streets or who closed their saloons on Sunday. Many people looked on policemen as crooks and grafters who were contaminated by their constant association with prostitutes, pimps, and pickpockets. In short many civilians regarded policemen either as public servants who too often were unfaithful to their duty or as troublesome and potentially dangerous antagonists with whom the less one had to do the better. In this atmosphere then, policemen tended to spend much of their free time with other officers, hashing over the rumors and wondering which way the lines of power and influence within the department were flowing.[4]

The geographical and social isolation of American policemen molded their performance in a number of ways. There was little or no lateral movement from one department to another; customarily a man spent his entire career in one city. There was no police counterpart to the process by which DuPont recruits from Union Carbide or Harvard from Columbia; a man could not establish a reputation in one department and use it to secure higher rank and more pay in another. Nor did policemen interact with members of other large organizations within their own cities. No one moved from being principal of an elementary school to captain of a police precinct. Consequently, police departments became highly inbred. Customarily new blood entered only at the lowest level, and men usually spent a considerable number of years in the ranks before attaining command positions.

In these circumstances, tradition became the most important determinant of police behavior; the emphasis in most departments was on doing things as they had always been done. Innovation was frowned upon, and the veterans impressed upon the rookies the reasons why things had to be the way they were. By the time a man got to be a supervisor, any new ideas he may have had as a rookie had been drilled out of him. Older men indoctrinated the rookies through the advice they gave, the stories they told, and the praise or blame they bestowed for any particular action. In New York, policemen spent up to seven hours a day in reserve in the station houses in addition to their nine hours on patrol. By mutual consent religion and politics were not discussed, but the swapping of stories and the comparing of experiences went on constantly. In these sessions, rookies learned the traditions of the department and what was expected of them as policemen. As one reporter put it in the 1890s, "the section-room in a police-station is a great place for traditions. There walked the ghosts of men notorious in their time, whom the town has forgotten absolutely, and the stories about them affect the manner of grip with which the policeman swings his club, or the temper in which he blackmails disorderly women."[5]

The discussions in the section-room were often interrupted by fires, parades, riots, and strikes. In these instances, policemen no longer worked alone but as a collective body, and it was just these occasions that made for the most hostile interaction between police and civilians. In parades and fires, the police had to keep people out of the line of march or away from the fire so that the firemen could do their work. So while there was some conflict of interest between the desires of the spectators and the job of the police, it was not a very serious one.

This was not the case in labor disputes, where in many cities the police intervened on the side of the employers so that the business could keep operating despite the strike. Strikes meant long hours of extra duty for which no overtime was paid, and many policemen had no use for either strikers or strikebreakers. Strikes introduced elements of disorder and unpredictability, both of which were threatening to policemen who liked to see things in an orderly and predictable pattern and routine. Policemen's pay and work schedules were set by law or ordinance, not as a result of individual or collective bargaining with an employer. If policemen were going to improve their lot, either individually or collectively, they did it by lobbying and other political—not trade union—activity. More money and better pensions came from legislative action either at City Hall or in the state capital.

For these reasons policemen were not likely to identify with the aspirations of labor, especially with new immigrants like Jewish garment workers or Slavic steel-mill hands. There were both class and ethnic differences between the secure native, Irish, and German officers and many workers. Especially estranged were those who had only recently arrived in this country and found themselves the most disadvantaged in the labor market and the most persecuted by the police. On New York's Lower East Side, a scene of constant labor conflict, Jewish spokesmen called the police "Black Hundreds" in memory of conditions in Czarist Russia.[6]

Other aspects of the complex police function were not so controversial. Few people wanted the police to ignore thieves and those guilty of bodily assault, and there was general agreement that the force had to act quickly and energetically to suppress rioters and restore order. During the course of the nineteenth century, large cities gradually became more orderly places. Roger Lane has examined available statistics for the state of Massachusetts which show a decline in felonies from 1835 until the end of the century. While serious crimes dropped, the number of arrests rose as the organized police brought in a considerable number of persons charged with drunkenness and other less serious offenses. Lane's data suggest that we may have to modify or scrap our usual association of increasing urbanization and increasing crime, because it does not seem to be true for serious crimes in one major industrial state in the nineteenth century. The number of riots also dropped in the latter part of the century. Before the Civil War street disorders were endemic in American cities; indeed it was their frequency which helped to overcome the reluctance to establish organized police forces.[7]

The creation of organized, uniformed departments did not eliminate all disturbances. The New York police had to cope with several serious riots in 1857 and the especially violent Draft Riots of 1863. The Draft Riots grew out of the economic and social tensions between the city's white working class, especially Irish immigrants, and Negroes. Conflicts over such gut issues as jobs and housing exploded in July 1863, when the national government introduced conscription to raise troops for the Union Army. The draft created such deep bitterness because the Emancipation Proclamation had expanded Union war aims from simply the preservation of the Union to include the abolition of slavery. Opposition politicians and publicists stirred up white working-class fears that emancipation would mean a flood of black migrants from the South coming north to take away their jobs and assault their women.

The police bore the brunt of suppressing the riots because most

military units had been shipped to Pennsylvania to repel Lee's invasion. For four days the police battled mobs in various parts of the
city, struggled to protect the downtown area, the center of the city's
political and economic life, and sought to prevent takeovers of arms
depositories. The police treated the riots as a serious threat to the
well-being of the city in particular and the Union war effort in
general. The superintendent of the department, John A. Kennedy,
narrowly escaped death at the hands of rioters on the first day of
the disturbances, which convinced his associates that the rioters had
to be suppressed with gun, club, and military artillery when available. The rioters were responsible for at least eighteen deaths, including those of three policemen, but there are only rough estimates
available of the number of rioters and bystanders killed by the police
and the military. The toll may have reached several hundred. Some
writers have contended that one thousand to two thousand persons
died in the riots, estimates which seem clearly excessive.

In later years New York police officials always referred to the
Draft Riots as the high point of their historical experience, their
finest hour, when their courage, devotion, and faithfulness saved the
city from anarchy and destruction. Politicians who had been critical
of the police now gave strong support. Slum dwellers who bore the
brunt of police clubs and bullets during the riots might not have so
favorable a view, but they had no way of counteracting the praise
heaped on the police by the respectable and propertied.[8]

In the post-Civil War period ethnic group conflict sometimes resulted in individual and group acts of violence and disorder—in 1871
the religious and communal hatreds of Catholic and Protestant Irish
led to the killing and wounding of more than one hundred people—
but increasingly these conflicts became ritualized in vaudeville
sketches and ethnically supported prize fighters. Vaudeville and box-
ing served as safety valves in which the tensions of urban life could
be dealt with by humor or fought out by single champions. The
comedians' dialects and the shamrocks and Stars of David on
fighters' robes are out of fashion now, rejected as stereotypes perpetuating ethnic divisions. In the decades from the 1880s to the 1930s
they may have served a positive purpose in providing ritualistic outlets for the expression of group identity.[9]

In any event, American cities for the most part were decidedly more orderly places in 1900 than in 1850. The possibility of violence in connection with labor disputes remained, and race riots increased in number and intensity after 1900, but daily urban life became more predictable and controlled.

Older cities had passed through the first stages of disorderly growth. In the pre-Civil War years, conflicts between immigrants and native Americans led to repeated outbursts of violence. In contrast, American cities absorbed millions of newcomers in the years after 1900 without the social and political strains attendant upon Irish immigration of the 1830s to 1850s. In those decades, a city's physical form mixed land uses and social classes in highly volatile combinations. Natives and immigrants, factories and residences crowded together in the limited area of the walking city. By 1900 land use became more specialized with the emergence of a large central business district where major retailing concentrated. Other parts of the city served as areas for heavy industry or warehousing. Residential areas also became more specialized as improved transportation in the form of horse cars and electric trolleys greatly enlarged the physical area from which people could conveniently commute from home to work. In the process social classes separated themselves from one another; the more established now lived at a greater distance from new arrivals. Areas in transition from one social class or ethnic group to another experienced tension and social strain, but in general physical distance reduced points of conflict.

More developed urban organizational and institutional life also promoted order. Work groups and other social clusters provided a sense of integration and belonging. Immigrants established benefit societies, churches and synagogues, and social clubs to ease the transition from the European village to the American city. Also the police had acquired experience in dealing with potential sources of violence. Juvenile gangs abounded in slum neighbourhoods, but seemingly their sense of decorum, and police intervention, kept violence from reaching the levels common in the 1850s.[10]

The police who patrolled northern and western cities to maintain order reflected the immigration of a previous generation. First- and second-generation Irish-Americans made up a disproportionately heavy percentage of policemen by the 1890s. According to official figures, which may have underestimated the total, men of Irish birth comprised more than one-quarter of the New York force as early as the 1850s. The first Irishman on the Boston force occasioned a great outcry—most members came from rural New England—but by 1880 Boston had one hundred Irish policemen. The next decades brought substantial increases in that number. Chicago, Cleveland, and San Francisco had more Irish police officers than the Irish proportion of the cities' populations would warrant. One disgruntled observer, John Paul Bocock, published a testy article in 1894 entitled "The Irish Conquest of Our Cities," in which he noted the places where either the chief of police, the chief of detectives, or both were Irish. The list included interior cities like Denver and Omaha.[11]

Even after the tides of immigration shifted from northern and western Europe to southern and eastern Europe, Irish preponderance in police forces remained. In the 1920s men of Irish birth or parentage made up more than one-fourth of the police forces of Buffalo, Chicago, Cleveland, and Detroit, far greater than the Irish proportion of the total populations of these cities. Arthur Niederhoffer estimated that in the early 1960s forty percent of the New York police force was of Irish origin at a time when the comparable figure for the city's population was perhaps ten percent. In a study of sergeants in the Chicago police department also made in the early 1960s, James Q. Wilson found that a disproportionate number of them were Irish, and furthermore that the Irish sergeants were more likely to come from police families and were more likely to spend more of their free time with other policemen than were sergeants of other ethnic backgrounds.[12] Even in Akron, Ohio, which has never had a very large number of Irish residents, among the great names in its police history are John Durkin, who was born in Ireland and served as chief for thirty years, Steve McGowan, and Frank McGuire. In nearby Cleveland, Chief Fred Kohler, American born of a German father, fought a running battle with many of his Irish subordinates who objected to taking order from a "damned Dutchman." The feeling against Kohler was especially bitter when he transferred the popular Lieutenant Bill O'Laughlin to a less desirable position.[13]

Ethnic and religious antagonisms permeated many departments. Some forces such as Cleveland's had recurrent conflicts between Catholics and Masons, and the Irish in New York held back the advance of newcomers. If they could not prevent the appointment of Italians and others to the force, at least they could make promotion difficult. Like other large organizations, police forces developed contending factions which rivaled for power and prestige in the form of desirable assignments and command positions.[14]

Yet in the nineteenth century these matters were not settled intramurally, at least not totally. Police forces were not autonomous; political figures outside the department often made the key decisions on promotions, assignments, and disciplinary matters. In New York before 1895 the board of commissioners decided these matters, not the commanding officer of the department, then known as the superintendent. George Walling, who spent thirty-eight years on the force, eleven of them as superintendent, published an interesting autobiography in 1887, two years after his retirement, entitled *Recollections of a New York Chief of Police.*

Walling lamented that he was in the worst of all positions, that of having responsibility, in the public eye if not in law, without power. "Time and time again have I attempted, one way or another, to have fuller power placed in my hands, but for the last four years during which I was superintendent, my position was that of a mere figure-head. What I claim is, that a man who is held responsible for the actions of certain subordinates in any public department, should have absolute control over those under him as to assignment and transfer." If a subordinate defied him all Walling could do was to bring charges before the commissioners, who, if they chose, could simply ignore them.[15]

Policemen and their political backers constantly invoked whatever support they had for promotions and desirable assignments. Some men sought soft berths, desk jobs; others wanted to be where the action was. The corrupt wanted to have beats with the most saloons and brothels to raise their outside incomes; the family men wanted to be as close to home as possible. The transfer then could be a most potent method of rewarding one's friends and punishing one's enemies.

People outside the department also pressured administrators to make certain transfers. In New York City in the 1890s, green goods men, confidence men who bilked would-be distributors of counterfeit money by selling them only useless paper, changed their base of operations every time a particular captain was transferred to a new precinct. Gamblers, saloonkeepers, madams, and pimps had to have a sympathetic captain in charge of the precinct. They couldn't operate with an "untouchable," a "crusader," or a "100 percent copper." Rather they sought a man like Alexander S. "Clubber" Williams, who gave New York's most fashionable red-light district its nickname when he was transferred there in the early 1880s. On learning of his transfer, he told a reporter that he had been living on salt chuck long enough, now he was going to get some of that tenderloin. The West Thirties became known as the Tenderloin, a name adopted for the major vice areas of other cities.[16]

Williams took a "liberal view," as he described it, of brothels and gambling houses, as long as they contributed to his wealth and featured his brand of whiskey. By the early 1890s, he owned a house on East Tenth Street and an estate at Cos Cob, Connecticut, which had among its effects a fifty-three foot long steam yacht. New York's Captain Timothy Creeden had to borrow $15,000 to secure his promotion, but his first assignments were to precincts with limited potentialities for graft. His creditors therefore arranged his transfer to a more lucrative precinct so that he would be able to pay his just debts in a reasonable time. Captains like Williams and Creeden used their precinct detectives, or "wardmen," as they were known in New York, as collectors. The captains did not take money directly but rather employed these "bagmen." The wardmen usually kept twenty percent of what they collected and were guaranteed the captain's protection in case of trouble. When captains were transferred from one precinct to another they tried to get their wardmen transferred with them.[17]

If transfers could be very advantageous to some policemen, they could be devastating to others. A man who incurred the wrath of his superiors could be transferred from one end of the city to another. Any change in a department's power structure or in the outside political forces which controlled the police could result in wholesale transfers.

The activities of William Devery, New York's Chief of Police from 1898 to 1901, illustrate the point. By statutes of 1895 and 1897, many of the powers of assignment and discipline formerly exercised by the board of commissioners were given to the chief. Devery became chief as a result of his association with Tim Sullivan, a major political power on the Lower East Side with extensive interests in gambling and prizefighting. Any policeman who raided one of Sullivan's gamblers was likely to find himself patrolling the cemetery or exiled to "Goatville" in the north Bronx, which was still rural at the time. In little more than a year Patrolman Jeremiah Moran served in 126th street in Manhattan, Oak Street in lower Manhattan, and Astoria, Flushing, and Whitestone in Queens. He stopped unpacking. As part of a complicated political battle involving rival factions of Democrats as well as Republicans, Devery at one point transferred two deputy chiefs, six inspectors, and twenty-two captains.[18] In Cleveland, Chief Fred Kohler transferred sixty men at once, sending men from preferred jobs out "to the woods," as Siberia was known in the Cleveland Police Department, and bringing men of his own choosing into the downtown area.[19]

Thus, the shake-up, or mass transfer, could be a good indication of the lines of power within and without a police force. If commanders did not want to issue direct orders as to their policy on bookmakers and saloonkeepers that remained open on Sunday, they could easily convey their desires through their use of the transfer. For the patrolman, unless he was exceptionally stubborn or a notoriously slow learner, the moral was clear: if you want to get along, go along. Policemen who did not want to have anything to do with the "world of graft" could manage assignments that kept them out of the red-light districts; those who believed that collecting from saloonkeepers and gamblers was "clean money" or "honest graft" in the famous phrase of Tammany's shoe-shine-stand political philosopher, George Washington Plunkitt, often found their way into these areas.

The transfer could be one mechanism of reward and punishment; another important one was promotion. In many big city departments in the late nineteenth century, promotion depended upon political influence and money. A man could become a captain or higher only if he had strong political support and, in some instances at least, he had to raise a great deal of money. Timothy Creeden again is a case in point. Rumors had circulated for years in New York that captaincies had to be paid for and that they were expensive. In 1893 the New York *World* carried a story, without any names being used, about a sergeant who paid $15,000 to become a captain. The following year Creeden admitted to the Lexow Committee that he did have to pay this much for his promotion to a representative of one of the police commissioners. The price was as high as it was because another candidate had been willing to pay $12,000. As a captain's salary in the 1890s was only $3,000 a year, Creeden obviously had to collect from illegal enterprises in order to make his investment worthwhile.[20]

Ambitious policemen also found it valuable to join the right political clubs and to make themselves useful to the district and ward leaders who controlled their professional destinies. A turn-of-the-century policeman was not part of an independent or autonomous professional or bureaucratic agency. Rather the police were part of the political apparatus, and impartial police administration was the last thing the politicians wanted. Their interests were best served by a system open to their personal intervention and manipulation, a fact which had important consequences for police discipline.

The nature of police work made discipline a major problem. Policemen usually worked alone or in small groups, and there were endless opportunities for them to spend their time in saloons rather than on patrol, or to shake down peddlers and small businessmen, or to be too free with their clubs in dealing with drunks and rowdy juveniles. Supervisors interested in raising the level of police performance, or at least seeing that patrolmen remained on post, had limited means at their disposal. By the end of the nineteenth century, the New York department had a thick book of rules. It prescribed in minute detail proper methods of patrolling and making reports. Anyone guilty of violating the rules could be brought before the commissioners, and if found guilty punished in some way.

However, the statutes governing police tenure stated that policemen could be removed from the department only for cause and that there had to be a hearing on the charges brought against them. The courts interpreted this hearing broadly, making it a quasi-judicial procedure in which policemen had the right of being represented by counsel and one which the courts could review both as to fact and procedure. And when policemen began to have a percentage of their salaries deducted for the pension fund in the 1890s, the courts took this to give them a vested interest in their jobs and therefore restricted removals even further to protect that interest. Occasionally the commissioners removed a man from the department only to have the courts reinstate him, sometimes with back pay. After the Lexow inquiry and the election of a reform administration, Theodore Roosevelt and others tried to get a police reorganization bill which would allow the commissioners to remove men from the department without court review. The police fought this successfully; they were convinced that court review alone protected them against arbitrary and capricious administrators.[21]

A policeman under charges could invoke other defenses before matters ever reached the stage of court review. Like ambitious men, erring officers also sought the company and support of powerful politicians to protect themselves. The career of Alexander "Clubber" Williams is again relevant. By 1887 Williams had had 358 formal complaints lodged against him for a variety of offenses, ranging from neglect of duty to gross corruption and brutality. The commissioners had fined him 224 times. But Williams never suffered any major penalty because of the strength of his political connections. He and his friends beat back attempts by grand juries and others to remove him from the department. The same report which totaled the charges and fines against him also announced his promotion from captain to inspector. With the four-man board, if a police officer under charges could secure the votes of two of the commissioners he was safe. Two commissioners once voted for Williams' removal from the force, but he had the two supporters he needed to remain in office. In 1895 the reform-minded Roosevelt board forced him to resign. One of Williams' subordinates had testified against him before the Lexow Committee, and he decided not to fight.[22]

Commissioners and administrators relied on fines to punish breaches of discipline. Fines often hurt the policeman's family more than anyone else, while for the major grafter they could be written off as a minor cost of doing business. In some departments administrators punished policemen more often for violation of the rules than they did for crimes like assault or blackmail. On the administrators' side, it was easier to make a case for rule violation than for other offenses, and such a charge did not involve serious morale questions. Charging a policeman who had used his club with assault would bring all his colleagues to his defense, whereas fining him a day's pay for a rule violation would not pose such a threat.[23]

While departments often had strong internal rivalries and factions,

whether political, religious, ethnic, or personal, members banded
together against any outside attack. In New York, policemen committed perjury as a matter of course to protect each other against
civilian complaints. A policeman accused by a civilian of some
transgression could usually find a brother officer willing to swear that
he was somewhere else or doing something else. In order to maintain the morale of their organizations, supervisors usually accepted
a policeman's word before a civilian's, although many policemen
believed that they could not expect justice in disciplinary proceedings.[24]

Under the best of circumstances, on-the-street supervision was a
difficult business. Supervision and supervising the supervisors could
generate more distrust and ill will than positive benefits. In New York,
roundsmen had the responsibility to see that the patrolmen were
really patrolling, but how was one to know that the roundsman was
doing his job? One method was to count the number of complaints
he made against patrolmen, and patrolmen often believed that the
roundsman "dropped one" on them just to keep the captain off his
back, just as a contemporary motorist thinks himself the victim of
some sort of numbers game when he gets a ticket. A particularly
hated instrument of supervision was the "shoo-fly," a man sent out
in civilian clothes to check on the performance of the patrolmen.
When Theodore Roosevelt served as a police commissioner in New
York in the 1890s, he made a good many trips through the streets
at night with his friend, the reporter Jacob Riis. Those patrolmen
they found in the saloons rather than on the streets had to appear
at headquarters in the morning.[25]

Close supervision of one sort or another might keep policemen on
the streets; whether it could solve the problems of discipline and
evaluation is something else. Closer supervision might eliminate
some of the more flagrant derelictions of duty, but as in most work
situations the closer the supervision, the more concern the worker
has for satisfying the supervisor than for doing his job. In too many
instances policemen adopted the position that when under close
supervision and a bulky book of rules the easiest way to stay out
of trouble was to do nothing. The standard became the avoidance
of error rather than doing a good job.[26]

There are still major problems in setting and maintaining standards of quality control for functions such as policing and teaching. Can a supervisor rate a patrolman by the number of arrests that he makes or a teacher by the scores students make on standardized exams? In both cases an attempt to apply such a standard could easily lead to frustrating the purposes for which police forces and schools exist. A large number of unnecessary arrests would not keep the peace peacefully, just as concern only for exam scores induces rigid and mechanical teaching; both, however, would give the supervisor some quantitative measure, even if neither measures anything very useful. In policing, teaching, and a number of other service occupations and professions, evaluation depends on a variety of imprecise and not very satisfactory indicators and ultimately rests upon the judgment of those responsible for making the evaluation. But at the turn of the century a great many citizens did not trust either the intelligence or goodwill of police administrators, and the result was the spread of civil service procedures for police appointments and promotions.

Chapter 5

Civil Service, Municipal Reform, and Urban Police

Civil service reform was the great cause of upstanding middle- and upper-middle-class men in the late nineteenth century. From the 1870s on, patrician reformers struggled to outlaw the spoils system of political appointments. They hated the "low politician" and the political machine and wanted to restore respectability and their own kind to the conduct of municipal government. Their great watchwords were honesty, efficiency, and business government. They were fond of saying that there was no Democratic or Republican way to clean the streets or manage a police department—just an efficient or inefficient one.[1]

The reformers conceived of the city as a corporation responsible for the provision of certain services and believed that municipal governments should be rated as to how effectively they provided them and at what cost in taxes. Like most people they wanted a high level of service and low taxes, although many of them had a quite restricted view of what cities should provide their citizens. The business minded wanted those services that most directly aided their enterprises or increased their level of security and well-being, like good fire and police protection; they did not approve of cities embarking on a wider range of social services for the less well-to-do.

To achieve these goals they wanted to end the traditional ties between office holders and political district leaders by making appointments on the basis of competitive examinations rather than political endorsement. They wanted an educated and disinterested civil service. The patricians strenuously objected to the fact that New York and other cities were being run by men who talked out of the sides of their mouths. They wanted to sever the relations between police, politicians, and saloon and brothel keepers. Aspirants for public jobs who had to pass examinations were more likely to share reformers' values or at least so the latter believed. Such applicants would have more formal education, more concern for the public interest, and think about the city as a whole rather than their own section of it. In a word they would share the view that public office was a public trust. On police the reformers stressed the impartial administration of justice and even-handed enforcement of the law. They wanted to curb patronage appointments, assignments, and promotions and to make police departments stand for the moral imperatives of middle-class American Protestantism.[2]

The first tentative steps toward fulfilling these aims came in the 1880s, when a number of departments introduced civil service procedures for appointments and promotions. The politicians, however, found ways to circumvent the civil service laws and to retain their traditional influence in appointments. Written tests were often of the essay type to give the examiners the widest latitude in grading, and the medical and physical exams could be and were carried out in a discriminatory fashion, with special consideration given to those who had political support. One man in New York who had been rejected twice for syphilis passed on the third try, and candidates sometimes grew miraculously to reach the minimum height. In New York prospective policemen could secure application blanks from either the police commissioners or the civil service board; the chances for appointment were distinctly better for the men who originally went before the police commissioners. The last line on the examination for patrolman was a disclaimer that the applicant had not paid any money to anyone. This convinced many candidates that they were expected to pay. The civil service rules stipulated that for every open place the civil service board would certify three men from whom the police commissioners could then choose one. The commissioners were not bound by the rank order and could skip over the top man on the list, the one with the highest exam score, and choose someone lower down. In these ways, political influence and paying for promotions lasted long after the formal adoption of civil service procedures.[3]

Historians often use the term Progressive Movement for the first two decades of the twentieth century when many of the trends that had been under way since the 1880s or 1890s, such as civil service reform, reached fruition. Also by the first decade of the twentieth century, municipal reform had a broader scope. "Reform" encompassed several quite different proposals and ideas. One was simply to throw the rascals out. A second and ultimately much more important one was to change the structure of municipal government to reduce lower-class and special interests. The civil service program became intertwined with a larger program to eliminate "politics" from the government of cities, to make urban government a matter of administrative efficiency rather than political conflict. To the merit system for appointments to public office would now be added methods of choosing executives and council members that would make it more likely that they would come from the business and professional classes. Many smaller cities and towns adopted the city manager form of government where executive responsibility rested with a nonpartisan professional who was hired to run the city government, much as a corporation's board of directors engages a chief executive officer.[4]

The city manager form usually involved nonpartisan at-large elections for members of the City Council. In such an election candidates ran without traditional party labels, and the Council was elected from the city as a whole rather than having each man represent a district or ward. The purpose of at-large elections was to curb local and lower-class influences. Most lower- and lower-middle-class candidates would be known only in their respective neighborhoods; they would not have a following in other sections of the city or the credentials to appear as community-wide leaders. It would be unlikely that a Polish saloonkeeper or an Irish undertaker could win the support of a downtown newspaper as being representative of the city as a whole, whereas a lawyer or prominent businessman could have a city-wide reputation and secure newspaper endorsements.

Another popular form was the commission pattern, whereby the voters chose a number of commissioners, usually five, each of whom had responsibility for a particular function such as public health or safety. Both the city manager and the commission forms sought to end the fragmentation of power that had been characteristic of nineteenth-century city government, where mayors fought city councils and administrative boards often were independent of both. The commission form declined in popularity because unqualified people were elected as commissioners and squabbling among commissioners impaired governmental efficiency. The city manager form avoided these pitfalls and became the preferred structural innovation. Reformers believed that the political machines had developed at least in part because of the diffusion of power and responsibility and that the machines performed a useful function of coordination but in an underhanded way that subverted the ends of good government. Their goal was simultaneously to get coordination to fix power and responsibility, and to avoid government by party organizations, professional politicians, and the lower class. Structural transformation stressing administrative responsibility and nonpartisan at-large elections hopefully would accomplish these ends and make respectable and impartial law enforcement and police administration more likely.

The elites who supported these structural changes often spoke of achieving greater democracy by taking government away from the party organizations and the professional politicians and restoring it to "the people." But "the people" is an abstraction, and when we go behind the rhetoric to look at the impact of these structural devices, we see that they were often anything but democratic, if by democracy we mean a system of government in which the voices of all men and all groups have a good chance to be heard.

While the structural reformers may have talked about democracy, they were often more interested in efficiency, honesty, businesslike government, and fearless and impartial law enforcement, which were the last things many of the people wanted. Efficiency and businesslike government might mean cutting the public payroll, increasing the work load, and decreasing the job security of municipal employees. Thorough law enforcement could mean no beer on Sunday, and impartiality would destroy the value of contacts and connections. The elites valued centralization and distrusted localism. They wanted uniform standards for schools and police precincts throughout the city and had little patience with the neighborhood and block focus common among the lower classes. Centralizers deplored the fragmentation and the difficulties in getting any city-wide action inherent in a locally oriented political system. Cleveland, with its thirty-three wards and council members for a city of less than 800,000 people, is a classic contemporary example. Proponents also claimed that these structural changes would enable citizens to have more direct influence on government, that no longer would the political machines come between people and government. Supporters of the bosses, on the other hand, viewed them as mediators rather than roadblocks.

As a general rule this new pattern of urban government was more likely to be found in smaller and more homogeneous cities where the newspapers and the chamber of commerce could claim to speak for most of the politically aware and articulate people. Larger and more diverse cities resisted these changes. The big city, say over 250,000 people, was more likely to have a diversity of classes and ethnic groups among its population. The census reports showed that the larger cities, with some exceptions such as Los Angeles, consistently had a higher percentage of foreign born than did most smaller cities. Big cities had more of a two-party tradition than smaller cities, which tended to be Republican in the North and Democratic in the South. The metropolises of the nation had more complex class structures and probably more overt class consciousness than did smaller communities, where the rhetoric and the conception, if not the reality, of a classless society tended to be more prevalent.

For these reasons, therefore, most big cities continued to use the mayor-council form of government and ward elections which made more provision for local interests and allowed the political arena to serve as the vehicle for the reconciliation of conflict. City councils, elected by districts, would have to reach some sort of accommodation between those areas which wanted more policemen and those which wanted a park instead and would have to balance the competing demands upon the city's resources.[5]

Some of the larger cities did make basic changes in their charters during these years. An elite group in 1909 pushed through a new charter for Pittsburgh which severely restricted local influence and increased the power of the upper-middle class in the city's government. Two years later a similar change was made in the city's school system. Detroit in 1917 adopted a new charter which created a much smaller council and again one with a predominantly upper-middle-class membership. Los Angeles had a small council, elected at large. Some big cities, like Cincinnati and Cleveland, even adopted the city manager system, although Cleveland later gave it up.

The more usual form of charter change for the big cities was the achievement of home rule by which the cities could write their own charters and thus be free from some of the more outrageous practices of the state legislatures in the nineteenth century. However, as the normal processes of urban growth now led to a considerable number of people and jobs moving out beyond the political boundaries of the city, home rule proved to be a mixed blessing since it allowed independent suburbs to resist annexation to the central city. Suburbanites could thus enjoy some of the advantages of the metropolitan area while escaping some of the liabilities. This trend was well recognized before the first World War.[6]

Even where charters remained basically unchanged, cities still felt the impulse of urban reform movements. The civil service system became stronger and less open to partisan manipulation than it had been in the 1890s. This is not to say that the system succeeded in isolating completely the politician from the appointment process; it did not, but in many cities the parties did have less influence in staffing the public service.

Experts and observers of police administration thought the civil service system of some value as far as initial appointments were concerned; they did, however, question whether most departments had a sufficiently long and sufficiently rigorous probation period. For the first six months or year of service a policeman could be removed from the department if he showed his unfitness for the position, but most departments did not weed out those who lacked the qualities necessary to be good policemen. In later years organized police associations made removal even during the probationary period difficult if not impossible.[7]

The biggest weakness of the civil service system came in regard to promotions. How did one test for leadership qualities? How much weight should one give to academic abilities in looking for a police commander? How much emphasis should be given to experience? Did a man with fifteen years as a patrolman deserve a higher rating for promotion than a man with ten years' experience? What provision should be made for a spectacular arrest or an individual act of heroism? Should one "good collar" outweigh five years of keeping a beat peaceful? We shall return to some of these questions as they raise basic issues about the nature and function of police work as a whole. Our present purpose is to consider them in relation to the public faith and trust in police administrators.

Most major cities made competitive examinations a primary determinant in promotions. New York required examinations for all uniformed ranks except chief, although later promotion exams stopped at the rank of captain. Some cities chose even their chief by competitive exam. Observers such as Raymond Fosdick, who studied a number of police departments in both this country and Europe, contended that this system put a premium on test taking, not on the ability to do the job. It seems almost self-evident that the only way one can tell whether or not people can do a job is to set them to doing it and then watch their performance. By this reasoning those best qualified to judge a man's administrative potential would be those with whom and for whom he worked. A promotion policy resting upon judgments by superiors and colleagues implies that this judgment can be trusted, that it is informed and not swayed by extraneous considerations.

But trust is precisely what was lacking. Reformers and citizens generally believed that too many police commanders were influenced more by political affiliation, religious and ethnic ties, and money than they were by a professionally sound assessment of another's capabilities. For this reason the lawmakers limited the administrator's freedom of action by substituting the judgment of the makers and graders of examinations for his. Despite the letter of the law, political influence remained strong in promotions, even more so than in initial appointments. Police commanders exercised too much power in too many sensitive areas for outsiders to be indifferent about them, and politicians and others constantly sought to get "their" policemen promotions and the right assignments.[8]

During this period of the structural transformation of American municipal government most cities abolished their police boards in favor of a single administrator. The single head, whether called commissioner, safety director, or chief of police, would provide the fusion of responsibility and authority for the police that progressives thought essential for all government agencies. Throughout the last two decades of the nineteenth century, mayors, commissioners, and others connected with the New York Police Department argued that the department required one commissioner rather than the hydra-headed board. The board, especially the bipartisan one, impeded rapid and decisive action and made the whole process of reward and punishment a matter of elephantine balance of conflicting political influences. Those dissatisfied with police performance believed that power and responsibility had to be conferred upon one man, and that only a single commissioner responsible to the mayor could maintain an honest and efficient force. To make this change more palatable to the party organizations, they coupled this proposal with one to establish a separate board of elections which would exercise the controversial powers over the election process and reduce the police function to preserving order at the polls.

The change to a single commissioner came only after repeated police scandals and sensational investigations such as those conducted by the state legislature's Lexow and Mazet committees. In 1898 a Tammany mayor and members of the police board combined with pliable Republicans to force out an honest chief of police in favor of one of the great scoundrel cops of New York history, Bill Devery. In 1900 and 1901 independent investigators found systematic police protection of prostitution on the Lower East Side, where the prostitutes used children to pass out their business cards and men could hardly walk through the streets without being accosted and almost assaulted. One independent raid on a gambling house turned up a number of prominent players, including a police captain. In this atmosphere the legislature in 1901 abolished the police board and substituted a single commissioner, appointed by the mayor for a term of five years but who could be removed either by the mayor or the governor of the state.[9]

In ensuing years other cities abandoned the board for a single administrator. Boston made the change in 1906, Cleveland and Cincinnati in 1908, Birmingham in 1911, Omaha in 1912, St. Paul in 1914, and Buffalo in 1916. By 1920 only fourteen of fifty-two cities of more than 100,000 people which at one time had boards governing the police retained them.[01]

With the passing of the boards, American police forces were administered either by professional chiefs of police who had risen through the ranks or nonprofessional commissioners. In small and middle-sized cities the professional chief sufficed, while the larger cities also had a civilian commissioner or safety director whose powers varied from that of general supervision to actual command of the force.

Leonhard Fuld, whose *Police Administration* appeared in 1909, and Raymond Fosdick, who published *European Police Systems* in 1914 and *American Police Systems* in 1920, contrasted unfavorably the American system of choosing heads of police with the European. In Europe, especially England and Germany, police administration was an honored and respected career which attracted university graduates and former army officers. In both countries the head never came from the rank and file; administration was thought of as a demanding office which required a broader education and point of view than could be found among policemen. The model was that of the army, which recruited its officer corps separately from its enlisted men. The class stratification implied in such a procedure did not bother scholars and reformers who were convinced that the basic problems of American municipal government derived from the lack of formal education and respectable social standing among politicians and office holders.

Fuld and Fosdick wanted police heads to be professionals who could command the respect of the community and who would administer their departments with a concern for the values of integrity and impartial law enforcement. If such men held the reins of power they could be trusted with broad and essentially unfettered control over their subordinates. Fosdick emphasized the care with which European cities chose their police heads and then the security of tenure and the high prestige, salary, and status that they enjoyed.[11]

American cities, on the other hand, suffered from poor appointments, often politically motivated, and a resulting lack of public faith and trust. The chiefs who came up through the ranks rarely transcended the quality of their respective departments. While they might have the value of long experience and know the policeman's art, they often had limited administrative ability. Too many chiefs were simply fifty-five-year-old patrolmen. These chiefs allocated manpower on a kind of hit-or-miss basis and had little sense of how to delegate authority to keep themselves from being buried in routine. The civilian commissioners generally were nonprofessionals who served for limited terms and could be and were removed with each change in political fortune.[12]

Some chiefs and commissioners did manage to rise above mediocrity and routine and make a significant personal impact upon their respective departments. Often they were able to do so because of the support they received from mayors who themselves were men of great ability and innovative persuasion. Two examples of heads who did manage to have substantial influence on their organizations are Commissioner Arthur Woods of New York and Chief Fred Kohler of Cleveland.

Woods came to control New York's police during a reform phase of an almost cyclical pattern of Tammany control, a damaging investigation followed by a reform administration, which in turn was followed by another Tammany victory. During periods of Tammany domination, district leaders like Tim Sullivan of the Bowery made the key decisions on police. Repeated investigations disclosed a systematic involvement of the police with the underworld and its Tammany overlords. These investigations led to reform movements which occasionally unseated Tammany but only for one term. In 1894 the Lexow inquiry triggered a union, or fusion as it was usually called, of anti-Tammany groups which elected William L. Strong, a respectable Republican businessman, as mayor. Strong made Theodore Roosevelt one of the members of the police board. Similar revelations of corruption in the Tammany-dominated department in 1899 and 1901 brought about the replacement of the board by a single commissioner and the election of another reform mayor in Seth Low.

Low, a stiff and unbending man who had previously been mayor of Brooklyn and president of Columbia University, appointed to high positions men listed in the social register and generally viewed his job as cleaning house. When he ran for reelection in 1903, his opponents carried signs, "To Hell with Reform." As one shrewd Tammany man put it, many of the voters didn't like corruption but they couldn't stand reform.

Enforcing the law meant restricting behavior many people thought harmless, and here was the great dilemma of the reformers. How could they be true to their own standards of the sanctity of the law without making themselves thoroughly unpopular? How could they try to modify the letter of the law, which decreed the Sunday closing of saloons, without opening the way to systematic police bribery and corruption? When they did try to clean house, they alienated enough voters to bring Tammany back. And when Tammany returned so too did the old pattern of police performance, with some modifications. Charles F. Murphy, who became leader of Tammany in 1902, realized that spectacular police scandal was dysfunctional, that it aroused and combined Tammany's enemies and made reform victories possible. Murphy tried to keep police graft within acceptable limits, but he did not always succeed.[13]

In 1912 a major police scandal erupted with the murder of gambling house proprietor Herman Rosenthal and the involvement of Lieutenant Charles Becker in the case. Becker was the head of one of the vice or strongarm squads, so-called because much of their activity consisted of putting axes through the locked doors of suspected gambling houses. This position gave Becker great power over the proprietors, who had to pay to remain unmolested. Sporadic police raids served as a collection device, a reminder to the gamblers that they had best pay their dues promptly. Rosenthal had paid for protection and subsequently was raided in spite of the promise of immunity. Rosenthal then talked to District Attorney Charles Whitman. In July 1912 he was shot late one night in front of a hotel by four young gunmen known as Gyp the Blood, Whitey Lewis, Dago Frank, and Lefty Louie. Whitman used the testimony of underworld characters like Bald Jack Rose to link Becker with the slaying. In an incredible trial conducted before Judge John Goff, who in 1894 had been the counsel of the Lexow Committee, Becker was found guilty of plotting the murder and hiring the gunmen. The Court of Appeals set aside the conviction because of Goff's intensely prejudicial conduct of the case. Goff hated crooked cops and seemed intent on railroading Becker. Whitman did not give up and succeeded in convicting Becker in a second trial. The newspaperman Herbert Bayard Swope played a major role in keeping public opinion aroused against Becker.

Whitman's reputation as a crusading district attorney put him in the governor's chair, so Becker's appeal for clemency from the death sentence resulting from the trial prosecuted by District Attorney Charles Whitman came before Governor Charles Whitman. Not surprisingly, Whitman rejected the appeal and Becker was executed on July 30, 1915. There is a strong possibility that Becker was framed; Whitman's case rested upon the testimony of people whose credibility was suspect, to put it softly, and it required an exceptionally willing suspension of disbelief to accept some of the tales told in court.[14]

The case generated an investigation of the entire police department conducted by the Curran Committee of the Board of Aldermen, whose revelations helped spark another fusion movement, which elected John Purroy Mitchel as mayor in the fall of 1913.

Mitchel, still in his early thirties, was a typical reformer in his upper-middle-class orientation and his concern for efficiency. He believed that if city government were sufficiently honest and efficient there would be no need and no future for the Tammany-style machine. How remote this view was from the perspective of many of the voters became apparent in 1917, when Mitchel lost his bid for reelection despite an unprecedented campaign expenditure of more than a million dollars.

When he entered office in January 1914, he regarded the police commissionership as his most important and most difficult appointment. He tried to get Colonel George Goethals, the army engineer who had supervised the building of the Panama Canal, to take the job. Goethals said that he would consider accepting only if the commissioner had absolute power to remove members of the department without court review and to promote promising younger officers more rapidly. Mitchel then had introduced into the state legislature the so-called Goethals Bills to abolish court review and shorten the time in grade required for promotion.

The issue of court review highlighted the tense state of the relations between the police and the reformers. The police always looked upon the reformers as their implacable foes. The reformers' insistence on clear lines of authority and responsibility limited the policeman's ability to find alternate channels to get what he wanted. If his superior would not grant a desired transfer voluntarily, he might do so if enough political pressure were applied. Absolute power of removal in the rule-ridden department would reduce a policeman's job security and, if Tammany returned to power, would give the district leaders and the spoilsmen unparalleled power over the police. Moreover the reformers' insistence on no graft would eliminate what many policemen considered legitimate sources of income. So the police fought the Goethals Bills vigorously and managed to preserve court review of attempted removals from the department. For similar reasons policemen also opposed complete home rule for New York City. They wanted to keep lines open in Albany so that if they ran into stormy weather in City Hall they would have an alternative haven.[15]

Goethals did not accept Mitchel's offer and the mayor turned to Arthur Woods as his police commissioner. Woods, a Harvard graduate, had taught at Groton School and previously served as a deputy police commissioner. Woods gave the New York Police Department one of its best administrations from 1914 to 1917. He was an able man and he had the support of the mayor. Neither Woods nor anyone else could ever eliminate completely police graft and corruption, but he did keep it to a minimum.[16]

In 1918, after he left police headquarters, Woods delivered a series of lectures at Yale, subsequently published under the title *Policeman and Public*, which give an excellent picture of his conceptions of police administration.[17] This little book is still worth reading for anyone who wants to understand the nature of police work in the United States and the difficulties of carrying out that work. Woods viewed the function of the administrator as training and motivating his men to keep the public interest foremost. To most citizens and most policemen, the public interest was a rather nebulous concept and one that could easily be lost sight of in the welter of conflicting private interests. It was in the public interest that sidewalks be kept free of snow and ice, but a patrolman could easily justify not issuing a warning or summons to someone he liked or who was generous at Christmas. Later perhaps someone else might break a leg because of that unshoveled sidewalk.

Such an incident is only a minor example of the constant judgments policemen were called upon to make. Should a man carrying a parcel at 3:00 A.M. be made to identify himself and disclose the contents to the man on the beat? What does a policeman do when someone comes shouting in the street that he has been robbed and demands that a man nearby be arrested? How does a policeman interpret the prohibition against builders' obstructing the sidewalks or streets? Too often policemen decided that the safest course of action was to do nothing, to avoid the possibility of a mistake and ensuing disciplinary action. In regulatory situations some men used the letter of the law to conduct shakedowns, such as making builders pay for the privilege of violating the letter of the law on obstructed sidewalks. It was the administrator's job to encourage policemen to take positive action when the public interest required it and to restrain them from abusing their regulatory power to line their own pockets. The premium then was on sound judgment for both the man on the beat and the superior.

Woods held to his position on the maintenance of the public interest in connection with police performance in political demonstrations and labor disputes. The function of the police in these situations was to keep order to protect life and property, not to take sides. As long as a strike was legal, it did not matter to the police who won. Woods' attitude, supported by Mayor Mitchel, contrasted with previous strikes where the police intervened on the side of management and acted more as strikebreakers than as impartial preservers of the peace. His policy was to let both sides know what the rules are clearly and plainly and then enforce those rules impartially. More than anything else he wanted to prevent the use of thugs and hooligans as "private detectives" in strikes and lockouts. If the police did their job, neither side should have to resort to such men, whose presence vastly increased the possibilities of violence. Similarly in political protest meetings in Union Square and elsewhere Woods avoided a massive police presence which might bring about riots. Instead he sent his men circulating through the crowds in plain clothes urging calm and attempting to radiate good cheer. Contemporary departments facing student protests could well follow this example.

In his personnel policies, Woods stressed the necessity of earning his men's respect by judging them fairly and being available to hear their legitimate grievances. It is hard to say how policemen responded to his leadership. He seemed to have the respect of a good many, but he did have difficulties with organizations like the Patrolmen's Benevolent Association and especially the Lieutenants' Benevolent Association and its president, Richard Enright. The PBA was formed in the 1890s as a quasi-labor union to agitate for salary increases, to improve working conditions, and to protect job security. Mitchel and Woods never fully accepted the legitimacy of such employee organizations. Woods wanted to deal with individual policemen who felt aggrieved; he did not want to recognize these organizations as the representatives of the rank and file. Mitchel at one point said that the organizations would have to be strictly benevolent, that

is not engage in anything resembling trade union activity in order
to continue functioning. However, he did not raise any serious objections when the associations fought the Goethals Bills in the legislature and succeeded in defeating them.[18]

To a considerable extent the PBA had become a captive of Richard
Enright's Lieutenants' Benevolent Association. Enright joined the
police department in 1896, became a roundsman in 1902, and a
sergeant in 1905. He was reported to be a favorite of William
Devery, chief of police from 1898 to 1901 and later first deputy
commissioner. In 1907 the legislature raised roundsmen to sergeants
and sergeants to lieutenants. Enright, who had been active in the
roundsmen's association, then became president of the newly formed
Police Lieutenants' Benevolent Association, an office he held until
1918, when he became police commissioner. A shrewd police politician, Enright used the lieutenants' association to keep his name
before the public and to challenge the commissioner's leadership.
The association held an annual banquet which Enright used as a
forum to attack reformers in general and reform police commissioners
in particular. Enright wanted a professional chief to be the real
director of the police rather than constantly shifting civilian commissioners who might be "theorists." According to Enright and many
other policemen, Woods' attempt to limit strongarm methods and
arrests on suspicion impaired police efficiency. The patrolmen's and
lieutenants' associations continued to lobby in the legislature to
frustrate reform legislation.

Woods and Enright crossed swords over the issue of Enright's
promotion to captain. Under the previous commissioner, Rhinelander
Waldo, Enright had served as acting captain in charge of the bureau
of repairs and supplies at police headquarters. On taking office
Woods had said that he would promote no man that he thought
unfit, and he passed over Enright for promotion three times even
though Enright had first place on the captains' list. According to the
civil service rules, a man passed over three times went to the bottom
of the list. Woods apparently objected to the scope of Enright's
political activity and the lieutenant's attempts to undermine his
leadership and the reform administration generally. Woods also
claimed that men with desk jobs had an undue advantage in pre-
paring for civil service exams in comparison with their colleagues

doing the tough work out on the streets. Many of the rank and file thought Woods' action arbitrary and contrary to the principles of the merit system, and, more important, many members of the department were more in sympathy with Enright's conception of police work and the proper role of the department than they were with Woods'.[19]

In 1917 the police benevolent associations, along with other groups of civil service employees, actively opposed Mayor Mitchel's bid for reelection and helped the Tammany candidate John "Red Mike" Hylan. When Hylan took office he made Enright his police commissioner, a post he held until 1926. Hylan and Enright ran the police department in the interest of the Tammany district leaders. Transfers, discipline, promotions, and police policy all coincided with Tammany's interests. It was not until another serious scandal, exposed by the Seabury inquiry into the police and other Tammany departments during the administration of New York's famous playboy mayor, Jimmy Walker, that the situation was reversed. Fiorello La Guardia won the mayoralty in 1933 and worked hard to transform the police.[20]

Woods' career as commissioner is an indication that a reform civilian commissioner was only as strong as the political support behind him, and that a reform movement which stressed honesty, efficiency, and thorough and impartial law enforcement was likely to find its political base eroding fast. Moreover, the relations between Woods and Enright indicated that a commissioner had no easy job establishing control over his own department. In fact in many ways this was and still is the commissioner's most difficult task.[21]

The Cleveland Police Department was less than one-tenth the size of New York's, so its administration was a much simpler matter. Fred Kohler ran the department for ten years, from 1903 to 1913, virtually unimpeded. Kohler was a different kind of police administrator than Arthur Woods, just as Cleveland's Tom Johnson was a different kind of reformer than John Purroy Mitchel. Unlike the Harvard-trained Woods, Kohler was no scholar. In today's terms he was a dropout, a tough kid, handy with his fists, who knew poverty and hardship. He held various laboring jobs until in 1889 at the age of twenty-five he used his political connections to become a policeman. During the 1890s he was closely associated with a rising

Republican, Robert McKisson, who succeeded in becoming mayor of Cleveland. Kohler rose with McKisson to become a lieutenant and later captain. He gained the reputation of being something of a wild man, a tough cop who made gamblers and brothel keepers blanch. Just as in New York, raids in Cleveland made sure that the gamblers paid the right people and gave proper political support. But a Kohler raid was no ordinary affair. He was not content simply to break into an establishment, he broke it up. Axes crashed into gilt-edged mirrors, smashed walls, and splintered furniture. The very mention of a Kohler raid brought the gamblers into line.[22]

In 1901, Democrat Tom L. Johnson won his first term as mayor of Cleveland. Johnson was a self-made millionaire from Kentucky who had developed into a thoroughgoing urban reformer. A disciple of the single-tax philosopher Henry George, Johnson had an expansive vision of what a city could be. To a greater extent than Mitchel, his conception of reform went beyond honesty and efficiency. He thought of the city in terms of the quality of life of its citizens, and he did yeoman work in spreading his philosophy of the possibilities of urban life and urban responsibility to the people of Cleveland. To him, reform was making available cheaper streetcar service, public baths and parks, promoting woman suffrage, fighting for adequate taxation of business, and working for utility franchises that would protect consumers' interests. The city was not simply a corporation for the provision of services; hopefully Cleveland could be a community that would promote the development of all of its citizens. Johnson did not conceive of the city solely as a place of individual economic opportunity, but as an organic entity which manifested its concern for social welfare and social justice.[23]

Johnson wanted the police to leave the saloons alone on Sunday; what made a few beers permissible on Saturday afternoon and immoral on Sunday? He did not want raids on gamblers and brothels; he knew that the raids served only to raise money for the police and their political masters. He wanted a police force that would concentrate on essential matters of crime and public order.[24] During his first year in office Johnson took the advice of some of his supporters who said that Republican Captain Kohler was erratic and politically untrustworthy and had him exiled to the "woods." But as time went on, the mayor came to think that maybe Kohler was the man to give him the kind of police force that he wanted. He brought Kohler back downtown as head of detectives and in 1903 made him chief of police, a post he held for the next ten years.

Kohler proved to be a controversial and tempestuous figure as chief. Despite the fact that he was a career policeman, he did not have much use for his colleagues. Sociologist John McNamara described the police as a "punishment centered bureaucracy," a description that certainly fits the Cleveland department under Kohler. He especially disliked the Irish, who made up a considerable portion of the force. He transferred a good many men out of downtown and used his favorites to spy on the other men. He returned to patrol duty all of the detectives he inherited and replaced them with his informers. The way to the chief's favor was to break the traditional policeman's code of silence and solidarity and be prepared to inform on one's fellows. He verbally flayed men whose shoes were unshined or who had grease spots on their uniforms. He gave Johnson a police force that minimized shakedowns and restricted public vice without closing the town tight. The Kohler and Johnson technique was to station a policeman in front of saloons, gambling houses, and brothels where other crimes were committed. The policemen simply asked all who were going to enter their names, addresses, and places of business. Under this policy of "police repression" there were no raids, and Cleveland's "tenderloin" steadily shrank in size during the Kohler years. The police did not bother saloons on Sunday as long as they were visibly closed—that is, their front doors were locked and the blinds drawn; Johnson and the police had no objection if the customers entered through a side door.

Kohler announced his most famous innovation, dubbed the "golden rule" policy, in December 1907. Kohler adopted a policy set by Samuel "Golden Rule" Jones, Mayor of Toledo, and his police chief, Perry Knapp, although Kohler characteristically claimed it was his original idea. Rather than arrest drunks and other minor offenders, the police were either to escort people home or let them go with a warning delivered on the street or by the desk officer in the station house. Vagrants would be taken to the city line and there deposited. Kohler defended his policy vigorously against skeptics in and out of the police department in Cleveland and before the annual meetings of the International Association of Chiefs of

Police. Policemen spent too much of their time dealing with petty offenders; the police courts threw out a good many of the cases brought before them; and an arrest for a normally law-abiding citizen could damage irreparably his reputation and well-being. The chief noted that in 1907, before the golden rule policy became operative, the police made 30,418 arrests, but that in 1908, under golden rule, the force made only 10,095 arrests. Despite this drop of 66.8 percent in the total number of arrests there were more felony arrests in 1908 than there had been in 1907, 1,000 to 938. The police had more time to concentrate on major matters, and the good citizen who happened to have too much to drink did not suffer unduly because of it.[25]

Opponents of the policy responded that the police were not and could not be a reformatory agency, and that bypassing the normal correctional channels of court and workhouse eliminated these opportunities for reformation. Kohler's view that court and workhouse rarely reformed anybody seems more realistic in the light of subsequent experience. Also involved here is the question of how much discretion the police should exercise. One of Kohler's critics, W. J. Norton, took the position that the police should not attempt to discriminate between incidental or habitual offenders or between those violators who should be escorted home and those who should be arrested. His argument does not show much faith in the average policeman.[26]

> They [the police] are ignorant, untrained scavengers of the social body, and when told to occupy the pastor's post, naturally they drop the scavenger's job, sit in the pastor's chair, but do none of his work, because they can't. The plan of our government grew out of wise experience, and it seems better to allow the patrolman to carry out his special function of maintaining order, and to permit the courts to pursue their functions too, deciding upon methods of correction and feeding the machinery that grinds out the correction.

As previously noted, Kohler did not have much faith in most policemen either, but the chief, as an experienced officer, knew that no force and no individual member could make an arrest for every violation he encountered. It would be physically impossible to have complete law enforcement. Police departments as organized bodies and policemen as individuals had to set priorities and exercise discretion, and Kohler's golden rule policy amounted to a set of guidelines and standards for the exercise of that discretion in the making of judgments as to which violations merited an arrest and which did not. The chief pointed out, with considerable justice, that it would be easy for any police force to amass a large number of arrests; whether life and property would be any more secure as a result would be questionable. The President's Commission on Law Enforcement and the Administration of Justice reported in 1967 that one of the major weaknesses of American police departments was their unwillingness to make policy. They permitted discretionary situations to be guided by unexamined tradition or individual whim. Fred Kohler took the risk that so many police administrators have avoided of devising, articulating, and defending policy. He took a good bit of heat as a result, but he did improve the level of police performance in Cleveland.

Warning people out of town has a long history as an American police practice. Vagrants, prostitutes, and other undesirables have been told to get out of town or suffer arrest, or if arrested and taken before a magistrate, have been given the choice of leaving the city or undergoing a term in the workhouse. Kohler made this a group rather than an individual policy, but his practice of dumping vagrants at the city line ran into considerable opposition from the affected suburbs, East Cleveland and Lakewood. Often vagrants discharged from the Cleveland wagons were loaded into East Cleveland's and driven back to Cleveland's Public Square. One group of unfortunates made the trip four times in one day.

Kohler carried on a number of running feuds during his years as chief. Theoretically the chief reported to the board of public safety, which by Ohio's uniform municipal code of 1902 consisted of two men, one from each of the major parties, appointed by the mayor with approval of two-thirds of Council. Matthew B. Excell, the Democratic member of the board, had no use for Kohler and would have liked to restrict his authority; but Mayor Johnson supported the chief, who exercised the major powers of discipline and transfer over the force. For years Kohler carried on a verbal fencing match with Police Prosecutor and later Judge Manuel Levine. The conflict could almost be anticipated because of their respective roles; the chief complained the courts did not back up the police, and the judge thought the police highhanded and arbitrary. Moreover, Levine had come to this country as an adolescent; by dint of hard work and study he became an attorney, but he never lost his sympathy for the poor and the oppressed, a sympathy Kohler did not share despite his own youthful experience with deprivation.

In 1910, a difficult year politically for the chief, Levine managed to embarrass Kohler mightily. The great Tom Johnson lost the mayoralty in 1909 to an unimpressive but popular Republican, Herman Baehr, and politicians wondered how Kohler, who although a Republican had been so close to Johnson, would fare. Apparently Kohler's enemies worked for Baehr in the campaign. The chief had civil service protection and could be removed only for cause by the civil service commission. Kohler opened the door by a speech he gave at the police chiefs' meeting in Birmingham, Alabama, in May 1910. The chief intelligently analyzed the failure of correctional institutions to do any reforming and the evils that flowed from the indiscriminate mixing of prisoners. Judge Levine was impressed by the speech, many of whose phrases and sentences seemed familiar. He traced them to an article published in a sociology magazine a few years before by Roland Molyneux and showed that Kohler had simply lifted some of the article for his speech without giving any credit. The public reaction to Kohler's embarrassment led his opponents to bring a number of charges against Kohler and attempt to remove him from office. The campaign to oust Kohler had been under way for some time, but the timing of the introduction of the charges was influenced by the plagiarism disclosure. The charges ranged from drunkenness to abuse of authority to "gross immorality," but in a four-day trial the chief and his attorneys impeached the credibility of many of the prosecution witnesses—one of whom was a prostitute known as Trixie Valentine—and Kohler was vindicated.

The chief continued to make enemies within and without the police department, and his behavior grew increasingly erratic. In 1912 he was caught in compromising circumstances with the wife of a traveling salesman, and in 1913 the civil service commissioners convicted him of conduct unbecoming an officer and removed him from office. By this time his former supporters, including Mayor Newton D. Baker, decided that Kohler had to go. His career was not over. He subsequently won election as a county commissioner on a Republican ticket, and in 1921 won the mayoralty election. Theodore Roosevelt had once called Kohler the best police chief in America, an accolade he cherished until his death in 1934.[27]

Fred Kohler has been discussed at such length because his career illustrates a number of the dilemmas facing police forces in American society. He had a long tenure, ten years, he had the political backing during much of that time to run the department as he saw fit, and he had the will and the energy to take charge. Scholars and theorists of police administration such as Raymond Fosdick and August Vollmer, who was the long-time chief in Berkeley, California, stressed the need for sufficient time and political support for a police head to improve a department. In his report to President Hoover's Wickersham Commission, Vollmer argued powerfully and persuasively that the single biggest drawback to good morale and effective functioning of American police departments lay in the short and uncertain tenure of the chief administrator. The chief had to know police business thoroughly, so he should be a professional rather than a civilian; he should know his city to make sound decisions about different policies required in different areas; and he should know his department to separate the good men from the grafters who knew how to make things look good, and to be able to make proper promotions. Passing over a good man in favor of a plausible second-rater could soon destroy a department's morale.[28]

But what of the problems of police despotism, of the arrogance of power? Certainly many of Fred Kohler's subordinates thought themselves the victims of arbitrary transfers and disciplinary actions. What happened to the names and addresses that policemen collected outside brothels and gambling houses? Kohler was Cleveland's best known man-about-town in his years as chief, and a veteran reporter said that as far as he knew Kohler never paid for a drink, a meal, or a theater ticket. When the former chief died in 1934, he left a safety deposit box with close to half a million dollars worth of bonds and other securities. If the chief were granted the power to control the force as Vollmer urged, what was to prevent him from using that power to advance his own financial and political interests? Even if a man were scrupulously honest, security of tenure might breed insensitivity to the needs and problems of others and encourage him to believe in his own infallibility. For these reasons many Americans insisted that the police head not have this sort of power and autonomy. The police were necessary, but they could not be allowed to become autonomous; they had to be carefully watched so that they would not become instruments of despotism.

Vollmer's proposal assumed an agreement on the proper functions and role of the police, but this is precisely what did not exist. The people of large and diverse cities differed strongly on what constituted correct police performance. Ministers and church-goers had one conception; gamblers and sporting men another. The police did not have a unified constituency which had clear expectations of what the police were supposed to do, and most big city departments had to try to thread their way through a maze of conflicting pressures. Close the saloons on Sunday, leave them open, shut the gamblers down, keep the conventioneers happy, run the prostitutes out of town, have girls available—these were the contradictory messages the police received.[29]

How could a chief or commissioner operate like a stable professional in such a situation? In many cities, political campaigns often turned on the role of the police; and a new mayor usually meant a new commissioner or chief. In those cities where the mayor had absolute power of appointment and removal of the commissioner or chief, the kind of man he put at the head of the police told a good bit about his political beliefs and associations. It indicated whether he wanted a clean administration—no graft—or whether he was more concerned about the needs of the political organization and its underworld connections; whether he was prepared to try to suppress vice or accept it as inevitable.

The reformers' conception of good government as the outgrowth of the concentration of power and responsibility held true only if they controlled key positions. When a Richard Enright succeeded an Arthur Woods, the interests of Tammany district leaders took precedence over other considerations. The structural reforms of civil service rules and revamped administrative structures could satisfy the reformers' aspirations only in homogeneous communities or where a single interest predominated. Otherwise, centralized control would shift back and forth in its orientation depending upon the relative electoral fortunes of bosses and reformers. The legal authority employed by Arthur Woods to shape up the department was used by Richard Enright for quite different purposes.

Moreover, administrative initiative and civil service protection for the rank and file were incompatible. Policemen of various ranks could ride out demands for innovation knowing that reform commissioners seldom lasted very long. Tammany's George Washington Plunkitt referred to reformers as "morning glories" who wilted or faded away in the heat of day. Plunkitt and his fellows put in more than a full day every day. They were in politics as a business and a way of life.[30] So too were policemen constants. Politicians and policemen knew they would spend their active years in sustained contact and that reformers threatened the self-interest of both. While civil service procedures reduced some of the politician's power over the policeman's working life, they also reduced policemen's receptivity to reform leadership. Increasingly, the police could follow their own lead, independent both of the party organizations and innovative administrators. They did not achieve complete autonomy, at least before World War II. Overall they remained more closely tied to the political organizations than to reform aspirations, especially in those cities which did not adopt the structural devices of the progressives.

Policemen, politicians, saloonkeepers, and gamblers formed part of the same social world. Sometimes they spent their boyhood years together, with some members of boys' gangs becoming policemen and others bookies' runners. Even where such prior contacts did not exist, cops found that the civilians most ready to associate with them socially were those in the rackets.[31] The retirement dream of more than one policeman was to own a saloon in a drinking man's neighborhood. Such men would pursue numbers bankers, horse parlor operators, and saloonkeepers open on Sunday reluctantly if at all. The imposition of prohibition created the widest gap in our history between the formal demands of the law and the behavioral patterns of the majority of urban people and policemen alike.

Chapter 6

Alcohol and Other Drugs

In recent years historians have taken another look at prohibition and concluded that it was not simply the result of the envy of the "boobs of the Bible Belt"—as satirist H. L. Mencken would put it—who refused to let the cosmopolitan urban population have any fun. An integral part of the Progressive Movement, prohibition was interlocked with many of the diverse attempts at political and social regeneration of the first twenty years of the twentieth century. For those who wanted clean government, eliminating the saloon would eliminate a big source of political corruption. Saloonkeepers poisoned municipal politics by bribing policemen to let them violate the law, by getting potential voters drunk, by acting as ward heelers and recruiters for political machines, and by undermining the virtues of sobriety and right thinking.[1]

The reformers' concern for efficiency in government paralleled a major movement for efficiency in business and in education. The theory of scientific management associated with the engineer and productivity expert Frederick Taylor stressed control of costs and precise measurement of output. Taylor wished to increase workers' efficiency and improve them morally by providing superior rewards for superior service, thereby encouraging diligence and self-control. A drunken worker could not be an efficient worker, and as machinery became more complex and expensive, employers demanded sobriety among their labor forces. The most famous example was the railroad rule that forbade the consumption of alcohol by workers on the job. Increasingly, managers wanted workers who did not drink off the job either. Businessmen were divided on the merits of prohibition, but the spread of workmen's compensation and employer liability laws increased the number who wanted to ban alcohol, at least for the working classes.

Some settlement house workers and social reformers supported prohibition because of their firsthand knowledge of the ravages of alcohol abuse on the lives and families of the poor. Social progressives wanted to improve the quality of family life and to give maximum opportunity for a better life to the children of the slums. A drunken husband and father or a gin-soaked mother condemned the family to poverty and degradation and almost guaranteed that the children would reproduce the life style of their parents. Some of the progressives realized that alcoholism might be the *result* of poverty and the slum environment as much as cause, and they argued that improving the quality of life would curb drunkenness. But because it was easier to go after symptoms than root causes, many social reformers supported prohibition as one step in their drive to make possible a better life for all.

Finally, there was the religious argument, especially strong among evangelical Protestant groups like the Baptists and Methodists. The use of alcohol was not only sin in itself, it also encouraged the commission of other sins such as adultery, fornication, gambling, and theft. Whole libraries of lurid subliterature predicted degradation and disgrace for any young man or woman who tasted liquor. The girls were doomed to ruin and the boys to be profligates and degenerates. It is easy to satirize some of the arguments used, but one must take seriously the depth of the belief that alcohol was incompatible with respectability and the good life, in the traditional Protestant rather than the *Playboy* sense.

There *was* an element of paternalism and repression in Progressivism in general and prohibition in particular. People were to be made to be decent, to conform to the role patterns of a society dominated by the values of hard work and deferred gratification. If exhortation and education did not get men to give up alcohol, then the law would have to be invoked. For many of the prohibitionists, the use of the law provided a way of validating their own values, of proving to themselves that what they believed was right. If the law and their own values coincided, this was proof that all right-thinking people condemned the same evils.[2]

Prohibition has sometimes been treated as a rural-versus-urban contest, with prohibitionist sentiment found in the countryside and small towns, while the large cities were wet. It is more accurate to conceive of the prohibition controversy as a struggle of social classes. The prohibitionist sentiment was strongest among middle-class evangelical Protestants, who made up a larger proportion of rural areas and small towns than they did of big cities. Wet strength lay in the numerically small upper classes who looked upon a meal without wine as a sign of barbarism and in the great immigrant masses to whom alcohol was an integral part of life. These groups, the highest and lowest social levels (excluding blacks who were systematically barred from the political process), made their homes in the large cities. Los Angeles had a very small percentage of foreign born for a large city in 1910—its population was heavily native American middle class—and Los Angeles was the only large city outside the South to vote in favor of prohibition. Within cities, peripheral areas where the more prosperous lived voted against saloons; the downtown and immediately adjacent areas where the bulk of the poor and the foreign born resided were towers of wet strength.[3]

Big cities, with their complex division of labor and high degree of specialization, were almost inevitably diverse and heterogeneous. In many ways, it was easier for the immigrants to cope with this diversity and heterogeneity than it was for the native-born middle class, which was accustomed to equating its views with the official ones, to seeing its values as universally valid. Many middle-class urbanites came from small towns where the old Puritan tradition of communal responsibility for individual behavior remained alive. To be indifferent to another's moral behavior was a breach of the covenant which should bind men together. Some immigrants wished to become assimilated into American society as quickly as possible. For other immigrants, society as a whole was either an abstraction or an arena. They lived their family and intimate social lives within the confines of the ethnic group and asked only that they be let alone to follow their traditions and build their institutions. When they went into the larger community it was to wrest a living from the social arena. They did not expect that all men shared their values; they did not necessarily believe that any one moral code should control the actions of all men and all groups. All that many immigrants asked from the society as a whole was enough money to live, to earn the wherewithal to maintain their group life and identity. In such a context, the prohibitionists' attempt to deny them the use of alcohol and close their saloons was an insult.[4]

For immigrants and workers generally, the saloon performed a complex of functions. It was a place to drown one's sorrows; it provided the forum for sociability; it served as a primitive labor exchange where men learned of job openings; and with the political clubhouse the saloon functioned as a meeting place where a man in trouble with or in need of something from government could find someone who could do something about it.[5]

Despite the opposition of the upper and lower classes, the Protestant middle class and the Progressives (there was considerable overlapping between the two categories) generated enough political strength to make prohibition part of the United States Constitution. After a series of triumphs on the local and state level, the prohibitionists decided to press for a national amendment and, in the circumstances of World War I with its extraordinary hatred of Germany and things German, succeeded in passing the eighteenth amendment. The great brewers almost invariably had German names and striking a blow against the liquor power could also be striking a blow against the Huns, as Allied propaganda referred to Germans in World War I.[6]

What doomed prohibition was the overwhelming evidence of the impossibility of enforcing it, and a significant change in the behavior pattern of the respectable middle class. During the 1920s many of the urban middle class abandoned the full range of beliefs and practices of the Protestant ethic. Social historians have noted the change of sexual mores, at least in the literature and movies of the decade, with the decline of the double standard and the demand of many women for a new sexual role. In the 1920s the image of the flapper was hardly that of staid housewife and mother of a large brood of children. The surplus of goods and the spread of advertising encouraged an atmosphere of consumption rather than simply production. Hard work seemed less its own reward, and movie stars replaced successful businessmen or achievers in the arts as popular heroes. For many of the middle class, alcohol came to be thought of as a touchstone of a sophisticated and smart way of life. The fact that prohibition made drinking deliciously illegal added to the attractions of alcohol. The depression which set in after 1929 turned people's attention away from the possibilities of moral perfection and toward the necessity of economic survival. Proponents of repeal claimed that bringing back beer and whiskey would end the depression, economically as well as psychologically. As a result of these social changes, prohibition lost a considerable part of its constituency, and the eighteenth amendment gave way to the twenty-first amendment which made alcohol legal again.[7]

Obviously, the impact of prohibition upon urban police departments was a highly significant one. American police forces had long suffered from their legal obligation to enforce unpopular laws, but never had they been charged with enforcing anything like the total prohibition of alcoholic beverages. The more unpopular the law, the more pressure on the police to ignore it, and the greater the temptation to bribery and corruption. Prohibition raised the level of corruption beyond previous levels and provided a new and very profitable business for organized crime. The great midwestern metropolis of Chicago provides the most spectacular case study of the impact of prohibition upon the relations of politicians, policemen, and illegal enterprise, in part because the vigorous reform tradition in the city assured maximum publicity for its transgressions.[8]

Chicago had a pattern of politically protected organized crime dating from the late nineteenth century. The two most profitable activities were gambling and prostitution. Those who controlled the wires from the tracks for up-to-the-minute odds and race results had a commanding position in gambling, while the chief protected prostitution area was the famous Twenty-second Street Levee. The men who ran these businesses, like Mike McDonald, Mont Tennes, James Colosimo, and John Torrio, had strong ties to local politicians and police commanders. Periodically, reform groups would generate enough pressure to bring about embarrassing investigations, sometimes at the state level. The usual response was to transfer some policemen, demote others, and crack down on vice activities through special squads. After such an upsetting interval, vice entrepreneurs, politicians, and police officers usually succeeded in reestablishing their normal and profitable relations. There was simply too much public demand for these services for the moral reformers to have their way for long. The gangsters also engaged in labor racketeering of one form or another, such as providing strongarm men for firms and unions engaged in disputes. The city also had a persistently high level of bombings carried out for a variety of reasons.

When the Volstead Act mandated national prohibition, organized criminals moved swiftly to take advantage of the new opportunity. Jim Colosimo was murdered the same year, and Johnny Torrio emerged as the leading figure in Chicago vice. Torrio shifted his primary interests from gambling and girls to the manufacture and distribution of beer. His second in command was a young man recently recruited from the Five Points gang in New York, Al Capone. Torrio entered into agreements with preprohibition breweries to supply his organization with beer. However, his most important asset was his ability to guarantee his subordinates and allies immunity from prosecution or harassment by the authorities. Bootleggers and distributors outside his control, like the O'Donnell brothers, suffered from terrorism and police repression. As the Torrio group consolidated its political base, it extended its gambling and prostitution activities even further. Torrio took advantage of the political divisions of the Chicago metropolitan area by basing many of his activities in various suburban communities like Cicero, Burnham, River Forest, and Stickney.

Torrio's success required the closest cooperation with the administration of Mayor William Hale "Big Bill" Thompson. However, in 1923, Thompson gave way to a reform Democrat, William Dever. Any change of administration complicated matters for vice entrepreneurs by upsetting previous relationships with politicians and police; a reform administration was a much more serious matter since it was committed to severing these ties. Competition among the bootleggers increased, no one could be sure of his political protection, and gang warfare rose sharply. By October 1926, according to the Illinois Crime Survey, 215 gangsters had been murdered by other gangsters, and 160 had been killed by the police. Torrio himself was caught up in a raid conducted by Dever's Chief of Police, Morgan Collins, and served nine months in jail. His conviction and sentencing indicated either that he no longer had the power of immunity for himself and his fellows or that he thought himself safer in jail. His prestige irreparably damaged, Torrio gave way to his former lieutenant, Alphonse "Scarface Al" Capone. In 1926 Capone's and other bootlegging groups reached a partial agreement on the distribution of territories, which broke down in less than a year.

In 1927, Big Bill Thompson, campaigning on a platform that promised a wide-open town, again became the mayor of Chicago. The bootleggers returned to Chicago from the suburbs, and the police department underwent a thorough revamping. Officers who had cooperated with the reform administration found themselves transferred to "the sticks" or tried before the civil service commission on exceedingly flimsy charges. Thompson, who boasted that he was wetter than the Atlantic Ocean, made good his promise of a wide-open town. The replacement of Dever by Thompson seemed to support the Tammany adage about the limited appeal of reform. The experience of the Dever administration also pointed up the dangers of instability. It was during the reform administration that the carnage among the gangsters reached its height, although the most melodramatic single incident—the St. Valentine's Day Massacre, when gangsters dressed as policemen machine gunned seven members of George "Bugs" Moran's organization—took place in 1929.[9]

Two groups of civilians interested themselves in reforming the Chicago police. The first consisted of those who wanted to eliminate vice or at least to keep it from being too blatant and too public. Organized in the Committee of Fifteen and other groups, elite moralists wanted to break the protection-for-pay relationships existing among politicians, police, and vice entrepreneurs. They were convinced that open and widespread gambling and prostitution and the nonenforcement of the liquor laws bred a disrespect for law and increased the moral and physical dangers to the young who were enticed by dance halls, betting shops, gin mills, and brothels.[10] Before World War I many moral reformers also concerned themselves with factory conditions, the working and living conditions of newsboys and others engaged in street trades, and the provision of public parks and bath houses. During the next thirty years moral reformers and social progressives split, to the point where those who crusaded against obscenity or alcohol ignored other issues or gave strong support to the economic status quo.[11]

Relationships between moral reformers and police were invariably tense. Even when the mayor and the head of the department in the persons of William Dever and Morgan Collins supported vigorous police action on morals laws, many of the rank and file of the force refused to go along. The amount of money available for corrupting policemen was simply too great for orders from the top to be obeyed down the line, and the social gulf between policemen and reformers prevented any lasting cooperation. Policemen and gangsters, on the other hand, inhabited the same social world. They came from the same neighborhoods and had similar boyhood experiences. Individual gangsters were not permanently immune from arrest and prosecution; yet the police had no intention of eliminating the "rackets." Cop and crook lived in a symbiotic relationship; their common boyhood associations were reinforced by their occupational interaction. They knew and needed each other.[12]

The second group of elite reformers concerned itself with police performance on crimes against persons and property. The Chicago Crime Commission and other such bodies were contemptuous of crusades against bootleggers and bookmakers and wanted police priorities to be set on robbers, rapists, and burglars. Businessmen who created and supported these organizations had much more concern for their safety and property than they did for the morals of young men and women growing up on the South Side. The Crime Commission and the police could reach accommodation on some issues at least. Civilians objected to the police practice of keeping the crime rate down by simply not reporting incidents, but the two groups could agree on increasing the number of men, adding new equipment, and making some administrative changes that would not threaten existing political patterns.[13]

The differences between the orientations of the two groups of elite reformers are shown in the reports published under their sponsorship within a few years of each other. The *Illinois Crime Survey* of 1929 devoted considerable space to the activities of the vice lords and their relationships with the police and the politicians. *Chicago Police Problems,* which appeared under the aegis of a prestigious Citizens' Police Committee in 1931, avoided these questions and concentrated on such matters as traffic control, administrative efficiency, and the need for more men. The staff of the committee under Bruce Smith, one of the leading independent experts on police administration of that time, established close working relationships with the police department and in effect agreed to avoid controversial issues, to stress administrative reorganization, and, most important, to press for the addition of one thousand men to the department. Increasing the size of the force would mean more protection for the property of the elite and would open up promotion and other opportunities for the men already on the force. The city administration did implement many of the proposals made by Smith after an interval during which the cooperation between the police and the committee broke down. The Chicago Police Department thereby underwent a thorough reorganization in the early 1930s to improve administrative efficiency. The number of units and individuals who reported directly to the chief was cut drastically and the span of control reduced to manageable limits.[14]

Chicago provided the most noteworthy example of the varying kinds of public concern over the police in the prohibition era, but elite groups in other cities also supported elaborate studies of the crime and police problems in their communities. The Cleveland Foundation financed a study of *Criminal Justice in Cleveland*, published in 1922. Raymond Fosdick, whose extensive studies of police organizations in both Europe and the United States have been previously cited, wrote the section on the police. Fosdick was appalled by the state of the Cleveland department, which had neither the organization, the personnel, nor the equipment to deal with the complicated police problems of a large, heterogeneous city. Despite Fred Kohler's vigorous tenure as chief, the department had not adapted itself sufficiently to the needs of a rapidly changing city. The force operated as if Cleveland were still a small town rather than the fifth largest city in the United States in 1920. The city had more than doubled in population since 1900, neighborhoods had changed markedly, and the city possessed a highly diverse social and ethnic mixture. Cleveland has been described, with considerable justification, as a series of ethnic villages; yet it was also a metropolis involved in complicated industrial, commercial, and financial activities. The police department grappled with the changing character of the city on an ad hoc, day-to-day basis. It had no planning staff, no long-range assessment of needs, and crept along in its old routine way while the city it served grew and changed dramatically.[15]

Cleveland's charter caused many of the problems in providing for both a safety director and a chief of police, each of whom reported directly to the mayor on some issues. Theoretically the safety director had authority over both the police and fire services, but the charter gave the chief of police some independent powers. Kohler had overcome some of these handicaps because of Johnson's support. The system made for a good bit of buck passing and cloudy lines of authority. It also created many possibilities for conflict in that both the safety director and the chief could feel that the other was encroaching upon his area of responsibility or attempting to undermine his position. The safety director was usually a political appointee, a friend and supporter of the mayor with little or no experience in police affairs who held office only as long as the mayor who appointed him. As a result there was little continuity in the safety director's office and inconsistent or indifferent leadership for the police.[16]

Fosdick found the situation no better among the career commanders of the force. Only the size of the department had changed. Decisions were made on the basis of tradition and memory, and the superior officers exhibited little "intelligence and imagination." Some of them worked hard, but they lacked the records and knowledge to do anything other than react on the basis of past experience to problems and situations as they arose. If their experience gave no guidance or was outmoded, they had little else to offer. As in other cities, commanders worked their way up through the ranks. Most came from working-class backgrounds with little formal education, and they lacked both the desire and the capability to make extensive changes in organization and procedure. Fosdick condemned the written exams administered by the civil service commission for promotion for not indicating the qualities of leadership needed for administrative positions. Moreover, as in other police departments, political influence and money were the surest roads to advancement. As one cynical Cleveland policeman later said, the only book an applicant for promotion had to own was a bankbook. Cleveland policemen polarized along religious lines between Catholics and Masons, and members of one group sought to retard the advance of members of the other. In the 1920s Masons controlled most of the top positions in the department although many of the subordinates were Irish. Not until the 1960s did a Catholic become chief of police in Cleveland.

Catholics did much better in the Cleveland fire department, which remains heavily Irish.[17]

Fosdick also criticized extensively the initial appointment process. The rules of the department stipulated that applicants had to be between the ages of twenty-one and thirty-five. In the years from 1914 to 1921 the majority of those appointed were over twenty-five, which meant that they would be in their fifties or older before being eligible for retirement. He wanted a younger group who would be easier to train and be more physically vigorous throughout their police careers. The civil service exams for policemen were not widely advertised—many men perhaps learned of them from their local politicians—and the tests did not guarantee even "ordinary intelligence" among those selected. Many men left the department within their first year of service because of disciplinary infractions, dissatisfaction with the low salary, or a distaste for police work. This high turnover impaired the efficiency of the department and raised administrative costs, especially if the new recruits were provided with adequate training before being sent on the streets. Fosdick approved of the establishment of a police-training school of eight weeks and urged that it be expanded. However, in Cleveland as in other cities, when there was a budgetary pinch, the training school would be one of the first things to be curtailed or eliminated.[18]

The performance of the men after appointment indicated a low standard of discipline and morale. In 1920 twenty-three members of the Cleveland Police Department were found guilty of being drunk while on duty. Only four of them were dismissed from the department. If the safety director decided upon dismissal or demotion, the man charged could then appeal to the civil service commission. In that year, the commission overruled the safety director in six of thirteen cases. Fosdick, in keeping with his philosophy of the centralization of power and responsibility, urged that one man have the final say. If a trial board found a man guilty and recommended demotion or dismissal, it would be the responsibility of the administrative head to determine the punishment without any appeal. He cited Boston as an example of a city where this system worked admirably.

Cleveland's detectives were poorly selected and supervised. Often a man became a detective for a daring or spectacular arrest without any consideration of his qualifications for the position. The detectives rated lower than any other group on the force on the Army Alpha intelligence test. Detective commanders spent their time on the newsworthy cases, especially where a trip to another city to return a fugitive was involved, rather than on supervising the work of their subordinates.[19]

Prohibition was no better enforced in Cleveland than in other large cities. Indeed, the police functioned as part of the control mechanism among bootleggers by giving some preferred treatment and cracking down on others. Some bootleggers were able to use the police to prevent unwanted competition; the officers involved were well compensated. The extent of bribery became part of the public record a few years after the end of prohibition. In December 1935, Mayor Harold Burton, who later served as United States Senator from Ohio and Associate Justice of the Supreme Court, appointed the youthful Eliot Ness as Safety Director. Ness, only thirty-two years old at the time, was a graduate of the University of Chicago who had served as a treasury department agent. He soon brought bribery charges against a number of Cleveland police officers. Captain Louis Cadek, long-time head of the vice squad, was found to have a cache of $109,000 and was sent to prison. Ness transferred all the men out of one precinct and brought bribery charges against eight officers, including Captain Michael Harwood, long known as the czar of Collinwood in the northeastern section of the city.[20]

Harwood, called Big Mike, the cop who couldn't be broken, reminds one of Alexander "Clubber" Williams of New York's police in the late nineteenth century. Both were physically powerful men who were openly and brazenly corrupt. Harwood knew all the local politicians, he operated questionable night spots in his own precinct, and he controlled all liquor operations in his section of the city. For years, Harwood had made no secret of his activities and openly defied his superiors, up to the level of chief of police and safety director.

Ness and Harwood fought a bitter battle which the Safety Director won when Harwood was convicted of bribery and sentenced to the state penitentiary. Big Mike had fought suspension, had tried to be placed on the pension rolls for physical disability, and went to great and expensive lengths to discredit the witnesses against him at his trial. He had an apartment bugged and hired women to lure witnesses to the place and to get them to talk. All in vain, as the jury found him guilty and successive appellate courts refused to overthrow the verdict.[21]

The Chicago and Cleveland patterns of police tolerance and protection of bootlegging could be duplicated in most large and middle-sized cities. The law could be enforced only in those places where a substantial majority of the population supported it.

The end of prohibition and the successful prosecution of a few crooked cops did not solve the basic problem. As society has become more diverse, more heterogeneous, and more fragmented, the tendency has been to employ the formal sanctions and controls of the law to replace the informal controls characteristic of simpler, more unified societies. Prohibition was the most extreme example of this trend, which has been growing since at least the middle of the nineteenth century. But the realization that prohibition was socially unenforceable did not mean that other attempts to control behavior through the formal mechanisms of the police and courts were abandoned. At the present day more than one-third of all arrests in the United States are made for offenses against "public order or decency" where there is no victim who has suffered either physical injury or property loss. In some jurisdictions "crimes without victims," such as drunkenness, account for more than half of all arrests.[22]

We are in the paradoxical situation that as there is less and less agreement on standards of morality among the population as a whole, there is more and more statute law attempting to regulate behavior. Of course, if all members of a society agreed on what constituted acceptable behavior, there would be little need for elaborate legal systems. Since people do not agree, the dominant groups write their moral values, or at least the values they want others to observe, into the formal law. As social standards change, the law usually lags behind, so that there is often a widening gap between what many people consider valid and what the law allows. A case in point is abortion. More and more people regard abortion as a matter to be settled solely by a woman and her doctor, yet in many states until the recent Supreme Court decision the legal situation was still so restrictive that only the well-to-do could secure abortions legally.[23]

Those hardy perennials, prostitution and gambling, remain enormously popular, although still against the law. In recent years, Newark, New Jersey, and New York City have had major scandals concerning police corruption relating to organized gambling. A similar scandal could probably be created in most major cities. Gambling appeals to many people, the profits are enormous, and many policemen who would shun accepting bribes from narcotics peddlers think nothing of letting bookmakers and numbers runners operate for a price—that is, "clean money." Men who grow up in an atmosphere where betting on baseball or putting a dollar on the numbers is part of daily life are hardly likely to adopt a moralistic attitude toward gamblers and gambling. Civilians from similar backgrounds are not going to support police crusades against bookies; and even when a systematic and pervasive pattern of police corruption is exposed, such as in the *New York Times* survey published in the spring of 1970, the general public reaction seems to be one of cynical or weary indifference or resignation. More recently the Knapp Commission in New York has reduced public lethargy and intensified demands for corrective action.[24]

In general, however, while Americans might evince alarm at the growing power of organized crime and the spread of its influence over legitimate enterprises, there does not seem to be much concern about the sources of the money used to move into other businesses. Gambling profits provide the wherewithal for men of criminal backgrounds and methods of operation to gain a foothold, and in some instances much more than that, in the world of legally approved business. Most policemen as well as most citizens do not seem to carry their analysis of the situation to this length. Most think of the immediate gratification of being able to gamble at will or the immediate extra income derived from letting people do it. Through hard experience policemen in several cities have learned that interfering with gamblers can bring unwanted transfers or other punitive action. In this area prudent men take no action that has not been directly ordered by their superior officers. In cities where organized crime is strong, police departments may have many incorruptible men, but they are not likely to be assigned to vice activities. Moreover, they are prevented by group pressures from informing on their fellows. Policemen who object to corruption often can avoid those assignments that bring them into continuing contact with gamblers and prostitutes. Those who are interested in the extra income seek out these assignments and in turn are acceptable to those being regulated. By this selection process those assigned to gambling activities, whether they are called the vice squad or plainclothesmen, in wide-open towns tend to be those most likely to be ready to do business with the bookmakers and numbers bankers.[25]

To date, the sexual revolution has not eliminated the market for the services of the professional prostitute. Call girls, bar hookers, and streetwalkers still flourish in American cities, and males often function as prostitutes to service the sexual needs of homosexuals. After several major prosecutions in the 1930s and 1940s, organized crime apparently left the field of prostitution. According to the President's Commission on Law Enforcement and the Administration of Criminal Justice, prostitution is too difficult to organize and control to be of prime interest to organized criminals, who find more lucrative operations in gambling, loan sharking, and the infiltration of legitimate businesses.[26] Prostitution is still a difficult problem for police departments. Generating evidence and gaining convictions in this area usually require that policemen pose as prospective customers, which raises cries of entrapment. In some cities a considerable number of policemen are assigned to this work, and the question can be asked as to whether the benefits to the community of their activity justify the costs involved.[27] Yet according to theatrical producer Alexander Cohen, the extent of prostitution and pornographic shops in New York's theater district has reached crisis proportions, threatening even further the economic stability of a precarious industry. Furthermore, prostitution often is connected with crimes that do have victims, such as fraud, robbery, and assault. Similarly, while drug use may be a "victimless crime," users do victimize others to pay for their habits.[28]

Narcotic and hallucinogenic drugs have been part of the American scene for a long time. As long as their use was concentrated among black and other minority groups, middle-class Americans showed little interest and concern. In recent years as drug use has become more common among white middle-class youth, social attitudes have changed dramatically. There is now increasing demand to separate marijuana from so-called "hard drugs" like heroin and to minimize the penalties for possession of marijuana. Some states are reducing the charge for a first offense from a felony to a misdemeanor; in a few jurisdictions a suspended sentence is standard for the first offense.

But the potential penalties are horrendous in a state like Texas, and lawyers work diligently to prevent their youthful clients from coming before juries consisting of older, not very permissive, people.

Obviously, social attitudes toward drug use as a crime are confused and in the process of substantial change. In the early 1950s, legislatures increased penalties for sellers of narcotics as a way of drying up the traffic. The profits were too great, and too many addicts turned to selling to support their own habits for this process to work. As middle-class collegians and high school students sought new ways to "turn on," legislatures wrestled with the dilemma of either laying themselves open to charges of permissiveness or living with the possibility that it might be their own children who would be liable to the harsh penalties, The current trend seems to be in the direction of considering marijuana in the same category as alcohol. Because marijuana has become so popular and the evidence on its harmful nature is either weak or conflicting, there is a good case for taking it out of the criminal category. There is little likelihood at the moment that marijuana will be legalized as most adults still think it more dangerous than alcohol, but more and more responsible people are arguing that we should at least consider the possibility seriously. John Kaplan's *Marijuana—The New Prohibition* is an excellent exposition of this point of view.[29]

In an ideal world human beings might find their lives so satisfying that they would not feel the need for any depressant, stimulant, or hallucinogen. In the real world a great many people do feel the need for such substances and experiences, and how can any law be enforced, no matter how noble in purpose, that a substantial portion of the community refuses to support? Like drinkers during prohibition, marijuana users do not think they are doing anything immoral.

Law-enforcement agencies have particularly difficult problems when there is a wide gap between formal requirements and behavioral patterns. If only a small minority engages in acts deemed criminal and deviant, there is strong support for the suppression of that minority. If the legally deviant group grows to include a large minority or even a majority of a given community, the enforcement problems become acute. We have seen this pattern previously in regard to gambling and liquor laws.

There does seem to be one great difference between marijuana and other vice laws. A good many policemen traditionally come from backgrounds where drinking and gambling are acceptable activities. I don't know of any studies of the use of marijuana or other drugs among police officers, but I suspect it would not be very large, at least among the older men.

Although marijuana has made inroads among "straight" youth, most people and the media identify drug use with the counter-culture which rejects those values of order, stability, competitiveness, and patriotism held by many policemen. In the 1920s, Chicago cops could identify with steel workers who wanted their beer; now the police and the "turned on" young perceive each other as enemies. Each sees the other as a threat to revered values. The police are viewed as enemies to freedom, spontaneity, and the equality of all men. Policemen are "pigs," hired clubs and guns of a discredited establishment. To the police, the "hippies," the "yippies," and the "crazies" pose substantial threats to social order, stability, and constituted authority. Dirt, disorder, and moral decay are what the police see among the disaffected young, and the sight does not please them.[30]

Certainly, the police cannot enforce the marijuana laws against all violators; they must be selective. Most college campuses enjoy virtual immunity from the criminal laws against possession and use, and white middle-class adults are rarely bothered. The three groups who do feel the weight of the laws are the alienated who by dress and hair style show their contempt for policemen's value system, juveniles, and black and Spanish-speaking citizens. These last two groups lack the ability to provide themselves with privacy and so are more likely to violate the law in a public place. There are always more police around in high-crime areas, which are also areas of black and Spanish-speaking concentration, and many marijuana arrests grow out of arrests for other offenses. Juveniles and minority group members are more likely to be stopped for other reasons, which in turn can lead to marijuana arrests. Juveniles in a car with faulty taillights might be stopped where a white adult would be ignored; the policeman operates on the assumption that a car driven by a youth might be stolen, and it doesn't hurt to check licenses and registration.[31]

Such incidents point up the fundamental dilemma the police face in regard to the marijuana laws. The illegal acts are usually committed in private or at least not in full public view, and there are no victims in the usual sense. The police are charged with enforcing these laws; they are also charged with observing the constitutional protection of individual rights. They cannot do both at the same time. Full enforcement of the drug laws would be possible only in a police state where the police would be allowed to stop and search at will and where there could be no question of police infringement of constitutional guarantees since there would be no guarantees. In this dilemma, the police do not express outrage at the task they have been given. Instead they complain about the constitutional provisions and court decisions which they see only as procedural blocks to the efficient conduct of their work. The difficulties associated with enforcement of the marijuana laws constitute an important source of police dissatisfaction with the constitutional structure, which they see as hindering the attainment of their occupational goals rather than as the framework within which they should operate. The temptation for the police is to bypass the structure.

Almost all marijuana arrests derive from searches made without a warrant. Such searches are constitutional only if they are made with the consent of the person searched or in connection with an arrest made on the basis of probable cause—that is, that the policeman had reasonable grounds for believing that a crime had been committed. These provisions have led policemen to testify that youths stopped for faulty taillights or in a routine traffic check made "furtive movements" as if they were trying to dispose of evidence, or that the officer saw traces of vegetable matter on the floor of a car at night which might have been marijuana. Often the courts take the policeman at his word, since the search, or at least the ones that get to court, did turn up evidence of illegal possession.

The fact that the search uncovered the existence of a crime leads judges to assume that the officer had previous probable cause for believing that the law had been violated. It is possible, however, that only after and not before he conducts the search does the policeman have reason to believe that a crime had been committed. He then has to fabricate a prior probable cause. No one can say how often such perjury takes place. The problem is that the contradictory job society gives the police of enforcing this law and observing constitutional provisions tempts them either to ignore the law or to lie. Those youth in the drug culture, who mistrust the police to begin with, believe that police perjury is widespread and seize upon every possible incident to support their case that the establishment is indeed rotten. To them every arrest is tainted, and the resultant hostility makes the serious gulf between police and people even worse.[32]

The police, of course, could simply ignore the law as many urban departments did with prohibition. They have not done so in all cases because of the cultural conflict already mentioned, and also because the marijuana laws give them an element of control over "troublesome" elements. It may not be an accident that the radical leader Jerry Rubin has been arrested several times on drug charges. In many instances where multiple crimes are involved it may be possible to get a conviction of marijuana possession when there might not be enough evidence to support another, possibly more serious charge. Furthermore, how many young men have had their hair cut to ensure a suspended sentence on a drug arrest? Despite the problems involved with the antimarijuana laws, problems as serious as those with prohibition, the police still enforce and support these laws at least partially in order to satisfy their cultural perspectives and some of their occupational needs. Society might well decide, however, that the costs involved in maintaining the possession and sale of marijuana as criminal acts far outweigh the possible benefits, especially in view of the seeming impossibility of enforcing these laws without infringing upon constitutional guarantees.[33]

Chapter 7

The Police and the Automobile

American cities have always grown by sending people and businesses into the surrounding countryside, thus changing rural or suburban land into urban. For a long time the process was restricted and limited by the constraints of a primitive transportation technology. In the 1820s, for example, all cities were walking cities in that virtually everyone had to live within walking distance of shop or wharf. Only the wealthy could afford carriages to carry them back and forth from their country seats outside New York or Philadelphia to the center of town. The first public transportation in American cities came in the late 1820s with the horse-drawn omnibus, a clumsy vehicle capable of carrying twelve to twenty passengers along such busy thoroughfares as New York's Broadway. The one-way fare of twelve and a half cents put the omnibus out of reach of the bulk of the population. Laborers making seventy-five cents or a dollar a day could hardly pay a quarter or a third of their income for getting back and forth to work. The omnibus, however, did enable the well-to-do to separate themselves somewhat from the noise, filth, and crowding of the most built-up parts of the city. Omnibuses also contributed to fearsome traffic jams in the downtown areas as they competed with carts and carriages for space in the narrow streets.[1]

Teamsters' curses and whips and the clop of horse hoofs on cobblestone paving made noise pollution an integral part of the urban environment. The crush of traffic cost businessmen time and money, while pedestrians put life and limb in jeopardy to cross major thoroughfares. The process could take up to a half hour in the case of New York's Broadway. City councils passed ordinances which no one seemed capable of enforcing. The maximum speed limit in New York City was five miles an hour, but judging from the numerous complaints about "furious driving," it was no better enforced than contemporary speed limits. The newspapers of the middle of the nineteenth century contained diatribes against traffic congestion and laments that the city was choking itself to death similar to those of the mid-twentieth century.[2]

In the 1850s the introduction of the horse-drawn streetcar made possible even more movement from the downtown areas. Horses pulled the streetcars on rails laid in the middle of the streets. Such vehicles could make an average speed of four to six miles an hour, which was sufficient for all but the largest cities. At the same time railroads began to provide commuter service for the well-to-do who chose to live in the suburbs of New York, Philadelphia, and Boston. New York, the largest and most congested of the nation's cities, built an elevated railroad beginning in the late 1860s. Steam locomotives pulled the trains, creating intolerable noise for those along the right of way and showering pedestrians in the streets below with cinders and oil. In the late 1880s Frank J. Sprague, a pioneering electrical engineer, solved the problem of moving streetcars with electric power. His system spread from Richmond, Virginia, to cities all over the country. Electricity made possible average speeds of ten miles an hour or better and also opened for development hilly areas which had been beyond the capacity of horses. Even before Los Angeles constructed the first of its famous freeways, electric trolleys and interurbans enabled the city's people to scatter over a very large land area in search of desirable home sites. In the 1890s electric elevateds appeared in Chicago, Boston, and Kansas City, and New York converted its "els" from steam to electricity.[3]

The transportation developments of the second half of the nineteenth century had profound effects upon the physical form and social geography of American cities. Cities now encompassed much larger land areas than they had in the days of the walking city. New areas welcomed annexation to the city to receive the benefit of such services as water supply and police and fire protection. Only in the twentieth century did most suburban areas in the Northeast and Midwest decide that they had more to lose than to gain in becoming part of the central city. The availability of relatively rapid and cheap transportation—the five-cent fare was standard no matter how long the ride—enabled the upper half of income earners to seek pleasant neighborhoods of low density in the outer reaches of the city or in nearby suburbs.[4]

By 1900, many cities had developed the now familiar social geography of the inner city as the residence of the poor and the recently arrived, while the better off lived with more space, light, and air in the periphery of the city or a suburb. Historian Zane Miller presents a threefold division of Cincinnati in 1900, which could be applied to a number of cities: the Circle, the inner city residential area of the poor and the deprived, surrounding most of the central business district; the Zone of Emergence, a peripheral area inhabited by those who had made some economic progress, often the second generation in the city; and the Hilltops, the fashionable area for those who had really arrived.[5] Some of the wealthy maintained homes in the central city, in areas such as Philadelphia's Rittenhouse Square, Boston's Beacon Hill, New York's Fifth Avenue, and Chicago's Near North Side along the lake. These enclaves of the wealthy abutted the administrative and financial portions of the central business district. Also they were located just a few minutes' walk from some bad slums, but the social isolation was still great despite the physical proximity.[6]

The physical spread of the city and the separation of social classes had great impact upon police departments. There were many more miles of streets to patrol and increasing problems in providing station houses and communications devices for the new areas. In New York the northern reaches of the city had to be patrolled by men on horseback who had contact with their stations only once an hour. Men who had displeased their superiors downtown could be exiled to "Goatville" to meditate on their sins. In Cleveland being transferred out to the periphery was known as being sent "to the woods"; the energetic and the ambitious wanted to be downtown where the action was. Policemen soon learned that an acceptable standard of performance in one area could get a man in serious trouble in another. Downtown areas wanted the saloons and the gamblers to be left alone; middle-class residential areas wanted strict enforcement of the vice laws. In some cities, police departments established, either formally or informally, protected vice areas, usually located in black or the most recent immigrant neighborhoods. Those with the least political power found themselves, whether willingly or not, the hosts and hostesses of pimps and prostitutes.[7]

Severe police problems came in those areas in transition from one social class or one ethnic group to another. Middle-class people resented the invasion of their neighborhoods by poor immigrants. The least mobile were the last to leave and the most bitter about the loss of their pleasant and homogeneous areas. In transitional areas different groups with sometimes conflicting life styles shared the same streets, and the police found themselves constantly called on to adjudicate disputes or being pressured to stop boys from playing ball or Italians from parading in the streets.[8]

Neighborhood transformation is an old story in American cities. Expanding businesses and public institutions and facilities have long encroached upon residential land, and neighborhoods have sometimes degenerated from fairly fashionable to semislum in a single generation. Every new transportation device or extension of older facilities hastened the process of change.[9]

While the processes of suburbanization and the physical separation of social classes and ethnic and racial groups began before the introduction of the automobile, its spread did make possible an enormous increase in the amount of land potentially available for urban and suburban development.

The growth of sprawling metropolitan areas made possible by the automobile has generated increased demands for interdepartmental cooperation or for greater consolidation or pooling of police services. In major metropolitan areas of the Northeast and Midwest, there are hundreds of separate governmental units, many of which maintain their own police forces. Most of these departments are too small to provide effective training or technical services, and advocates of greater governmental consolidation have long cited police as one of the areas of need. Those whose watchwords were efficiency, standardization, uniformity, and centralization pressed for metropolitan government fifty and sixty years ago. They cited the variations between police performance in Chicago under a reform administration and such suburbs as Cicero and the fact that gamblers driven out of Cincinnati or Louisville could easily reopen in Covington or Newport. Greater integration of police operations would smooth traffic flow and facilitate the capture of criminals who fled from one jurisdiction to another. However, as the bulk of the elite moved to the suburbs, they stressed instead the values of separatism, independence, and local control.[10] Local officeholders have also resisted consolidation unless there are tangible benefits involved. It is not surprising that a man might prefer to be chief of a ten-man force than a sergeant in a larger department. For a patrolman, on the other hand, a large department would provide more opportunities for promotion and for varied assignments.

Despite the roadblocks, some progress has been made. The Los Angeles County sheriff provides police service to a number of communities by contract. The Chicago Police Department makes its technical facilities available to surrounding communities. States should probably take the initiative through incentive grants to encourage the formation of larger departments in metropolitan areas to provide greater integration and more effective police work.[11]

Conversely, minority groups increasingly demand local community control of police. They want schools, police, and other agencies to be sympathetic to and involved in the life of the community. Bureaucratic inaccessibility and direction from a remote and unfeeling headquarters is cited as one of the more pernicious examples of the powerlessness of the ghetto. In the past local control was condemned as control by local politicians, and no one yet seems to have solved the problem of finding the authentic voice or voices of the community. Reformers of the Progressive period saw centralization as the answer to the cozily corrupt relations between local precinct commanders and local criminals. Now minority spokesmen attack centralization for promoting bureaucratic rigidity and insensitivity to black aspirations.[12] The police, and the political and administrative structure generally, will have to balance the operational and technical advantages of centralization with a greater rapport with the local community. Now that government blankets citizens' lives, no one can feel free unless he has some say in the governmental decisions that affect him. The very difficult problem urban planners face, intellectually and then in practice, is to find ways and means to provide for this local involvement without damaging the interests of the city or metropolitan area as a whole.

The conflict between centralization and decentralization predates the automobile, which again simply enlarged the battlefield by making possible low-density, multinucleated metropolitan complexes encompassing thousands of square miles. Even within the political boundaries of one community, the amazing multiplication of automobiles generated severe police problems. From 1900 to 1930, the number of automobile registrations in the United States rose from 8,000 to more than 23,000,000. This phenomenal growth posed challenging new responsibilities for urban police departments in regulating traffic, limiting parking in downtown areas, and trying to keep the killed and maimed to a minimum.

In the absence of mechanical means of regulating traffic such as stoplights, more and more men had to be shifted to traffic duty to spend long hours in the middle of intersections controlling traffic by hand and arm signals. Departments found that many patrol posts went uncovered because of the demands for traffic regulation. Gradually engineers developed signal systems and electrically controlled stoplights to reduce the burden somewhat, but the growth of the volume of traffic kept police forces running to stay even. Cleveland in the mid-1920s detailed about 15 percent of the patrol force to traffic duties, which left a severe shortage of men for patrolling beats. Many areas adequately protected in 1910 had almost no men on patrol some years later.[13]

The introduction and spread of the automobile obliterated the distinction between the law breaking and the law abiding. Almost everyone who drives and looks for a place to park violates some law or ordinance some time. Policemen now found themselves arresting some of the most prominent people in their communities; men and women who had formerly considered policemen as guardians of their persons and property now became the objects of undesired police attention. The arrest records for Akron, Ohio, in the early twentieth century show the usual run of drifters and derelicts, drunk and disorderly, punctuated by names of the first families and the best addresses in town arrested for violating the traffic laws.

The automobile thus created considerable tension between the police and the middle and upper classes who traditionally supported vigorous law enforcement. Policemen had to impose sanctions on people above them, sometimes far above, in the social and economic scale. Officers who had been conditioned to demand respect from the lower-class groups they usually controlled could not use the same methods with prominent businessmen and professionals who objected to being stopped for moving violations or given a parking ticket. A lower-class individual who abused a policeman could expect to be dealt with by force and violence; middle- and upper-class people expected cops to treat them with respect and deference, not the other way around.[14]

Students of police administration such as Bruce Smith thought that the hostilities engendered by traffic control provided one major reason why police forces in the United States lacked a favorable political climate to grow and develop into truly professional organizations.[15] Departments tried to minimize ill feelings stemming from traffic laws by treating automobile violators differently. In Akron a traffic arrest did not require the person to be searched whereas other offenses did. Departments later began substituting summonses for arrest and then warnings instead of summonses; but the basic problem remained.

An additional source of tension arose with the institution of ticket fixing. In a number of jurisdictions, the ability to "fix" or "square" a ticket became the dividing line between those with some power and influence and those outside the pale. Politicians and police officials found an additional source of patronage and power in saving violators from the consequences of their actions. In some small cities, the chief of police can fix a ticket, although he may not be inclined to do so if the policeman reports that the violator was also abusive.[16]

Most people believe that the traffic laws are not enforced in any fair and equitable manner and that anyone stopped for speeding is the victim of a capricious and arbitrary act. The driver knows that he is only one violator out of hundreds if not thousands of lawbreakers and he objects to being singled out and punished. Otherwise staunch advocates of law and order do not want the law enforced against them when they are speeding or guilty of other violations. Their attitude is reinforced by the manifest impossibility of uniform and equitable enforcement of the traffic laws in any given jurisdiction; when one examines the situation existing between different cities, the results are even more startling.

Boston, Massachusetts, and Dallas, Texas, in the early 1960s were both cities of approximately 700,000 in population. In 1964 the

Boston police wrote 11,242 tickets for moving violations, while the Dallas police issued 273,626 such tickets, a difference of 1 to 24! Bostonians do use public transportation more frequently than people in Dallas; still the variation seems inexplicable simply on the basis of the volume of automobile traffic.[17] The key variable in the vastly different levels of traffic enforcement in different cities, sometimes cities located next to each other, is the attitude of senior police commanders toward traffic enforcement. In the absence of pressure from the top, most policemen will act only on serious violations such as driving while intoxicated or grossly exceeding the speed limit. Traffic stops can involve the policemen in tense and often demeaning relations with civilians. If a driver offers a bribe or boasts of his "clout" with the chief or whines that he is innocent and then becomes blustery when he realizes that the traffic officer is not going to give him a ticket, he attacks the policeman's self-esteem. The temptation then is to avoid such encounters.

If commanders want ticketing, however, they can get it. The most effective way is to make traffic enforcement a specialized responsibility. It does not require much specialized knowledge or training to enforce the traffic laws, but it is easy to check on the performance of a specialized unit. All the commander has to do is to keep track of the number of tickets issued. This would not be a good measure for officers with general duties who could point to other responsibilities as the reason for low productivity. The traffic officer does not have this excuse. The policeman must prove he is efficient by keeping up with his quota, thereby becoming involved in tension-producing relationships with the public.

But in other ways, traffic is a desirable detail; and a policeman will keep to the level of ticketing expected by his superiors to hold that assignment. The traffic officer works on his own a good bit. He is free of close supervision as long as he maintains his quota, and policemen soon learn of those troublesome stop signs that will produce a high level of violations to maintain the "greenie a day that keeps the sergeant away." Traffic policemen also do not have to involve themselves in domestic disputes and tavern brawls, which are unpredictable at best and dangerous at worst.

Police commanders can establish their own norms on traffic enforcement because most civilians are not interested in the *general* policy of the department. They are often very concerned about specifics—the teenagers dragging on the next block or doing something about a son's first speeding violation—but they have little knowledge of or interest in the overall patterns of police activity. Indeed, most civilians probably are not even aware that there is such a thing as a general policy on traffic laws and that there are such wide variations in enforcement practices between different departments.

The existence of these wide variations does raise questions about equal protection of the laws. There seems to be no logical reason why police commanders should have so much discretion about the intensity of law enforcement in traffic except that few civilians support full enforcement. As in the case of Sabbatarian restrictions and the liquor laws during prohibition, most citizens do not pattern their behavior according to the formal dictates of the law and are pleased when no policemen are around to enforce that law. By default society leaves it largely to police commanders to determine how vigorously the law should be invoked. Commanders probably make their own decisions on general enforcement policy as a result of their personal beliefs and experiences.

There is some evidence, however, that the population composition of a given city does have an impact on police department policy. Cities with a highly mobile population are more likely to have stricter traffic law enforcement. Officers may act on the assumption that a more mobile population requires more formal law enforcement because the informal controls of a more stable society are absent. Moreover, such cities are more likely to be governed by efficiency-oriented city manager systems.[18]

The city manager system came into being to reduce political influence in municipal government and to make government a matter of efficient administration rather than political bargaining and negotiation among competing interest groups. The city manager system presumes a high level of homogeneity among the people of a given city or a population so mobile that it has not had the time to develop political interest groups. Conversely, the more stable the population, the more likely it is that competing interest groups will have developed, groups that have their own ideas on law enforcement and other policy matters and the organizational weight to make those views felt. In this case, police commanders and other administrators would not have so much freedom of action to set policy as they desired. They would have to be aware of the conflicting demands within their constituencies and temper their actions accordingly.

The police not only had to help keep automobile traffic moving, they also had to deal with the problems caused by cars after they had arrived at their destination—in a word, parking. The parking situation had become acute in downtown Chicago by the mid-1920s. In 1910 the city had only 12,000 registered automobiles; in 1926 it had 341,000, an almost thirty-fold increase in sixteen years. Chief of Police Morgan Collins asserted that "Parked cars cut the street width in two, slow up all traffic, strangle business and delay everyone, while only a few car owners are benefited." In January 1928, therefore, the city prohibited parking on downtown streets. Merchants wailed of impending disaster, but most found that the bulk of their customers came by public transportation, so they were not immediately affected.[19]

As public transit lost customers and automobile registrations continued to climb, even in the depressed 1930s, the problem became more acute. In the years after World War II suburban shopping centers with their mammoth parking lots took away much of the retail business formerly concentrated downtown. However, the parking situation remained serious as more and more people drove to their central city jobs. The solution, if it can be called that, in many cities has been to replace outmoded buildings with parking lots, which certainly do not do anything for the aesthetic character of the city while adding to the volume of automobile traffic and resulting air pollution.

The enforcement of parking regulations provides a good illustration of the manifold pressures under which American police work. One was the problem of self-image. August Vollmer, a perceptive police administrator and writer on police affairs, noted in 1936 that policemen hated to write parking tickets. They thought it a child's job and not real police work at all. And there was always the possibility that the owner might appear when the ticket was being written and create an unpleasant scene.[20] In recent years many cities have hired women as meter maids to tag illegally parked cars and free patrol officers for other duties.

Parking regulations, like so many aspects of police work, can easily become subjects of intense political controversy as various groups and individuals struggle to write their interests into the law or, failing that, to mold its enforcement to conform with their desires. The incompatibility between rapid automobile movement, the limitations of streets, and the desire of citizens to have maximum freedom to park puts intense pressure on police.

For years, garage owners in New York City demanded that the police enforce the ban on overnight parking in the streets. Automobile owners, organized in such groups as the AAA, protested against unnecessarily "rigid" and "harsh" enforcement of the law and eventually prevailed by virtue of their superior numbers. Of course, the garage men won also as the growth of auto traffic transcended the ability of the streets to contain cars even with many double parking.

New York's garment district with its heavy truck traffic could not function at all without massive evasion of the parking rules. Policemen have been seen working hard to get one truck maneuvered out of an illegal parking place so that another could get in. A street pattern and physical layout geared to water and rail transportation cannot easily cope with an automobile and truck technology. The police remain the whipping boys for all those who feel aggrieved in the continuing struggle to provide maximum freedom of movement with maximum access to one's destination in a heavily built-up area.

The automobile also introduced a fearsome source of accidental dismemberment and death. More Americans have been killed in automobile accidents of one kind or another than in all our wars combined. The slaughter reached mammoth proportions as the number of car registrations grew into the millions. Americans who had grown up in a preautomobile age often had difficulty in adjusting to the speed of automobile traffic. The newspapers of the 1910 to 1930 period are filled with stories of men and women who stepped off a streetcar right into the path of an oncoming automobile or who moved off a sidewalk without looking. In a sense millions of adult Americans were like children in that they had no experience and no comprehension of the relationship between distance and the time it would take an automobile to travel that distance. The construction of safety islands helped streetcar riders but at the expense of impeding auto traffic. Time, experience, and the disappearance of the streetcar reduced the toll somewhat, but other traffic accidents continued to take a high toll.[21]

Citizen groups often demanded that the police enforce the traffic laws as a method of curbing the slaughter and reducing the danger of death and dismemberment on the highways and streets. However, there is little evidence that police enforcement rates have any impact on the incidence of traffic violations or the number of accidents. Cities with high rates of ticketing seem to have just as many accidents as those with lower rates, with little direct relationship between police activity and traffic safety. However, some police administration experts believe that enforcement can reduce the number of serious accidents.[22]

Police departments want to retain traffic laws and the responsibility for enforcing them, but generally for nonsafety reasons. These laws provide good reasons for stopping, searching, and often harassing rowdy juveniles and others considered undesirable. If there is no other way to get at some troublemaker, a parking or moving violation can provide an occasion. Traffic stops often involve searches which turn up evidence of some other crime, although as previously noted, this is a gray area, one productive of considerable tension between police desires and court restrictions.[23]

The love affair of the average American with his automobile and our reliance on truck transport are not diminishing in intensity; if anything the United States will be more than ever a nation on wheels for the foreseeable future. The gasoline shortage of the winter and spring of 1974 shows some signs of abating. Whether the shortage itself is merely a temporary condition or whether the easing is temporary still remain to be seen. Police departments will still have to cope with the ambiguities and contradictions of law and behavior in this area, although there may be more demands for uniformity in police practice and for greater compliance with judicial restrictions on search and seizure.

The automobile transformed the nature of police patrol as well as generating police problems. The first step in improved police mobility came in the 1890s as part of the bicycle craze of that decade. Changes in design made bikes safer and faster. People saved their money assiduously to use them to ride to work or for pleasure jaunts on Sundays. Theodore Roosevelt and his colleagues on New York's police board created a bicycle squad, which eventually included one hundred men, to deal with runaway horses and cover a larger patrol area. As automobiles became more common, departments used them to distribute men on patrol posts or take in prisoners. Akron had an electric patrol wagon for these purposes by 1900. By 1910, the automobile flying squad was common; its purpose was to rush men to points of need. Until the development of patrol car radios, the full potentiality of automobile patrol could not be realized. Detroit broadcast police calls over regular radio channels in the late 1920s, while Cleveland was the first city to provide its cars with two-way radios operated on a special frequency. Even before radio, advances in communications technology in the form of telephones had a significant impact on police performance. In contrast to the situation where anyone needing a policeman had to find one on the streets or go to the stationhouse, the spread of the telephone allowed citizens to mobilize police services quickly.[24]

The combination of telephone, radio, and automobile patrol has cut possible police response time substantially. Response time is critical to effective police performance. The President's Commission on Law Enforcement reported the results of a Los Angeles study which indicated that in those criminal situations where an arrest was made, the average response time was 4.1 minutes. In cases where no arrest was made, the average response time was 6.3 minutes. More than one-third of all arrests were made within one-half hour of the commission of the crime and almost half of all arrests came within two hours.[25] Computer systems can now monitor response time as well as keep track of what units are available to handle calls. The Chicago Police Department received nationwide publicity in the early 1960s for the splendor of its equipment and the speed with which it operated. New York has an advanced communications and control network known as SPRINT.

The availability of this equipment does not always indicate a willingness to use it to fullest capacity. Cleveland's police do not check response time with the computer. The department has long been under attack for one reason or another, and members see no reason why they should develop information which could be the basis of public criticism. This defensiveness leads the department to resist any monitoring of its activities and to maintain as much control as possible over its information or, as in this case, to refuse to develop readily available information.[26] In addition, commanders under pressure to get the crime rate down can most easily achieve that goal by underreporting. In many instances police agencies do not encourage full filing and recording of complaints because it will only make them look bad. The more complaints not cleared by arrest, the more inefficient the department seems. Since the police cannot prevent crimes or solve most of them after they occur, despite the public's expectation, the simplest way to cope with the situation is to discourage complaints and keep the number to a minimum. Policemen will report crimes more readily if complainants are of higher status or deferential to the officers involved.[27]

Radio has spread from the cars and motorcycles to the individual policeman on foot. More and more the policeman's equipment consists of gun, club, and radio. Other police officers attributed the effectiveness of New York's Tactical Patrol Force, an elite group sent to trouble spots, to their communications. They were the first to be equipped with extensive individual radios. "When you need those guys they're there," was the way one officer put it. Without individual radios, a patrolman was lost to his superiors as soon as he left his car or motorcycle. Now headquarters can maintain contact with the men in the field much more easily. This is probably most important in those situations where large numbers of policemen have to act in coordinated fashion. The radio has also liberated the patrolman from the demands of the call box where he had to ring in at specified times to show his superiors he was actually patrolling his beat. Some commanders have kept call box reporting because there is no guarantee that a man with a radio is where he says he is.

One drawback of the shift from foot patrol to radio-dispatched automobiles is that policemen now have less contact with citizens in nonadversary situations. Foot patrol is expensive and inefficient in most areas; still the man on the beat could maintain the kind of communication with citizens that kept both aware of the humanity of the other. This may be a romanticized view, one that mists over the harsh features of the past and retrospectively endows it with positive points that were not apparent to people at the time. Yet it seems probable that putting policemen in containers, which cars are, and physically separating them from citizens has to have an impact on police-community relations. Most policemen and citizens come in contact only in specific service, order-keeping, and law-enforcement situations, many of which have an adversary quality. The policeman has to make judgments about people he does not know. He has to make these decisions on the basis of visible signs of dress, demeanor, and status; rarely does he have personal knowledge of the individuals or families involved. Increasing scale and technological efficiency thus have negative side effects in limiting the range of communication between policemen and civilians, although it would be unjustifiable to attribute the police-community relations crisis of our time solely to technology. Furthermore, there is no question that people needing police service now have a generally better chance of receiving that service within a reasonable time than they did two generations ago.

In the late 1960s former Commissioner Johannes Spreen of the Detroit police tried to combine the mobility of the machine with the personal interaction of the foot patrolman by putting his men on scooters. Scooters were also used to some extent in New York, where Spreen served before going to Detroit, and a few other cities. The scooters are a twentieth-century equivalent of the bicycle policemen of the 1890s, although if we do not solve the ecological problems of the internal combustion engine or find an acceptable substitute, we may all be riding bicycles again. The Baltimore police department has recently taken to bicycles to patrol the city's numerous alleys.[28]

One of the perennial questions involving patrol cars is whether they should be staffed by one man or two. Many police administration experts argue that the one-man car has many advantages besides the obvious saving in manpower. One man will be more alert; he will not be involved in idle gossip or spreading the latest department rumors. It might even be safer as well as better community relations because the one man will be more careful and less prone to use force and bluster than two. Many policemen have not been convinced by these arguments. They want a backup in case of trouble, and a partner who can testify for them in case a civilian lodges an unwarranted complaint. The present-day pattern is mixed. Some smaller cities use exclusively one-man cars, especially on the day shift, while some larger cities vary with one-man cars in quieter districts and two-man cars in the more active areas. Other cities use two-man cars almost exclusively.[29]

At the end of the 1920s, the presidential commission on Recent Social Changes appointed by Herbert Hoover noted more than one hundred ways that the automobile had transformed American life. Many of these changes directly affected police problems and operations. As Americans became people usually visible only from the chest up, the policeman's chief occupational deformity shifted from flat feet to lower back fatigue. A nation on wheels required a patrol force on wheels. In his *Police Systems of the United States*, originally published in 1940, Bruce Smith noted that many police forces became so enamored of their cars and technology that they ignored basic problems of administration, training, and supervision. Technology could be fun, new hardware could induce the same sort of euphoria as new toys for children, and its display could reassure citizens about the quality of its police department. No doubt it made possible better police service; whether individual departments fulfilled that potentiality is another question. An emphasis on equipment could be a means of bypassing tough issues of personnel and management. Technology could speed a policeman to an area of need; what kind of job he did when he arrived would depend on other factors, ones not especially susceptible to technological innovation. Ultimately the quality of police service would be most influenced by the quality of recruiting, training, and managing conducted by individual departments.[30]

Chapter 8

Bureaucratization

During the twentieth century, police departments have become increasingly bureaucratized through a combination of their own efforts to reduce outside influence and reform desires to eliminate political interference in police affairs. Bureaucracy is a system of organization which stresses specialization of function, uniform salary, appointment, and promotion policies, and the ability to fill a role rather than personal qualities or connections. Bureaucrats can be considered as interchangeable parts who fill certain slots in an organizational chart; one bureaucrat can be substituted for another, and as long as both are competent to play the assigned role, the organization does not notice any difference. Bureaucrats interact with each other not as full persons but as roles; Joe doesn't talk to Jim so much as the assistant comptroller reports to the comptroller or the sergeant to the lieutenant. The emphasis in a bureaucracy is on developing the skills to perform the assigned tasks, to further the aims of the organization by playing the role assigned not to a person but a slot. The most successful bureaucrat is the one who can master ever more demanding and complex roles as he moves up the organizational ladder. The individual achieves his sense of worth and fulfillment by subordinating his needs to those of the organization. The organization's goals must be his goals, and he acquires prestige and esteem not only by virtue of his place within the organization but also by the organization's position in society. To have a low-status position in a low-status organization is to be doubly cursed in a bureaucratic society, which unfortunately is the position of patrolmen in many American police departments.

By the seemingly inexorable logic of Parkinson's law, the adminis-

121

trative staff needed to run police departments has grown steadily. More and more employees are needed in headquarters and staff positions to oversee and support the men on the line out on the streets. There is a surprisingly—to the uninitiated—large gap between the number of men in a department and the number patrolling the streets at any given time. In the early part of the century policemen worked ten or twelve hours a day, six days a week with one or two weeks furlough in a year. Now the forty-hour week is standard in most departments with much more liberal vacation provisions. New York policemen now receive vacations of 27 working days after three years service. New York's former commissioner Howard R. Leary told the *New York Times* that his department simply lacked the manpower to cope with the city's problems of crime and public order.[1] Increasing bureaucratization and the changing work schedules of a more leisure-oriented society have reduced the effective strength of most police departments, although the case can be made that the greater level of specialization and supporting services in big city departments makes each man more efficient than in past decades. But the policeman does not produce a product; he provides a service, and in the nature of things it is difficult to increase the productivity of service occupations. Better communications can get the man more quickly to the point of need and better equipment might help him perform his duties more effectively; still he is involved in interaction with people and a speedup there would be counterproductive. Providing for people's varied needs takes time and empathy, neither of which lends itself to assembly line procedures. Despite the communications revolution in policing, cops have managed to avoid overrushing.

In the early years of organized police departments, appointments and promotions did not follow any prescribed pattern. Some cities elected their commanders and sometimes even the patrolmen. In other cases there were no formal eligibility requirements for promotion so that a man could be appointed to a senior rank without having any service as a patrolman. Over time election and immediate conferral of senior rank disappeared and departments followed a bureaucratic pattern of entry at the lowest level with a requisite amount of time in grade necessary before promotion would be possible. The law prescribed minimum standards for appointment and increasingly tied promotion to satisfactory performance and the ability to pass formal exams. In the language of the sociologist, the law tried to substitute universalistic, rational criteria for particularistic, individual criteria. The civil service laws supposedly substituted what you know for who you know.

Civil service reformers believed that eliminating the spoilsman and the politician from police appointments and promotions would enhance the professionalization of the police and make possible impartial, efficient law enforcement. If the ties between the police, the underworld, and the politician could be severed, vice and graft would disappear, the political system would be cleaned up, and the police would impose middle-class standards of propriety upon the urban population. It was for these reasons that a Charles Whitman could use the Becker-Rosenthal case to put himself into the governor's mansion at Albany. In the eyes of many middle-class New Yorkers in 1912, Charles Becker was not simply a cop who took graft but a threat to the very foundations of civilization.[2]

For their part, the police implacably opposed many of the reformer's proposals. While moral reformers wanted the police to emphasize vice law enforcement, policemen saw their function as the maintenance of order, keeping the peace without invoking the letter of the law, and dealing with those who harmed the person and property of others rather than harassing bookmakers and saloonkeepers.[3] The police also objected strongly to some of the specific means moralists proposed to ensure that the departments enforce the vice laws. The New York struggle between reformers and organized police over court review of police removals has already been noted. The reformers wanted to maximize the administrator's leverage over the department to make it responsive to his will. If power and responsibility could be centralized, then citizens would know whom to blame if the crime rate rose or vice laws went unenforced. The reformers conceived of the police as a disciplined force directed to stamping out evil and making the values of an elite prevail throughout the city. Policemen, for their part, worried about job security. If administrators had such absolute power, there would be nothing to prevent arbitrary and capricious removals. Policemen were not willing to trust the goodwill of an administrator as the sole guarantee of their livelihoods.[4]

Policemen and others who wanted to limit the freedom of action of the top administrator could also call upon the traditional fear of police despotism and the dangers of unlimited power in any public sphere. In some departments disciplinary action had to run an involved gamut through the police chain of command, subject to review by the mayor and/or a civil service board and ultimately by the courts. The elaborate procedures and review safeguarded the men from arbitrary removal; they did little to make departments responsive to the nominal leadership. American police departments, which employ uniforms, weapons, military titles, and military traditions like saluting are often quite unlike the military in the limitations placed upon administrative or command discretion. This is not to imply that a commander cannot make life uncomfortable for his subordinates; he can and often does. But the pattern of law and often custom has been to limit top leadership's tenure and power.[5]

Moreover, policemen knew that reformers tended to last only for one term. When the reformers lost out, as when Seth Low lost his bid for reelection as mayor of New York in 1903, Tammany came back. If there had been absolute power of removal, all those policemen who had cooperated with the reformers could be removed by Tammany. Something like this happened in Kansas City, Missouri, where each change in party control in the early 1920s meant that those policemen hired by the previous administration would be fired as an economy measure and then new men would be appointed. Even by the reformers' own values, freedom of action for the administrator worked only if they controlled the top positions.[6]

In their drive to protect their job security, organized police bureaucracies, along with other public employee groups, lobbied for legislation to limit administrative discretion. For example, the law providing for good behavior tenure for policemen had phrases like "written charges" and "formal hearing" as necessary steps in any removal proceeding. Policemen insisted on the right to be represented by counsel and to make the hearing a formal judicial proceeding. They were aided in their quest by citizens who believed formal civil service procedures the best mechanism for securing a disinterested, professional bureaucracy and weakening the power of the political machines. Those interested in the reform of municipal government faced a formidable dilemma. The structure that would allow the good man the maximum power to achieve the goals of good government would also permit the self-seeking scoundrel to advance his interests at the expense of the public welfare. Limiting administrators' freedom of action to protect against abuse of power encouraged rank and file resistance to innovative leadership. The police were not simply side-lines observers in this instance. Their interests were best preserved by stringent restrictions upon administrators' authority. In the final analysis what the police wanted, and what to some extent they have achieved, is *autonomy*, the freedom to do their jobs and maintain their prerogatives with minimum outside interference.[7]

The involved relationships between political parties, civic groups, and the organized police bureaucracy have led to a considerable reduction in external control of police affairs. Reformers wanted to eliminate politicians from having any say in police appointments and promotions, and policemen succeeded in preventing administrators from gaining a totally free hand on discipline. The law and the courts provide some protection for policemen against arbitrary ad-ministrative action, although the powers of discipline and transfer give commanders strong controls over their men's working lives. But overall, in recent decades, the power of the organized bureaucracy has grown tremendously. Groups such as the Fraternal Order of Police and the Patrolmen's Benevolent Association exercise consid-erable influence both within many police departments and at city halls and state legislatures.

At the same time that its own political power has burgeoned, the bureaucracy has learned to condemn any outside concern about the police department as political interference and to ride out any inter-nal demand for drastic change.[8] Textbooks and manuals on police administration of the 1930s and 1940s, such as Bruce Smith's *Police Systems in the United States,* warned vigorously about the "savage threat" that political interference had on the morale and efficiency of a police force.[9] In cities like Los Angeles and Chicago, police scan-dals paved the way for administrators like William Parker and O. W. Wilson who embodied the model of professional impartial law en-forcement and who would brook no political involvement in their professional decisions.

In a large and complex department, however, it might prove easier to eliminate political interference at the top than lower down the line. The commissioner or chief might under certain circumstances, such as the aftermath of a major scandal, demand and receive a "free hand." But he cannot always prevent his precinct and district commanders from developing or maintaining substantial understandings with the local political power structure. The commissioner may find his subordinates more involved in the political life of their districts than he is at the higher level. Commissioners also find that lack of political influence in police affairs can also mean lack of political support. No political interference can mean no outside help for the administrator who wants to move his department in new directions or who wants to break established patterns of power and influence within his department.[10]

New York is unique because of the complexity of the city and the size of its police department, about 30,000 members. But some of its problems exist on a smaller scale in other major cities. A recurrent theme in New York's police history is the great difficulty an administrator has in capturing control over his own department. Superintendent George Walling, who retired in 1885, complained bitterly about his inability as superintendent to control his subordinates. In the 1890s Theodore Roosevelt chafed at his lack of ultimate disciplinary power. Commissioner Howard Leary granted a long interview to the *New York Times* in the spring of 1970, not long before he resigned, where he emphasized that it is much easier for the commissioner to identify problems than it is to mount the resources to deal with them. If the commissioner looks to City Hall and the mayor for help, unless of course he is simply asking for more men and more money, he is vulnerable to the charge of a political sellout, of allowing politics in police affairs. If he tries to go it alone, the bureaucracy can ignore his directives or undercut them.[11]

On paper the commissioner has formidable powers of control and discipline; in practice he finds that his resources are limited. The bureaucracy represents a voting bloc of impressive size and political sophistication; many businessmen and other citizens want to retain police goodwill, and in a time of fear of mugging and crime in the streets generally, the police can present themselves as the protectors of society who must not be tampered with politically. Small businessmen in Akron, Ohio, display signs in their shop windows, "Support Your Local Police: Keep Them Independent." For these reasons the bureaucracy can stop or greatly modify any attempt to transform traditional police practices and prerogatives. Commissioners have found they have a difficult enough time surviving in an atmosphere of constant crisis, and that no matter what their initial attitudes toward graft, corruption, and brutality, they have been forced to spend most of their time defending their departments.

The police bureaucracy has worked hard and successfully to ensure that police commanders including the chief or commissioner will come up through the ranks. "Promotion from within" and "the value of career service" are two of the bureaucracy's most cherished slogans, and in many instances police groups have succeeded in making these slogans into unofficial law at least.[12]

Controlling the sources of top leadership in this way is one of the more important goals and achievements of the bureaucracy in its drive for autonomy. Policemen, like most people, prefer to move along in accustomed ways rather than being receptive and alert to whatever new directions a particular commissioner might try to insist upon. And making sure that the commissioner is "one of their own" helps to guarantee more of the same rather than anything new and different. When Mayor John Lindsay wanted to move the New York Police Department in new directions, he went outside the city for his first police commissioner. But he minimized the challenge to the bureaucracy by appointing Howard R. Leary, who had twenty-six years of experience in the Philadelphia force at all levels from patrolman to commissioner.

Leary survived as long as he did in the jungle that is New York City politics because of his considerable political abilities. The commissioner recognized the power of the Patrolmen's Benevolent Association and cultivated a satisfactory relationship with its head, John Cassesse. Liberal elements in the city objected to this relationship as the association seemed to be the embodiment of all that was backward and obscurantist in the police establishment. But Leary realized that the formal powers of the commissioner's office would amount to nothing without a political base. He could receive some help from the mayor, but the rumors are that Leary and Lindsay had their differences, perhaps an inevitable result given their respective roles. Where does the police commissioner's primary loyalty lie—to the mayor who appoints or the department he heads?[13]

Even if the commissioner and the mayor have identical conceptions of the police function and proper police performance, the commissioner would still have to seek internal alliances. The mayor simply cannot help him in the difficult task of gaining control over his own department. The head of the Patrolmen's Benevolent Association can provide some help in this area; the cost to the commissioner is that he must forego some of the formal powers of his office and pay heed to the bureaucracy's conception of its role. In reality, therefore, the commissioner's formidable formal powers remain mainly on paper unless he has the political skill and the internal allies to make them effective. Leary often spoke about "reorganizing" and "modernizing" the department, which was a polite way of referring to increased centralization and expansion of his authority; but he was careful not to threaten his working relationship with police organizations.

New York's recent commissioner, Patrick V. Murphy, concentrated on police commanders, the bosses, demanding that they curb corruption and "cooping"—sleeping or otherwise malingering on duty—within their commands. Murphy was especially concerned about possible police relationships with narcotics dealers and suppliers. The new commissioner also disregarded seniority in making top appointments. He received favorable national publicity, although he seems to have generated serious internal opposition. He had the strong support of Mayor Lindsay, and with persistent revelations of corruption and time-wasting combined with the city's crime rate, he had substantial external support. However, Murphy resigned in the spring of 1973.[14]

In many departments, the head, whether called chief, commissioner, or director of public safety, serves at the pleasure of the mayor or can otherwise be easily removed. His tenure is distinctly less secure than that of the men under him, who are nominally subject to his control and direction. Cleveland, under Mayor Carl Stokes, had something of a revolving door in the top leadership of the police department. Stokes, one of the few black mayors of a major American city, had difficulty finding men who could retain his confidence and that of the police at the same time. This may have been an impossible task, given the differences in background and political philosophy between Stokes and most Cleveland policemen, but it is hard to be effective at the top without rank and file support. No mat-

ter what the formal powers of control and discipline may be, civil
service protection and internal cohesion against outside threat reduce
the administrator's ability to run his own department.[15]

City Hall and other external groups who want to make substantial
changes in police performance encounter the police code of solidarity, which makes policemen overcome their internal differences and
conflicts to resist outside pressure. Cleavages between patrolmen and
superior officers, between the uniformed and the detective force,
between Catholics and Protestants, and among supporters of different
aspirants for top jobs are forgotten in the face of outside pressure.
Such solidarity has long been part of American police life. As previously noted, policemen are sometimes willing to commit perjury to
protect each other. One of the standards burned into rookies is that
they are not to talk about department business to outsiders; anyone
who reveals anything that might damage the department in general
or a fellow officer in particular faces serious internal consequences.

Such cohesion and solidarity reduces the administrator's control
over his own department by making it difficult if not impossible for
him to use tactics of divide and conquer. He cannot easily play off
one group against another in such a situation, nor can he find many
men willing to testify about illegal or injurious behavior by fellow
policemen. Such "stoolies" are shunned by their colleagues.[16] In
extreme situations the administrator can be faced with attacks of
"blue flu," massive sick calls by policemen, an orgy of ticket writing,
or the opposite, a refusal to issue summonses, thereby cutting the
community's income. The civil service procedures and job security
for the rank and file, combined with most police administrators'
political vulnerability, make the commissioner's or chief's task more
often one of maintaining the status quo and keeping scandal to a
minimum than of embarking on new and innovative programs. The
administrator finds that he has to live with a certain amount of
corruption and hopes that it does not explode in his face. On charges
of police malpractice and violations of civil liberties, most heads
defend the practices of their respective departments, not only because
they agree with them as a result of their own police careers, but
because they must defend them to retain any degree of control over
their organizations.[17]

As previously noted, defenders of civil service procedures believed that these would eliminate "politics" from police affairs. They did not, at least until the 1940s in most American cities, and to the present day in a good many. Ambitious young policemen could see no reason why they should wait long hard years for promotion and desirable assignments, especially when political friends and supporters could advance the process considerably. So policemen often actively sought alliances with influential political figures. They looked for a "rabbi" or a "hook," the New York terms for an influential patron either within or without the department, who could help in promotion and good assignments, known as "milking the tit," or in protection from disciplinary action. Often the very men who pressed for "no political interference" in police affairs sought such intervention when it would advance their own careers. The paradox is more apparent than real, for what many policemen hoped for was freedom from undesired external control under the guise of eliminating politics, while at the same time retaining the freedom to seek desired outside alliances. Of course, it was not always possible to have one's cake in the form of no outside control and to eat it in the form of political help for a promotion. Still people tried, just like those citizens who press for a high level of public services and low taxes at the same time.[18]

The most carefully drawn procedures in the world could not prevent some political influence from creeping in, especially if the system were to have any flexibility at all. The more inflexible the procedures to eliminate the spoilsmen were made, the more those already in positions of power could resist demands for change. The alternative to political involvement was greater bureaucratization with all that meant in terms of immobility and increased resistance to breaking routine and setting forth new methods. Most American police departments until the 1940s and 1950s were only partly bureaucratized, and a strong amount of political influence prevailed. In the attempt to limit if not eliminate this influence police forces became more bureaucratized. The result is that while critics complained of political interference and control of police forces throughout much of our police history, in the last decade or so the bulk of the complaints have shifted to charges of excessive bureaucratic immobility and isolation from community desires. In the early 1960s scholars like Nathan Glazer, Wallace Sayre, and Herbert Kaufman charged that the New York police had become a closed system, more intent on preserving traditional practices and prerogatives than in serving the city. The political moves to reduce politics vastly promoted this process.[19] Police and the general public regard any involvement of elected officials in police affairs as political interference.

Mayors sometimes encourage this trend by boasting about their keeping hands off the police. There are other benefits in this strategy than simply a feeling of virtue. A hands-off policy means that the mayors can disclaim any responsibility for police operations. Anyone unhappy or aggrieved is sent to police headquarters to seek satisfaction; there is little point in a mayor who has vowed to maintain police autonomy listening to citizen grievances against the police. Thus "no political interference" may not always be self-sacrificing. A mayor may give up police patronage or influence, but by so doing he also gives up any political responsibility for the police. A scandal-marked administration or one coming into office immediately afterwards finds this strategy particularly attractive. Major police scandals in Los Angeles and Chicago led to administrators like Chief William Parker of Los Angeles and Commissioner O. W. Wilson of Chicago who would brook no political involvement in their professional decisions. The mayors of these cities thereby escaped some of the consequences of policy making. If one objected to the LAPD, attack Chief Parker, not Mayor Yorty.[20]

The police bureaucracy has used "no political interference" as a strong negative slogan in its drive for autonomy. Autonomy promotes the avoidance of evil by keeping the police "free from politics." A more positive argument was that police work, if not yet a profession, should become one. A hallmark of a profession is the claim that only its practitioners have sufficient expertise to judge its performance and evaluate its members. By definition, the members of a profession are set apart from the rest of society by virtue of their specialized training and experience, and if a profession is going to perform its social role and live up to its responsibilities, it must have autonomy. It must control entry and police itself; nobody else is capable of doing it. As could be expected, the movements for police bureaucratization and professionalization have run on somewhat parallel tracks, although conceptually and to some degree operationally they often conflict, and it is to the subject of professionalization that we now turn.[21]

Chapter 9

The Professionalization of the Police

Many facets of American life have become professionalized since the latter part of the nineteenth century. As the economic and social order became ever more complex with the extension of the division of labor, the spread of industrialism and urbanization, and the development of large organizations, more and more occupations claimed for themselves professional status. In contrast to the pre-Civil War period, when it seemed undemocratic to demand specialized training in order to practice medicine, occupational associations now demanded licensing procedures which would separate the quacks from the qualified. Physicians, lawyers, engineers, nurses, social workers, and teachers tried to raise their status and their income by stressing the value of their services to society and by insisting that performing these services properly demanded education, skill, a rigid set of work standards, and a particular code of ethics. In many instances professional or would-be professional groups enlisted the aid of the state in establishing licensing standards which would give the occupational association control over entry into the field. The associations also claimed that they alone had the credentials to judge the practices of an existing member and demanded that in effect they had to police themselves; laymen simply were not qualified. Many groups drew up elaborate codes of professional ethics which, not surprisingly, they have often been reluctant to apply against particular members; no one can be sure when he or she might be next.[1]

Nineteenth-century policemen could not claim professional status, nor is there much evidence that they were interested in it. In most cities, entry into the department demanded political connections, not education. Standards of performance revolved around staying out of trouble. The prudent man soon learned that in sticky situations, unless the people involved were black or other obvious outcasts, the safest course was to do nothing. Positive action against the politically potent could easily result in an unwanted transfer or other punitive measures.[2]

Policemen could and did insist upon the value of their experience, that while almost anyone could become a policeman, the man who had been on the force for any length of time had developed sense, skill, and judgment in the instantaneous decisions he could be called upon to make at any time. Policemen insisted that only men who had dealt with quarrelsome drunks or who had come upon a robbery in progress could judge whether the use of club or gun was justified in a particular case. Their school was the street, and only men who had attended that school by pounding a beat could evaluate the quality of police service. In the twentieth century, larger cities have developed elaborate police-training schools. Still, the most important part of the rookie's education comes after he has left the academy.

Just as in the nineteenth century, experienced men go to great lengths to teach the new recruits, to mold them in the traditional values and practices of a particular department. In this way, the old hands help the newcomers; they also help themselves by ensuring that the new men will not damage the reputation of the department or the well-being of their colleagues. William Westley, in his study of a midwestern department in the late 1940s, emphasized the importance of the socialization of the rookies by the veterans, just as Cornelius Willemse did a generation before. The same theme was found in the early segments of the popular television program "Adam 12," only now the rookie and the veteran rode together in a radio car. The principle is the same, even though the setting might be different.[3]

This process of on-the-job training, of indoctrinating new men into the traditionally sanctioned practices, often frustrates the formal educational effects of departments. The police academy might teach one conception of the policemen's role, a more professional one; the old hands in the precincts are likely to undermine these values and to downgrade the credentials of academy instructors. In this way a traditional "tough cop" approach can continue despite "professionally-oriented" formal training programs.

Nor does the process of socialization cease with the end of a tour of duty. Policemen form a social as well as an occupational group. Because of their unusual working hours, their daily involvement with the underside of society, their power to arrest, their responsibility to control other people's behavior, and the cynical attitude they develop toward people in general, policemen have largely been isolated from civilians. In some instances this isolation is imposed by civilians who don't want to associate with policemen. Andrea Kornmann, who wrote a little book about the police in the 1880s under the pen name of "A Policeman's Wife," complained that the other people in their building did not want to have anything to do with her when they learned her husband was a policeman. Often the isolation was self-imposed, as policemen came to believe that their work experiences gave them a view of life and society that civilians could not match. H. L. Mencken, who began his career as a reporter in his native Baltimore in the 1890s, once remarked in a sympathetic essay that policemen lived social lives as circumscribed as that of Supreme Court justices. Their social lives, then, reinforced their occupational cohesiveness and increased the importance of tradition and group solidarity.[4]

Often the demands for breaking away from tradition and substituting professionalization came from outside police departments, from scholars and reformers who wanted to break the hold of the past, which they saw as perpetuating police graft, toleration of commercialized vice, and discourtesy and excessive use of force against civilians. They wanted a new image for police work, one that would escape the negative consequences of the past. Raymond Fosdick's survey of European police forces for the Rockefeller Foundation and his later work on American police emphasized the superiority of European police because of the higher standards and lengthy tenure of senior police administrators, who were men of professional stature and were granted professional recognition. Fosdick also approved of the English practice of recruiting London policemen from the countryside, direct from the farm whenever possible, who could then be molded in the desired image of a London "Bobby." The disadvantage of this and similar practices is that English policemen may be even more separated from the rest of the community than American.[5]

Fosdick, Raymond Moley, Bruce Smith and other scholarly writers of the 1920s conceived of professionalization as an antidote to political interference and manipulation of police forces. Only a truly professional force could be an effective crime-fighting agency, and unless American police departments upgraded their standards and performance Americans would be engulfed in a rising tide of crime. These writers gave the stamp of scholarly approval to the popular picture of the 1920s as a time when bootleg booze and gangsters' blood flooded the streets of American cities. Chicago came closest to fitting the stereotype, which was exaggerated at best and positively misleading at worst. Yet historically, what people think is true is usually more important than what is true, for they act on the basis of their beliefs.[6]

In the 1920s and early 1930s, crime and its control occupied an important position among political issues, and professionalizing the police seemed to be one answer to the problem. Reduce the politicians' influence, train and educate policemen and especially senior administrators, and create a favorable public climate for the development of a professional force: these were the prescriptions of the promoters of professionalism. Citizens' groups paid for surveys of a variety of police departments; the Wickersham Commission appointed by President Herbert Hoover devoted considerable attention to the police; and universities began offering courses in police administration.

Scholars and commentators were appalled at the low educational level and IQs of policemen and especially the senior officers. The Wickersham Commission reported that 60 percent of the police of that time, the late 1920s, had no high school education at all. In Kansas City, five of seven lieutenants and thirty-one of thirty-five sergeants never attended high school. In one way this was understandable, as the ranking men would be older and have come to adolescence at a time when most people went to work by the age of 14 or 15. The commission also compared the scores on the Alpha test employed by the army during World War I of freshmen at the University of California with members of the Los Angeles, Minneapolis, Kansas City, and Cleveland police departments. More than 90 percent of the freshmen scored in the B range or better. Los Angeles made the best police showing, with 27 percent in the B or better category, while Cleveland, at the bottom, had only 17 percent. The commission believed police recruits should score at least a B. In the Cleveland department, and no doubt in others as well, ranking officers scored lower on IQ tests than did the patrolmen. Older men may have scored less well because they had fewer educational opportunities; an alternative explanation is that more intelligent recruits left police work before they advanced to senior positions. Scholars worried that the status and conditions of police work were so poor that ambitious and capable young men who did enter it left at the first opportunity. Making police work a profession and raising its status would attract a better class of recruit. In a reciprocal pattern, an upward spiral if you will, a better image and better men would reinforce each other with the end result of superior police service.[7]

Naturally, many policemen resisted these trends which would put a premium on book learning and which would make extensive changes in patterns of performance and promotion. The policeman who had learned his trade on the streets saw no reason why he should go to any other kind of school, and the traditional "tough cop" scorned the college professors who presumed to tell him how to do his job. The patrolman who looked forward to promotion because of his political contacts or for making a "good pinch"—an important arrest which did not create negative political consequences—had little use for proposals to recruit higher administrators directly from the legal profession or the universities, or at least to require advanced academic training for candidates for promotion. The cynical patrolman who said that the only book needed to advance in the Cleveland Police Department was a bankbook expressed a certain folk wisdom.

But while most policemen scorned the pretensions of professionalism and supported business as usual, some energetic and ambitious police officers did wish to improve their image and raise the status of their calling. Cornelius F. Cahalane, a deputy chief inspector of the New York Police Department, wrote two books for police-training purposes. The first, entitled *Police Practice and Procedure,* concentrated on New York laws and practices because it was designed for use as a text in the New York police school. His second, *The Policeman,* originally published in 1923 and recently reprinted, covered police work generally; Cahalane believed from his own experience and visiting departments all over the United States and Canada that the basic problems and principles were similar. Cahalane produced a sensible and thoughtful volume in which he set forth the law governing police actions and the recommended procedure for handling various situations patrolmen would be likely to encounter. Cahalane, like most of the professionals, placed more emphasis on crime control and detection than he did on police peace-keeping activities. He says nothing, for example, about the domestic dispute, the family quarrel, which traditionally has taken up a great deal of police time and which is one of the most difficult police tasks but which only recently has been given the attention it deserves.[8]

August Vollmer was another of the early police professionals. Vollmer served for many years as the chief of the Berkeley, California, department and later taught at the University of Chicago and the University of California at Berkeley. In the late 1920s he wrote or supervised much of the Wickersham Commission reports on the police. In 1936 he published *The Police and Modern Society,* which surveyed police responsibilities for major crimes, vice, traffic, "general service," and crime prevention. The topics indicate the scope and thrust of the book. Vollmer gives some attention to the domestic dispute, all of a paragraph, in which he notes that such calls "may encroach seriously upon the time at the disposal of the police." The implication is that cooling family squabbles is not real police work, which is crime prevention and control, not keeping the peace.[9]

The movement for professionalism accelerated during, and as a result of, the great depression of the 1930s. The revelations of police behavior regarding prohibition and the reliance on third-degree tactics in securing information and confessions seriously impaired their prestige and public image. Police spokesmen set out to repair the damage by invoking the rhetoric of professionalism. Before the crash, policing had been a working-class job, suitable for "greenhorns," recent immigrants, and others with reasonably good health who valued a secure and steady job but who did not have much in the way of formal education or mechanical or technical skill. The depression changed that pattern. Police departments suddenly became attractive to young men shut off from other opportunities by the economic slowdown. In New York City, experienced patrolmen received $3,000 a year, a princely wage for the time and one in a job with maximum security. As a result, departments could be extremely selective in their recruiting, assuming that their cities had any money to add men or even replace those retiring or dying. Half of the men in the New York Police Academy class of 1940 had bachelor's degrees. In his book *Behind the Shield,* Arthur Niederhoffer, a member of that class who remained a policeman for more than twenty years before taking a Ph.D. in sociology, asserts that these men introduced a strong note of professionalism into the New York department. Their stronghold became the police academy, where they tried to inculcate their principles into the new recruits.

These principles included a sensitivity to the findings of the social sciences on crime and disorderly behavior, a reduction of racial and ethnic stereotypes, a respect for the letter of the law, and a commitment to the values of integrity and efficiency in police operations. The traditional approach remained common in the precincts, however, and Niederhoffer postulated something of a civil war in the department between the professionals and the traditionalists. The college-trained professionals had a distinct advantage in promotion exams, which the traditionalists resented, and many of them were Jewish, which generated antipathies in the proverbially Irish-dominated force. In recent years the movement for professionalism in New York has been arrested somewhat by the fact that the depression group has retired and few of the new men entering the department have any college training. With the return of relatively full employment during and after World War II, the police have reverted to their traditional role as a haven of security for working- and lower-middle-class youth.[10] The professional impulse will remain to some extent, especially with the availability of federal money for upgrading police forces.

Major scandals in the nineteenth and early twentieth centuries generated "throw the rascals out" reform movements; such scandals in recent decades have increased police professionalism. The most obvious examples are Los Angeles under the late William Parker and Chicago under O. W. Wilson.

Wilson, a protégé of August Vollmer's, succeeded Vollmer on the faculty at the University of California after having achieved a nationwide reputation for cleaning up the Wichita, Kansas, department. In 1960 Mayor Richard Daley brought Wilson to Chicago in the wake of a major scandal in a city and a police department where scandal was commonplace. In this instance, however, a professional burglar named several police officers as accomplices, which went beyond the usual "ice"—payments to allow illegal enterprises to function. Wilson exercised a firm hand in Chicago, reducing the number of police districts and cutting some of the ties between local commanders and local politicians. He established a large internal investigation division to curb police graft and pushed forward younger officers to break the power of a very senior group of captains who were the real heads of the Chicago Police Department. Wilson also modernized the communications and radio car operations to provide faster and more efficient service.

Like most professionals, the commissioner objected to court restrictions upon police operations. Wilson attacked strenuously the Escobedo decision, which voided a conviction based on a confession obtained when the suspect's lawyer was in the building but not allowed to see his client. He later wrote that "One of the problems we, as police, face is when sympathy for the unfortunate merges into favoritism for the criminal. . . . In this country, tolerance for wrongdoers has turned into a fad. What we need is some intolerance toward criminal behavior."[11]

Like Wilson, William Parker was born in South Dakota and later moved to California. He joined the Los Angeles department in 1927, acquired a law degree through night study, and worked his way rapidly up the ranks. In 1950, after a major vice scandal, Parker became chief of police. For the thirty-two years prior to his appointment the average tenure in the job had been two years; Parker remained as chief until his death in 1966. During his years in office, Parker fought a running battle with civil rights groups, liberals, and blacks. However, he had strong support among middle-class whites and conservative politicians like Mayor Samuel Yorty, although Parker's comments and conduct during the Watts riots of 1965 increased demands for his ouster. He told a news conference that the riots began when "one person threw a rock and then, like monkeys in a zoo, others started throwing rocks."[12]

Parker's impact on the police and the city of Los Angeles shows the strengths and the very real limitations of the professional style. Parker conceived of the police as a thin blue line protecting society from barbarism and Communist subversion. The police had to be

efficient, incorruptible, and dedicated to preserving social well-
being without expecting much in the way of economic reward or
public praise. Urban society was a jungle in which, without the
restraining hand of the police, the evil impulses of men would run
roughshod over morality and justice. Crime, in Parker's view, resulted not from economic and social conditions but within the
minds of men who had made a conscious decision to violate the
law. Criminal acts arose from the "fundamental concepts that distinguish animal from man and man from his creator." Man is a
creature of belief and will, and these are the sources of criminal
behavior. "Hunger, poverty, maladjustment, and other physical
problems do not incite crime—they incite beliefs that may produce
crime." If we are to control crime, we must change the beliefs of
those individuals who commit crime, for the criminal does not believe he is doing wrong. "However faulty his premises, however
weak his logic, however selfish his reasons and however transitory
his beliefs, he acts in accord with his own concepts." The majority
of people who have suffered from poverty and deprivation have not
become criminals, which was proof to Parker that individual con-
science outweighed social conditions in accounting for crime.[13]

In the chief's view, only the law and law enforcement saved society
from the horrors of anarchy. "If criminal acts are symptoms of a
conflict between individual morals and accepted morals, then the
problem can only be resolved by resolving the conflict. Either the law,
our artificial standard of morals, must be altered, or the individual's
standard must be brought into closer conformity with popular requirements. The two in conflict invariably produce crime." Parker
did not favor "decriminalizing" deviant behavior. "It is apparent that
our way of life cannot survive if we so relax and broaden our laws
that almost any individual's standard will conform with them. Such
a course would be little more than anarchy. Therefore the only alternative is to alter individual standards."[14] Any deviation from the
norms of society is the deviant's fault, and the police must act against
him accordingly. The police, then, had to enforce the law without
fear or favor. They were not simply to keep order; they were to stop
the commission of crime wherever possible by their physical intervention and to deter it by creating maximum possibilities of detection, arrest, and successful prosecution.[15]

Parker's position involves some obvious difficulties. His "rotten apple" theory of criminality and unfettered-free-will view of human nature hardly comported with the findings of the social and behavioral sciences that criminal and deviant behavior closely correlated with poor and deprived environments and resulting weak family structures. Certain inner-city areas have remained high-crime districts for a long time, regardless of the specific groups and individuals involved. Forty years ago they might have been Polish and Irish; now they are black or Spanish speaking. City after city shows the same pattern of high crime and delinquency rates in the decaying areas near the core, with progressively lower rates in the areas farther out from the center of the city. Something more is involved in the genesis of deviant and therefore criminal behavior than malformed consciences.[16]

Moreover, Parker realized that his brand of professional police performance lacked total public support. The history of police in the United States was something of a long, dirty story. "However bright the present and promising the future, the past hangs as a millstone about the neck of the professional minded police."[17] Too often, the voters, in their support of political machines which controlled and manipulated the police in anything but a professional manner, showed that they did not want energetic, efficient, impartial law enforcement. Paradoxically, the "crooked cop" then became a symbol of all that was detestable about the political system supported by the majority itself. The public demanded a police department subject to political influence and manipulation and then condemned the force for its crookedness. Parker emphasized the political and public relations problems of the police. "The real difficulty is not that of doing a good job; it is not even that of telling the public that it is being done. The most important and most difficult task is the securing of a market for professional police work—a public that will demand it, pay the cost of it, and stand behind it."[18]

The professional policeman found himself in the uncomfortable position of offering a service that society required for its very survival, at least by his lights, but which many people did not seem to want very much. Parker looked to the business community for support as a group that would have a vested interest in having the police succeed in their endeavor to control crime. "Police organizations over the entire nation look to the businessman to supply the same realistic thinking to problems of community law enforcement that they have applied to private enterprise."[19] The people who were not businessmen, who thought themselves not the beneficiaries of private enterprise but its victims, saw Parker and his police not as the defenders of the rights and liberties of the people but rather as an alien army of occupation protecting an exploitative establishment. Furthermore, many businessmen were ambivalent about the police. They wanted protection and service but they also wanted the police to look the other way on parking violations or commercial frauds. In a diverse, pluralistic society based upon the pursuit of individual gain and gratification Parker would have a difficult time finding widespread support for his moral absolutism.[20]

Like most professional policemen, Parker opposed any restrictions upon police methods. He acknowledged the existence of the Bill of Rights, referring to "those inalienable rights of individuals which are the greatest possessions of a free people." If police forces did not recognize these rights, they would be false to their trusts. The legacy of police brutality constituted part of the negative inheritance of police history. "We still suffer today from the abuse of power by those who preceded us in the police profession. I believe that to avoid these fatal errors we must know and recognize the legal rights of individuals and be fully cognizant of when the law permits us to invade personal liberty."[21] But the law should give the police wide latitude to use wiretaps and "bugs" and to conduct search and seizure. To Parker the guarantees of the Bill of Rights were not absolute but relative. (Note the contrast between this view and his attitude toward crime and criminals.) Wiretaps and bugs allowed the police to learn of and solve crimes that would go otherwise undetected; therefore the police should be allowed to use them, and those laws that prevented their use or barred the introduction of such evidence should be repealed. The Fourth Amendment guarantees against unreasonable search and seizure did not in Parker's view mean that the police had to secure warrants. The police could perform search and seizure which, if done by civilians, would constitute illegal trespass.

Any conflict between effective police operation and individual rights should be resolved in favor of the police; only in this way could society be protected. Evidence obtained illegally should still be admissible in court. It was not the police who suffered from the exclusion of illegally obtained evidence but society. The courts' concern for the rights of suspects and defendants represented a misplaced order of priorities. To Parker, the rights of society, exemplified in professional police practice, took precedence over the rights of the individual, especially one who was probably guilty of a crime. Crime and criminals constituted so grave a threat to the social order that the police had to be free to use methods objectionable to those concerned about the right of privacy and the right to speak freely without the fear of governmental eavesdropping.

Parker denied that local police would threaten tyranny and a police state. He thought it perfectly possible to set legislative guidelines for the use of electronic eavesdropping without violating the rights of the law abiding.[22] Many independent observers deny this assertion because a bug or wiretap picks up anything said on the phone or in the area involved, and because once the principle is granted it is impossible to police the police on the extent of their use of electronic eavsedropping. The political implications are frightening in that any dissenting individuals or groups could become victims of governmental snooping. The danger is greatest on the federal level, although local forces often engage in similar monitoring.[23]

Parker's conception of professionalism insisted that the police had the expertise, the responsibility, and the discipline to use eavesdropping and search and seizure in such a way as to benefit society. Therefore decisions on the use of these methods should be left to the police. Like physicians, policemen required autonomy. They could not do their jobs if they were going to be continually second-guessed by the courts and other civilians. Society had to *trust* its police to use the formidable powers of the law in a wise and equitable manner and not to trample on the rights of the innocent in the process. As professionals the police could separate the sheep from the goats, and the courts and civilian agencies generally should accept policemen's expertise and not throw roadblocks in the way of their effective performance.[24]

Two questions immediately arise: Should anyone, no matter how dedicated and incorruptible, be entrusted with the powers and scope Parker demanded? Secondly, do American police forces reach the standard required for the chief's view of professionalism? The first question involves the contrast between freedom and control, between respect for individual and group freedom and insistence on complete conformity and predictability. Parker leaned heavily on the distinction between liberty and license; the former had to be protected but the latter had no rights at all. But how is one to determine where one leaves off and the other begins? Perhaps more important—who is to make that determination? To Parker the answer was obvious: the law and the law enforcers.

As a result of their backgrounds and their work experiences, policemen view most departures from the norms of conventional, predictable behavior as immoral and potentially dangerous. Most departments recruit working- and lower-middle-class youths attracted by the security of a police career. They are usually conventional to begin with, and their conventionalism is reinforced by the atmosphere and standards of their organizations.[25] As rookies they are trained to be suspicious, to be on the lookout for anything that might indicate criminal or disorderly activity. They soon learn that any call or any situation that necessitates police action, no matter how ordinary or routine, can lead to verbal and physical abuse. Their preference is for perfectly ordinary and predictable behavior among the civilians on their routes; anything else is a potential threat and may be dangerous for them. In a society of "cop-haters," policemen develop a strong demand for respect, even deference. If the authority of the uniform does not induce respectful and deferential attitudes among civilians, some men are prone to let fist and club earn it for them. Men in uniform, motivated by the values of authority and respectability, look upon dropouts from the straight world with loathing and contempt. Not only do hippies break the law by begging and using drugs, but their whole life-style is a rejection of discipline, order, and control.[26]

Politically, policemen have long had a penchant for joining extremist, right-wing organizations. In the 1890s many of them joined the American Protective Association, a Protestant nativist group opposed to the rising political power of Roman Catholics. In the 1920s policemen in southern and northern cities became members of the revived Ku Klux Klan; in the early 1960s a considerable number of the Dallas police force were reputedly Klan members. In recent years the John Birch Society, the extremist organization whose head condemned President Eisenhower as a tool of the Communist conspiracy, has attracted many policemen, either as members or strong sympathizers.

The goals of these organizations comport with policemen's social backgrounds—upper-lower and lower-middle class—and their occupational demands for order. These groups have been strongly nationalistic and moralistic, sentiments which correspond with the beliefs of many policemen, who often have served in the military, who are strongly patriotic in the My Country, Right or Wrong tradition, and who have personal and occupational commitments to a particular moral code. Secondly, these organizations worked to stem the tide of unwanted social change, to preserve the status quo, and even to recover the cherished, if often mythical, values of the past.[27]

Both the American Protective Association and the Ku Klux Klan specifically directed their activities against new groups struggling for political power and economic and social advancement. The APA reached its peak of power and influence in the early 1890s, when Catholics began capturing political offices on the state and local level throughout the Northeast and the Middle West. Many Protestants conceived of this Catholic upsurge as an individual and an institutional threat. They feared the effects of Catholic officeholders on Protestant civil servants and the American pattern of church and state relations. (Contrary to popular belief, the tradition on church-state in the nineteenth century was not complete separation. Rather the state aided religious institutions, especially nondenominational or interdenominational Protestant ones, to perform charitable and welfare functions. Some Catholic institutions also received aid. The impact of the APA movement was to sever many of these ties, to ensure that Catholic politicians did not funnel substantial funds into Catholic institutions).[28]

As Kenneth Jackson has shown in his *The Ku Klux Klan in the City, 1915-1930*, the Klan attracted working-, and lower-middle-class Protestants who feared the "invasion" of their neighborhoods by blacks and new immigrants, mainly Catholics and Jews. The Klan made the biggest impact on rapidly growing communities where class and neighborhood lines were fluid and where the prospects of unwanted social change were greatest. Klansmen hoped to use political action, and occasionally intimidation and violence, to hold back the forces of change and preserve their status. To Klansmen, Catholics, Jews, and blacks threatened the dominance of white Protestants; but Klansmen were not those WASPs who could retreat to their suburbs and their country clubs and maintain a splendid isolation. The Klan recruited from the economically pinched and the socially marginal (policemen fit this description precisely) who did not have the resources to run away or to construct barriers against newcomers. They had to stay and either accept the newcomers or maintain a hostile posture and hope they could retard neighborhood transition.[29]

Unlike the American Protective Association and the Klan, the John Birch Society welcomes Catholic members; indeed Catholics make up a disproportionate number of Birchites. Regarded for so long as somehow un-American, many Catholics responded with a strident nationalism, a superpatriotism that made love of country almost, if not quite, the equivalent of love of God. However, Catholic Americanism has been a selective acceptance of American culture and tradition. Most Catholics have not been comfortable with the American tradition as exemplified by Thomas Jefferson, Ralph Waldo Emerson, and John Dewey, thinkers who rejected authoritarianism and exalted intellectual freedom. On the other hand, Catholics, with relatively few exceptions, have been enthusiastic supporters of economic individualism. Like most other Americans, they have equated freedom with economic opportunity and the ability to use property and dispose of income as one sees fit. In the grim years of the long cold war with the Soviet Union and later China, Catholics could point with pride to their long record of anticommunism and more than ever equate Catholicism and Americanism.[30] Working- and lower-middle-class Catholics, heavily represented in urban police forces, have combined with Catholic businessmen and professionals in this "crusade" against communist subversion. No one knows how many policemen are members of the John Birch Society, but observers close to the scene have been struck by the number of men who express sympathy with Birchite principles if they are not actually members. Similarly, many policemen supported George Wallace in his bid for the presidency in 1968.[31]

Policemen may be attracted to extremist groups because of their sense of public rejection, of being outcasts from the society they have sworn to protect and defend. The mainstream of American political and social life only occasionally reflects the cynical and apocalyptic view of society prevalent among policemen who see themselves engaged in a constant battle against barbarism and anarchy to protect people who are too stupid to see what is at stake. Policemen are action-oriented people, trained to take charge of a situation and exercise and impose their authority upon possibly resistant civilians. Such men would be likely to be impatient with discussion, debate, and the necessarily slow procedures of democratic government. Like the radical left, the extreme right is impatient with procedural rights and guarantees and seeks quick and total solutions. Policemen with their occupational suspiciousness, their guns and clubs, and their legal right to use sometimes deadly force are prone to support a politics based on a theory of conspiracy, to believe that their opponents are not only wrong but treasonous and immoral, and that drastic action is needed to save morality and social order.[32]

The point is that policemen are not disinterested professionals who can be relied upon to exercise caution and professional reserve in electronic eavesdropping and other infringements upon freedom of speech and association. Policemen as individuals and departments as organizations have not been neutral in their view of advocates of political and social change. In the period before World War II and in some instances after, police forces often functioned as adjuncts of the reigning political machine to discourage challengers and preserve existing power relationships. In recent decades, more and more departments have separated themselves from the political parties, but they continue to resist demands for political and social change coming from the left or the blacks.[33] The police have not acted as disinterested protectors of the rights and liberties of all groups. In the name of law and order, departments have sometimes violated the legal rights of unpopular individuals and associations. The history of union organization and strikes is a case in point. It does not seem likely in future periods of political dissent and racial turmoil that the police will be more neutral and "professional" than they have in the past. Both the beliefs and activities of policemen as individuals and the announced organizational goals of departments make anyone concerned about a free society leery of Parker's dictum that the guarantees of the Bill of Rights are relative and subject to "reasonable" police infringement.

Also, the quality of police recruit in many jurisdictions declined in the 1950s and 1960s, which makes the achievement of professionalism even more unlikely. The depression movement of well-educated men into police work disappeared after World War II, although a few departments, mainly on the West Coast, have raised their educational standards and induced college graduates to become policemen. For the most part, the cities with the most dire need find that they have a difficult time attracting qualified recruits. In New York City the educational attainments and IQs of police rookies dropped in the 1960s. In many cities, pay scales have not kept pace with inflation, and the economic security of a police career has been overmatched by increased insecurity in the form of injury and even death on the job.[34]

The spread of communications devices has lessened discretion for the individual patrolman—although in the nature of things his discretion is still very great—and increased the control of higher command. In the nineteenth century, New York's headquarters sometimes found out about what was going on in some of the precincts by reading the newspapers. The captain in his precinct was a despot, benevolent or not. In the twentieth century, information and communication systems have increased the control that the center—headquarters—can exert on the periphery, the precincts and the men on the streets. Centralization, then, has been one of the major themes of twentieth-century police history. Commanders have much more opportunity to know what is going on among their subordinates and to influence their actions.

The commander's desire for control runs counter to the individual policeman's desire for autonomy. To a considerable extent this is the normal human desire to keep the boss off one's back and to work at one's own pace and style. In addition some men who think of police work as a profession challenge the bureaucratic structure and the commander's (often quite nonprofessional in orientation) desire for control. The professional, whether in law, medicine, or academia, insists that he or she must have autonomy to render the best possible professional service, that the professional can do his work only if he is essentially free from bureaucratic control. Those who want to professionalize police work emphasize the importance of the police task in society, the vital nature of the decisions a policeman is called on to make, and the complex human interactions the job entails. The professional must have skill and the long training to make these decisions quickly and accurately in an often tense and hostile atmosphere and without being unduly harassed or second-guessed from above. Commanders want their subordinates to be responsive to their orders. The professionally-minded patrolman wants to act according to his evaluation of the situation and not according to some bureaucratic directive.

However, the professionals or would-be professionals do not agree on the priorities that should prevail in police work. A minority conceives of the police primarily as peace-keepers and general-service officers who deal with frightened, sick, and defeated persons to make urban life more bearable for them and for the more fortunate. The more usual professional model emphasizes the police as law-enforcers, as crime-fighters, the last thin blue line separating civilization from anarchy.

There is an even larger question, and that is the value of the professional model in the effective performance of the police role in urban society. Parker and the professionals like him stress the paramilitary nature of the police. They are involved in a "war against crime." Prosecuting this war demands the utmost in discipline, dedication, and devotion to duty. Commanders imbued with this philosophy impress upon their subordinates the seriousness of the task and try to make the department respond as a disciplined, well-drilled military organization. Commanders seek ways of evaluating the work of their subordinates in quantitative terms wherever possible, to rate the quality of their performance and their devotion to the goals of the organization in terms of numbers that can be defended to higher authority. A professional department keeps accurate records of criminal incidents and can pinpoint those places and times where the law is likely to be broken.[35]

Many professionals consider "aggressive preventive patrol" the best method of controlling crime in high-risk areas. The force saturates the area with cruisers to the extent possible, while the men assigned are under pressure to justify their presence by a large number of arrests and "field interrogations," which juveniles, who are often the subject, consider harassment or "rousting." Officers are encouraged to issue citations for traffic violations, which gives them the legal right to search cars for evidence of more serious crimes. The professional knows that black adolescent males are statistically the most likely people to commit crimes against property; therefore he gives such individuals special attention, attention which is often deeply resented. The professional is taught to be impersonal, to go by the book, to be an efficient and impartial *enforcer of the law*.[36]

The professional style thus emphasizes the law-enforcement function of the police. The police are to control and, if possible, deter crime through intense law-enforcement activity. In the light of this philosophy the policeman should be the energetic, incorruptible crime-fighter who uses the most advanced technological and scientific methods and devices to bring criminals to justice.

This conception of the police permeates most textbooks in the field and departmental training programs, but this is not the reality of policemen's working lives. Most policemen spend most of their active duty time in service and peace-keeping pursuits. They provide an important record-producing and record-keeping service for the insurance companies in automobile accidents. They direct traffic or provide ambulance service for victims of traffic accidents or heart attacks. They keep drunks from injuring themselves or others. They cool domestic and neighborhood disputes which have reached the violent stage, and the policeman soon learns that it does not do any good to arrest the aggressor since the aggrieved party will not press the complaint anyway. They break up barroom brawls or fights at high school dances, and they keep order at fires so the fire department can do its work.

These tasks are performed most effectively when no arrests are made. The policeman who can maintain and restore order without invoking the formal processes of the law has achieved a valuable social result. He has increased the ability of people to live together in urban society without undue conflict, and he has not saddled anyone with the terrible burden of an arrest record.

The police can perform these service and peace-keeping tasks; they cannot prevent and control crime. No one knows how to do the latter in any way that would be consistent with the existence of a free society. As James Q. Wilson has pointed out, the police as crime-fighters are in the same uncomfortable position as the staff of mental hospitals. No one knows how to cure mental illness on any scale, and no one knows how to prevent and control crime. If we judge mental hospitals and the police by some sort of quantitative efficiency record, whether it be of cures or the crime rate or the number of crimes cleared by arrest, the results are sure to be dismal.

When the police are judged in this way, they have an overwhelming temptation to fudge the figures in some way, and many crimes go unreported because the victims are convinced that the police cannot or will not do anything about it. Detectives often pressure or subtly reward a thief who confesses to a large number of burglaries since he makes the clearance rate look better. In short, the professional law enforcement conception of the police promises something they cannot really deliver, although the attempt raises serious community tensions and civil liberties issues.[37]

Pressure for quantitative evidence of efficient law enforcement inevitably generates demands that the police be allowed to bypass the law. In this sense law and order are not complementary but antithetical terms. Order, in the sense of crime prevention and control or completely conventional behavior, can best be achieved through bureaucratic and ultimately totalitarian means. The rule of law in a democratic society insists that each individual be treated with due regard to his constitutional rights and his dignity as a human being. The police reply that they cannot control crime without using wiretaps, bugs, and conducting stops and searches of suspicious persons or vehicles. Detectives want maximum time with suspects so that they may exercise their "black arts" in extracting confessions without the presence of an attorney. One observer has said that some detectives secretly welcomed the Supreme Court rulings in the Escobedo and Miranda cases limiting police interrogation since it gave them a good excuse with higher authority for a less than satisfactory clearance rate.[38]

In general, however, the pressure for police productivity forces the police to be antidemocratic and anticivil liberties. They cannot do their jobs, as they and most of society perceive those jobs, without infringing upon the rights and liberties of citizens. The police suffer from a high level of frustration because they feel their efforts are unappreciated and that they are "handcuffed" by the courts. Also when policemen make an arrest that is not followed through by the other agencies in the criminal justice system—the prosecutor and the courts—they will resort to harassment of violators rather than the formal instruments of the law. Unfortunately each unit in the criminal justice system pursues its own goals rather than those of the system as a whole. Tension and sometimes hostility between the various units—

the police, the prosecutor, the courts, and the correctional agencies
—is a serious and long-term problem.[39]

The real problem of the police is that they have been asked to
perform an impossible task, and any organization that has been
charged with unachievable goals is going to have serious morale
breakdowns. If we recognize that we cannot prevent or totally control crime in a society committed to freedom and economic individualism and which permits a high degree of economic and social
inequality, we shall do ourselves and our police a considerable
service.

The problem of crime is a very real one—one can no longer say
the fear of crime and violence in many of our cities is irrational—
and the fears and hostilities generated by crime or the threat of it
have made our cities less livable. But expecting the police alone to
eliminate or substantially reduce crime will probably be futile at best
and positively dangerous at worst by encouraging even more police
attacks upon civil liberties. Governmental policy should be directed
toward eliminating as much as possible the economic and social
conditions that breed crime and cutting the rate of recidivism—that
is, repeated crimes by the same individuals. Since such a large percentage of criminals are repeaters, successful rehabilitation efforts
will pay significant dividends. Unfortunately the correctional system
has long been more custodial than rehabilitative; American jails and
prisons do more to brutalize people than anything else. We have to
ask ourselves whether we want our cities to be livable places for all
our citizens and commit the intellectual energy and financial resources to approach that goal or not. Similarly, for those who do
break the law, we have to provide a fair and equitable system of
justice and correction.[40]

As stated, these ideals are platitudes, easy to accept as principles
and generalities but difficult to turn into policy and action. Getting
public and police to discard a conspiracy or "rotten apple" theory of
the genesis of crime and criminal behavior would be one important
step. Crime is overwhelmingly concentrated in those areas marked
by poor health, low levels of education, high rates of family dis-
organization, rundown and overcrowded housing—in a word the
slums. Adding more men to the police force and increasing their
firepower would be much cheaper than eliminating the slums; the

impact on the state of social well-being, including the crime rate, would be negative. Attempting to control the symptoms without getting at the root causes has the attraction of being cheaper and less demanding upon our minds and pocketbooks; the value of applying external salves to internal diseases is something else.

At the present time, demands for a repressive police rise in an attempt to prevent the pathology of the slums from spreading to downtown and middle-class areas. Many police officials contribute to this sentiment by their complaints against court decisions which "handcuff" them. Increasing police militancy is a dangerous phenomenon of our time, fueled by frustration and hostility toward criminals, the courts, politicians, and civilians who do not share the police view of the genesis of crime and disorder. Some officers claim that if they were only unleashed, given the resources, allowed to do their jobs, and backed up by the courts, society's fears would soon subside. One can only envision a constantly rising level of demands for more men, more weapons, more freedom of action, and less court and public restraint if the social conditions which lead to crime do not change. The police would have to run harder than ever to stay in the same place. In the meantime the social implications of such a policy would be frightening indeed.[41]

Not all police departments present the image of a dedicated group of professional crime-fighters and law enforcers. James Q. Wilson in his useful book *Varieties of Police Behavior* distinguished three types of police forces which he termed the watchman style, the legalistic style, and the service style. The watchman-style department restricts its conception of its role to the maintenance of order. It is not professionalized; there is a good bit of formal and informal political interference in police affairs; and there is little concern for enforcing the letter of the law, especially the vice laws. Promotions and desirable assignments often must be paid for, and there is little of the discipline and sense of urgency of the militaristic professional force. If this sounds like the description of the typical nineteenth-century force it should, for this was in fact the pattern of almost all American police departments until recent decades and still is in many cities.[42]

Its liabilities were and are obvious. There tends to be a cozy relationship between the police and the gamblers, and police morale is weakened by the pattern of political and personal favoritism that prevails on internal matters. Discipline may be especially weak since any action might lead to unpleasant publicity. If a large portion of a department is implicated in such corrupt relations, no one can enforce the law against the police themselves. Officers outside the network of payoffs have to turn their backs on what goes on around them and deny publicly that any such activity exists. Again, the initial source of trouble comes from outside the department itself in the form of laws against gambling and other behavior that many civilians and policemen believe morally permissible. But the rot can spread from beyond the laws making crimes without victims to the whole range of police behavior and activity. Can an administrator discipline a man guilty of brutality or shakedowns if the man knows his superiors are on bookmakers' pads? Moreover, what is the effect on a young patrolman who learns that his colleagues and commanders are often more interested in profiting from the law than enforcing it? It is hard to see how such a man could avoid becoming alienated and cynical about his organization and the society in which it functions.[43]

Nonprofessional departments also seem especially prone to use third-degree methods to extract confessions from suspects. The Wickersham Commission reported a widespread use of such brutality in the 1920s, in cities such as Buffalo, Cleveland, and Chicago. Departments with an ingrained pattern of corruption and political interference may have been more prone to use such methods as the quickest and easiest ways to achieve results. Such departments would not be inhibited by respect for the formal constraints of the law which prohibited third-degree techniques.[44]

On the positive side, the watchman-style department does not pretend to enforce the law fully, or to offer the possibility of the complete prevention and control of crime if only the courts stopped handcuffing the police. In the watchman-style department controlled by the political organization, the police may have protected the gamblers, but they also had to treat the voters with some respect. Their political masters insisted they had to be nice to the people, or at least that portion who participated in politics by voting if nothing else. The politically controlled department was tied to the community to this extent at least; it could not ignore all civilian influence and desires. Separating the police from the political organizations without substituting some other form of integration has widened the gulf between the police and the rest of society.

The politically controlled police had, and has, too many weaknesses to be taken as a satisfactory model, yet it does provide some important connections between police and people that the autonomous professional model eliminates. The goal for the future should be greater integration of police and people by involving civilians in many phases of police operations and involving policemen in the full life of the community. Only in this way can the police be an integral and integrated part of a democratic urban society.[45]

In the long run a proper conception of professionalism is the only answer to the problems of the police in a democratic society. No matter what their educational attainments or the limitations of their training, policemen are professionals in that they exercise considerable discretion in situations where their decisions have great impact on the present and future well-being of their clients. A dispatcher or commander tells a policeman where to go, but when he gets there he is essentially on his own. Professionalizing the police in the form of the best possible training for handling the sensitive human relations in which they must intervene and for instilling a high code of ethics is the only long-range solution for the development of civil relations between policeman and citizens. Professionalization also holds the only hope for curbing corruption and having the police perform according to the dictates of the law.[46]

In the nature of things there is no way that any department could provide sufficient supervision to eliminate all forms of police misbehavior, although effective supervision does cut the number of rule violations and infractions of the law on the part of policemen. One of the serious problems facing New York's department in the late 1960s was the high number of patrolmen per sergeant, 14 to 1, which made effective supervision impossible.

Sociologist Albert Reiss and his associates, in observing police behavior in four cities, found a surprisingly high number of illegal transactions in which policemen took money or goods in exchange for a favor of some sort. Roughly one in five officers observed violated the criminal law while on duty. These violations did not include any dealings with organized crime. These transactions took place when the policemen knew they were being observed by outsiders. About four in ten of the officers observed were guilty of serious violations of the departments' rules. One can speculate that in other circumstances the number might be even higher. Reiss concluded that "during any year a substantial minority of all police officers violate the criminal law, a majority misbehave toward citizens in an encounter, and most engage in serious violations of the rules and regulations of the department." The police form a subculture with its own standards of value and morality. "The likelihood of an officer accepting illegal exchanges is increased when such practices are institutionalized and legitimated by the police subculture and organization." The level of corruption and malpractice, then, can be influenced by police commanders and outside agencies. Better cooperation between the various units of the criminal justice system and more effective central supervision within the police department itself could lower the rate of violations.[47]

Paradoxically, the closer the external supervision the less chance there is for policemen to develop the skills and attitudes of professionals, which emphasize the internalization of work standards and codes of ethics. Supervision by the patrolman's superior officers and the other agencies in the criminal justice system, especially the prosecutor and the courts, expressed in command, control, and court review, is antithetical to the full flowering of police professionalism. Few people, however, in or out of the criminal justice system, are ready to trust police officers on the streets to operate in a professional manner and with a professional's code of ethics. One may be cynical and say that many of the members of recognized professions put their own interests ahead of those of their clients and otherwise act in ways that violate their codes. That the standards are often violated is true, but it is highly probable that principles and practices would be much worse if these standards did not exist. What now needs to be done is to socialize policemen in their occupational role in such a way that they accept and apply professional standards. This will not be easy, given the negative conditions of police recruiting in many jurisdictions and the climate in which policemen must work. Many citizens are all too eager to undermine and subvert standards of integrity and effective performance.[48]

Until professionalism becomes ingrained within our police organizations, we must encourage more effective supervision and the development of professional independence at the same time. Accomplishing either of these tasks would be difficult enough; doing both at the same time in an era of fiscal stringency may be impossible. We must try. Our police officers must become professional specialists in human relations. Historian Sam Warner once said that American society turns over its most difficult task, that of caring for all the varied needs of people in trouble or who are not self-supporting or self-sufficient, to its weakest organizations. Like other service agencies, police departments must be strengthened and their individual members raised to the level of professionals in training, skill, and status. They must be able to function in the interests of society as a whole and not simply to protect the traditions, privileges, and prerogatives of the organization and its members. Other groups in the community who work for police professionalism must not make the mistake of viewing the police department exclusively as a crime-fighting and law-enforcement agency. Complete law enforcement is neither possible nor desirable under current American conditions, and bureaucratic and ultimately totalitarian control of crime would be incompatible with a free society. What is needed at this time is a recognition that the police are a peace-keeping and general-service agency as well as law-enforcers and crime-fighters, and that in their work the police must be bound by the rule of law just as other citizens are. In this way perhaps the currently dangerously tense relations between the police and much of the community can be improved, although the prospects are not good in a period of increasing personal violence and group conflict.

Chapter 10

Police-Community Relations

Police-community relations have always been problematic in America's big cities. From their inception, American police forces have operated to shield the elite from the masses, to impose middle-class standards upon the poor, or at least to confine unacceptable behavior to the slums and red-light districts. If police were not as zealous in these tasks as some of the elite demanded, they received considerable criticism from "reform" groups. If police did act energetically to control the masses, they were regarded as tyrants and traitors by people they lived and worked among. Departments could never satisfy all of the elements of their diverse constituency; police performance that pleased one segment of the diverse urban population had to displease another.[1]

During the 1930s and 1940s, however, these conflicts and differences over police performance were not very severe. William F. Whyte's study of Boston's North End, *Street Corner Society,* showed an almost ritualistic pattern of relationships between the police, numbers bettors and bookies, and the "better elements." When moralistic pressure rose to a certain peak, an "untouchable" came into the neighborhood as the precinct commander and closed operations. After the heat died down, he was transferred to another post and business as usual resumed.

Neither side expected complete victory. The moralists did not expect that all gambling would be eliminated, while the numbers runners and bankers realized they would have to accept periodic arrests and occasional reform waves when business would be difficult and unprofitable. Policemen, customers, and numbers operators formed part of the same social world, while the moralists were outsiders. Yet officers knew they could not ignore the formal demands of the law entirely, and they had to maintain some sort of communication with those who wanted to alter their traditional practices.[2]

The most dramatic conflicts between police and civilians before World War II came in labor disputes. American society, with its emphasis on individualism and the primacy of property rights, proved the most resistant of any major industrial nation to the establishment of collective bargaining and union recognition. Employers often tried to maintain operations in the face of strikes, which made for violence on the picket line between strikers and strikebreakers. To such employers the police function of protecting life and property meant getting strikebreakers past picket lines no matter what means had to be employed, while strikers wanted the police to arrest "goons," to keep strikebreakers from coming into town, or at the very least to be neutral toward the dispute.[3]

Obviously it would be difficult to generalize about police performance in the thousands of labor disputes in cities large and small over a long span of time, but a few observations are in order. First, police despised strikes as potentially disorderly situations which increased their workload and exposed them to abuse and danger. Furthermore, contested strikes exposed the vulnerability of the police. Their function was to maintain the peace and good order of the community against the minority which refused to abide by the rules of the game. But what happened when the community split, when there was no agreement on the rules of the game, when desperate men prepared to fight for more money, or better working conditions, or union recognition, and equally determined men insisted that they alone had the right to make these decisions?

In grappling with the dilemmas posed by community polarization, the police tended to follow the lines of power and influence. In general, departments had no use for strikes and strikers, but the key variable in their performance seems to have been the community's attitude toward a particular dispute. If the authorities favored the workers or were at least neutral, the police remained neutral. If, on the other hand, political leaders and newspapers viewed the strikers as un-American radicals or a threat to a town's prosperity by making industry reluctant to locate there, then the police acted as agents of employers in their strikebreaking activities. The New York police clubbed many immigrant workers in the garment industry who tried to set up picket lines. The department long perceived anarchists, socialists, and Communists to be the fomenters of labor discord and responded accordingly.

Under John Purroy Mitchel, mayor of New York from 1914 to 1917, the police adopted a more neutral stance; but it was not until the mayoralty administrations of Fiorello La Guardia between 1933 and 1945 that neutrality became confirmed policy.[4]

The Chicago police provide one of the most notorious examples of antilabor bias. In the words of a noted labor historian, "The Chicago police had a long, notable, and dishonorable record of breaking strikes with force on behalf of employers in defiance of civil liberties." Harold Ickes, who served as Secretary of the Interior under Franklin Roosevelt, had a long and unhappy experience with the Chicago police during his career as an attorney and civic leader in the city. He wrote in July, 1937:

> I don't know whether any city has a worse police force than Chicago but I doubt it. I have known something about it for a good many years and I have had two or three clashes with it over invasions of obvious civil rights. . . . The Augean stables emanated delicate perfume compared with some of the odors that have been redolent in this Department in the past. From the time of the Haymarket riots [1886] in Chicago, police always justified brutal invasion of civil rights by calling those whom it manhandled "anarchists."

Ickes' letter was called forth by the behavior of the Chicago police on Memorial Day in 1937, when they charged, clubbed, and shot a group of peaceful strikers and their families outside the Republic Steel plant in south Chicago. Ten civilians died, most of them shot in the back as they tried to escape from the rampaging bluecoats.[5] It would be interesting to know how many of the survivors and descendants of that Memorial Day approved of the actions of the Chicago police department during the Democratic convention of 1968, when the targets were youthful, primarily middle-class dissidents.

In the great steel strike of 1919, police performance varied widely in different communities. In western Pennsylvania steel towns, where the companies virtually owned the community, the police, aided by mounted state police and militiamen, ran union organizers out of town and prevented any public gathering of more than three people without a permit, which would not be granted anyone in favor of the strike. In Cleveland, on the other hand, Mayor Harry L. Davis had the police turn back strikebreakers coming into the city. Until stopped by a court injunction, the police treated any potential strikebreaker as a suspicious person and presented the classic alternative of get out of town or go to jail.[6]

The police were not and are not solely a general public service, oblivious to questions of power and prestige; they often act as an instrument to protect the interests of the dominant groups in the community. In day-to-day life this principle is not particularly visible; people can believe the motto of the Cleveland police that "Our Men Serve All Men." In the crisis situation of a contested strike, serving all men was impossible. The police, like it or not, had to take sides and their action or inaction had important implications for the outcome of a strike.

In the years since World War II the police role has declined in labor disputes as federal law dictates the conduct of contestants and most companies have decided that the risks of continued operation in the face of strikes outweigh any possible benefits. This is not to say that labor relations might not again become a pressure point upon the police; that possibility is always present. For the recent past and foreseeable future, however, the most important conflicts facing the police are those involving clashing life-styles between alienated youth and more settled members of the community, and the tremendous problems surrounding the declining economic base and the changing racial composition of central cities.

In the last twenty or twenty-five years police-community relations have worsened considerably under the impact of massive social and economic changes.[7] The problems associated with racial distinctions and discrimination and poverty have become so concentrated in our cities that "urban problems" has become a shorthand designation of national social ills. Larger and larger percentages of the populations of older core cities are made up of the poor, the trapped, and the deprived as individuals and businesses with any choice seek suburban and exurban locations.[8]

Traditionally, cities have grown and developed at major breaks in transportation. The classic nineteenth-century city was a port, whether on the seacoast, the Great Lakes, or one of the great rivers, with extensive railroad connections. Businesses and individuals wanted to be as close to the major transportation and communication facilities as possible, and central city land appreciated in value constantly as the urban areas developed, thus putting a premium on intense use, crowding if you will.[9]

In contrast, current technology favors dispersion within metropolitan or megalopolitan areas rather than concentration in core cities. Industry finds the single-story, continuous-flow plant by far the most efficient; deliveries and shipments are often by trucks, which are most effective away from the congestion of the central city and near an interstate highway connection; and the labor force drives to work, which necessitates large land areas for parking lots. Increasingly only those businesses with large capital investments which they do not wish to write off or with specialized needs which require proximity to outside firms and specialists remain in the central city.[10] In addition, the combination of the automobile and various kinds of government subsidies, such as those for federally insured home mortgages and highway building, has permitted the rapid development of the suburban residential districts which have attracted good taxpayers from the core city. Cities such as New York, Newark, Cleveland, and San Francisco find themselves in a fiscal crisis as their revenue providers, taxpaying businesses and individuals, move outside the political boundaries and therefore the taxing power of the city, while the cost of providing municipal services keeps rising.[11]

Blacks have been escaping the hopeless poverty and discrimination of the rural South by moving to the cities, both southern and northern, since the 1890s. The movement increased considerably during the two world wars. Since 1940 the movement has reached mammoth proportions and shows little sign of diminishing. One hundred years ago, race was primarily a "problem" of the rural South; now the exclusion and deprivation that is the lot of the black lower class in the United States is our most serious urban problem. Technological changes in agriculture have made many southern blacks economically superfluous and therefore in danger of starvation as the activities that used to provide subsistence, if nothing more, no longer exist or are performed more cheaply and efficiently by machines.[12]

Unfortunately, the same trend has occurred in the urban economy as unskilled and semiskilled factory jobs have declined in number and those that do exist are increasingly found outside central cities. Thus blacks are trapped in the central city because of poverty and suburban housing discrimination at the same time that entry-level jobs are declining or moving out. Traditionally, people have learned of entry-level jobs either by applying at the plant gate or learning from a friend or relative that a firm is hiring. When the plant is twenty miles away such word-of-mouth information is hard to obtain. Even if one learns of a job, there is still the problem of transportation. Public transportation is usually not available, so a car must be financed and run on a beginner's wages. The combination of these trends has resulted in a serious unemployment and underemployment pattern among inner-city blacks. Unskilled women, both black and white, especially have a difficult time in locating and arranging transportation to decent jobs.[13]

Cities are thus caught in a vicious downward spiral of a declining economic and tax base and a continued immigration of unskilled, uneducated, and discriminated-against people who impose heavy burdens on services like welfare, schools, police and fire protection, and the courts and correctional system.

Many white middle- and stable working-class people see the contemporary urban crisis in simplistic terms. Blacks won't work; "they" have no morals; all they do is drink and fornicate, desert their wives, and neglect their children. This used to be a good neighborhood before "they" moved in. Few citizens are aware of, or at least most do not think very systematically about, the complex interrelation between economic and technological change, the long-standing exclusion and deprivation blacks have faced in this country, and the resultant cultural and behavioral patterns. As Lee Rainwater has brilliantly demonstrated in his *Behind Ghetto Walls*, lower-class blacks have adopted various strategies for survival and getting some gratification out of life under the conditions of extreme deprivation forced on them by the white majority. Negroes were slaves for their first two hundred years in America; then slavery was followed by a freedom which left them economically defenseless and subjected and segregated in every aspect of social life. The processes of urbanization and industrialization in the nineteenth century led to a decline in the status of blacks already living in Philadelphia and New York.

Poverty continues to be the lot of a disproportionate number of blacks whose incomes do not permit an American standard of living, that is, the level of consumption that Americans think right and proper. Those blacks who do achieve economic competence still face discrimination in housing and other institutions. Previous migrants to cities could look for expanding choices as their incomes rose. To date, blacks have remained restricted in housing no matter how respectable they are. For the poor, respectability is economically out of reach. The low and irregular income earned by men on the fringes of the labor market and consequently suffering from chronic unemployment and underemployment makes it difficult for them to fulfill the role of provider that American culture prescribes for adult males. Lower-class men economically unable to function as the head of a family assert their masculinity in heavy drinking and sexual promiscuity. The male role model present to lower-class boys in the ghetto is that of the hustler or the streetcorner man, not the stable husband and father. Boys grow up believing girls and women to be bitches who will drive a man out of the house because of their constant complaining about the amount of money he earns and how he spends what he does have. Girls are socialized to expect that men are irresponsible, that inevitably the man will leave, and that the woman will have to bear the burdens of running the house and raising the children by herself. These conditions of exclusion and deprivation, which recent programs like the "war on poverty" have scarcely touched, breed expectations of failure and betrayal on the part of men and women toward each other. Each looks for signs that the other is not fulfilling the role assigned, and when the prophecy comes true, the fatalistic attitude is fulfilled.

To achieve some gratification and to hold their losses to a minimum, men and women limit their commitments to each other. Lower-class blacks usually marry at a fairly young age. If and when the marriage breaks up, as is usually the case, the pattern then is for a series of temporary liaisons—girl friend-boy friend relationships in which the man provides companionship and some money in return for sexual gratification and food and shelter. Occasionally these relationships can be quite long lasting, but they usually are not. The central figure of the lower-class black family, then, is a woman, either the mother or grandmother, who is the essential source of authority and financial support.[14]

Too often, whites do not realize that these patterns of sexual and family relations are cultural adaptations permitting survival and some gratification, although with a great deal of pain involved, under the harsh conditions of poverty in a supposedly affluent society. Throughout American history, whites have kept blacks in slavery, segregation, and poverty and then condemned them for being servile and degraded.

The Kerner Commission rightly laid many of the ills of urban cores to white racism. Unfortunately, the commission was not very enlightening about the various forms racism takes in American society. Economist Anthony Downs makes a useful distinction between overt racism and institutional subordination. Overt racism involves discriminatory action directly because of color or racial blackground. As such it is easy to recognize and condemn, and increasing numbers of white Americans struggle to purge themselves of directly racist feelings and to avoid any implications of racism in their behavior. They do not always succeed. When a black family moves into the neighborhood or when a child in school gets in a fight with a black student, unsuspected racial feelings surface. Even though racial biases remain, it is not impossible to eliminate through legal means blocks to jobs and housing based on overt racism. At present the Nixon administration has abandoned any significant effort to enforce the civil rights laws, but the job could be done.

What is infinitely more difficult to deal with is institutional subordination, the lingering effects of past racism. Often whites are not aware of its existence or deadly effects. For example, an employer may open his jobs equally to all who qualify, but qualifying may be impossible for blacks barred from the kind of education or previous work experience required. Segregated housing means diminished public services and poorer schools, and the products of these schools cannot compete in tests designed for middle-class competence. Asking people who have been deliberately denied access to the symbols and instruments of middle-class culture to compete equally would be comic if it were not so cruel. Yet equality of opportunity has strong mythic support in American culture, even if so often denied in practice because of racial and class segregation and subordination. Anyone who grants free and open competition for jobs or places in medical school can congratulate himself on living up to the American dream, and those who do not measure up in the competition have no one to blame but themselves. But past decisions to keep blacks as low-skilled, low-wage proletarians by barring them from education and job training make a mockery of pretensions to equality of opportunity. Most white Americans do not perceive the issues in this way, and they are extremely hostile to anything that looks like preferential treatment for minorities. "We did it, why can't they?" is the motto.

The effects of present and past housing discrimination in urban areas are especially pernicious. Black children attend primarily black schools whose teachers and staff try to get transferred out at the first opportunity to "good schools" in white areas. The teachers who remain are either the dedicated minority or the rejects whom no one else wants. The latter determine the tone for the schools, which deliberately set out to destroy any kind of pride and initiative in the children or simply abandon any attempt to promote learning.[15]

Housing is also related to jobs. The new jobs are in the periphery of metropolitan areas, where the population is about 95 percent white; blacks are contained in the core of cities, where employment is going down. The *New York Times* reported that New York City lost 250,000 jobs between 1968 and 1972. Cleveland's officially announced unemployment rate is now 10 percent; the actual figure is probably significantly above that. Meanwhile some suburban firms have difficulty attracting enough unskilled and semiskilled workers. Racism, both overt and in the form of institutional subordination, promotes these imbalances.

For a long time a characteristic black response to white racism was self-hatred, the desire to escape the terrible dilemma of being black in white America by denying one's blackness. Those light enough to do so "passed" into white society; others tried to achieve the same results by using hair straighteners and skin whiteners. An intense religious life allowed many Negroes to cope with their daily lives. Alcohol and drugs helped others "to ease their troubled minds," but at heavy cost to themselves and those around them. In a community where money, prestige, and power was scarce, men struggled bitterly for what was available. To survive, people dealt with each other in exploitative and manipulative ways; finding a "hustle" became a characteristic method of "making it" in the ghetto. The competitiveness and mistrust engendered by these conditions encouraged violence and aggression. As part of the syndrome of self-hatred, the frustrations resulting from white denial of black dignity were often channeled into aggressive and violent behavior against other blacks.[16]

Many of the patterns of the past still persist, the heavy use of alcohol and drugs, for example, while others are intensified, such as the struggle for power and prestige among activists within the ghetto. In the 1960s, federal programs did raise the stakes for those who could claim the mantle of speaking for the community, even if the programs did little for most of the residents of the area. The census of 1970 shows even more black families headed by women; the present figure is 27 percent. But there are significant changes. For young blacks, racial pride has replaced racial debasement. Natural and Afro hair styles are in, and black has become a term of positive identification among people who seek their roots in Africa and in their music. Black nationalists see Afro-American history as that of a "colonized" people who must struggle against white domination here in the United States just as African nations overthrew European colonialism in the 1950s and 1960s. The demand is that the patterns of exclusion, deprivation, and subjection be ended NOW, no matter what the cost.[17] The nationalists do not speak for all blacks, but they do represent a considerable portion of younger and more militant individuals. Some of them do not refer to policemen as human beings who might be insensitive and corrupt but as "pigs," dehumanized creatures who are outside any moral community.

No one can defend even the rhetorical destruction of policemen as human beings, and the threat and reality of ambush of policemen has grown tremendously. According to the International Association of Chiefs of Police, 91 police officers were killed in the United States during the first nine months of 1971, many of them ambushed while on routine patrol. Ten New York City policemen were killed in the first eleven months of 1971.[18] Policing, which traditionally was a safer occupation than agriculture, has become more dangerous. Even more important, policemen's perception of threat and their feelings of anxiety have risen to the point where many are prepared to admit that they are just plain scared. Excessive fear and anxiety are hardly conducive to effective performance.

I do not wish to imply that black nationalists are responsible for all or even most of police deaths. What is disturbing, however, is that civilians who call policemen "pigs" and policemen who refer to minority civilians as "animals" are creating a climate in which the basic humanity of other people is denied. Calling and thinking about other human beings as pigs or animals makes it easy to treat them as if they were less than human.

Unfortunately, police have a long history of contempt, corruption, and brutality toward blacks. No other group in our society has suffered as much from the negative facets of our police history that Chief William Parker admitted.

In the South and the North alike, the police used both their formal and informal powers to maintain the subjugation of the Negro population. In Chicago and other cities, the protected vice area where the police left the brothels and the prostitutes alone was located in the black belt. Thus parents who wanted to shield their children from commercial and exploitative sex could not do so. The numbers racket flourished and flourishes openly in the black ghettos, and children by the age of four know what the game is all about. The major share of the enormous profits has gone to whites rather than blacks, from the policemen on "the pad" who are bribed to let the business operate to the top bankers and controllers who moved in after the repeal of prohibition closed off that avenue of illicit enterprise. Those Negroes with ambitions for respectability and a moral atmosphere in which to raise their children found their efforts thwarted by the combination of housing discrimination and police tolerance of illicit activity in their neighborhoods. If they complained, the indifference or hostility they received confirmed their powerlessness.[19]

Often the police seemed more interested in confining blacks and black crime to the ghetto than in protecting residents of the area. In New York until recent decades, some policemen supported saloon-keepers who refused to serve black customers, no matter what the public accommodations law said.[20] In many cities, especially in the South but to some extent in the North as well, the police took the view that if a black man kills a white, that's murder; if a white man kills a black, that's justifiable homicide; and if a black man kills a black, that's one less nigger. In short the police permitted or ignored criminal behavior as long as only blacks were involved. Most complaints against the police derive from their indifference to crime and disorder in the ghetto, not disrespect and brutality, although there are plenty of complaints on that score as well. Blacks who perceive their environment as chaotic and violent resent the police for not protecting them better. The Civil Rights Commission found in 1966 that in Cleveland the police took four times as long to answer calls in black neighborhoods as they did comparable calls from white areas.[21] The New York department traditionally used Harlem as a dumping ground for its incompetents and those who had incurred official wrath for some reason.[22] In most cities slum precincts like slum schools get the rejects of the system. The men who are the least·well educated, the least likely to be sensitive to minority cultures and frustrations, and the most prone to take a "tough" approach to police work and contacts with civilians patrol those areas which pose the most sensitive, dangerous, and complex police problems. Lower-class whites also face police harassment and insensitivity. In some ways they are worse off than the blacks because they have few organizations and spokesmen to make their case to the media and to other agencies.[23]

The ecological fact is that criminals prey most often on those nearest and most accessible to them, so the biggest sufferers from black criminals are other blacks who live in their neighborhoods. As indicated in the previous chapter, there may not be very much the police can do about crime and criminality, but they can indicate a greater degree of concern and sympathy and at least give ghetto residents a feeling that somebody cares and that something is being done. And police indifference toward crime and vandalism does encourage more people to engage in such behavior.[24]

The social conditions that lead to crime are beyond police control; they cannot do anything about low incomes and broken families. They can only try to keep the personal and social damage to a minimum. The spread of addiction to drugs, especially heroin, presents particularly vexing problems. Heroin addiction is endemic among black and Spanish-speaking youths in decayed urban neighborhoods; in the late 1960s addiction spread tremendously among servicemen in Vietnam and made substantial inroads among middle-class youth. Heroin addicts face the dilemma of not being able to hold a steady job while needing money, lots of it, to support their habits. Prostitution and theft are obvious sources, and many police officers see almost a one-to-one relationship between rising rates of addiction and increased burglary and robbery.

Narcotics control and the other crimes it generates is a frustrating business. If heroin becomes scarce, the price goes up and addicts must commit even more crimes to satisfy their needs. Addicts have mutilated themselves to secure hospital admission and therefore access to some drugs in time of famine. Police announcement of a seizure of a large cache of heroin may be a source of congratulation for the officers who achieve it, but it brings about headaches for their colleagues. In addition some policemen have succumbed to the large amounts of money involved and entered into corrupt relations with narcotics dealers. With the best will in the world, narcotics enforcement is still difficult, extremely time-consuming, and frustrating. Enforcing the law involves sticky constitutional questions, and there is the serious problem of what happens after arrest. No jurisdiction has enough treatment facilities for addicts, and there is a distressingly high rate of relapse when apparently cured people go back to the same environment in which they became addicted in the first place.

Narcotics and related criminal problems form one of the most dramatic instances of the truism that policemen are charged with picking up the pieces of the failure of the social order in general. Seemingly, society does not know how to prevent addiction in the first place or how to cure it afterwards. Heroin provides an escape from the despair and hopelessness of the ghetto environment or from the boredom and purposelessness that afflict large numbers of youth. No one has yet done much to solve these basic social problems and the related increases in criminal behavior.[25] Understandably, however, citizens demand some form of action against the greater possibility of being burglarized, robbed, or assaulted, and so the police are under great pressure to do something, even if there are no very clear ideas as to what actions would be both effective and consistent with the principles of a free society.

When the police do saturate a high-crime area and engage in aggressive preventive control in an effort to control crime, they greatly increase tension and hostility, especially in view of the technological and residential changes of the last quarter century. The foot patrolmen had much more of an opportunity to keep in touch with the values of the community and the more positive aspects of human behavior than the man in the radio car. The radio car patrolman interacts with civilians most often in an adversary situation. He lacks the other contacts that kept the relation between police and people from being simply that of combatants. The radio car man sees civilians only at their worst, when they are trying to escape the negative consequences of actions like speeding or when they are in trouble, drunk, defeated, or degraded. He must make his judgments on the basis of visible signs such as color, age, dress, and attitude rather than on his intimate knowledge of the people on his post.[26]

In high-crime areas, which now are those populated by blacks and the Spanish speaking, a large number of field interrogations and a high arrest rate are the evidence a patrolman offers to his superiors to show that he is on the job, that he is efficient. However, in so doing, he can further alienate the people among whom he works. Stops and searches in the ghetto, especially if accompanied by racial epithets or disrespectful language or attitudes, further impress upon the residents their powerlessness and their outcast position. The hostility young lower-class males exhibit toward the police means that they will fail the attitude test, which makes arrests more likely. A policeman is more prone to make an arrest in a discretionary situation if a juvenile expresses contempt and hostility toward police authority than if he is apologetic and respectful. In this vicious circle, police practices and ghetto responses reinforce each other in such a way as to intensify the hatred and contempt policemen and black youth feel toward each other.[27]

Physical brutality and the third-degree practices of beating confessions out of suspects are not so common now as they were at the time of the Wickersham Commission investigation in the late 1920s and early 1930s. What does remain is what one author calls "institutionalized malpractice," various procedures which violate the law or the constitutional rights or the human dignity of civilians. One form of malpractice is to make an arrest to cover an infringement of civil rights. Apparently such arrests are rare, but no matter how few there is no justification for them. If a policeman oversteps his authority and a civilian protests, the policemen then might make an arrest for resisting an officer or some other charge. The arrest then justifies legally any police activity, even to the point of using force to overcome unlawful resistance.[28]

More serious in the long run than any verbal or physical abuse a civilian might suffer is the arrest record itself, which will haunt the individual for the rest of his life. Blacks and other minority groups are much more likely to be arrested and the arrest is much more serious for them than for many whites in view of their difficulties in finding jobs. In many inner-city neighborhoods, relatively few boys reach their twenty-first birthday without some sort of a record, and employment applications often ask, Have you ever been arrested? Note: not, Have you ever been convicted? but simply arrested. A yes answer often closes any possibility of getting the job; so the police decision to make an arrest itself imposes severe penalties upon the individual, whether the arrest was warranted or not. An arrest in a discretionary situation may have a lifetime impact upon a boy whose major offense was that he was not sufficiently respectful and deferential toward the police.

Juveniles themselves are very much aware that for the same action one boy may get simply a chewing out while another winds up serving a year in jail; they also know that it is the policeman who makes the key decision of whether to invoke the process of the criminal law at all or to deal with the situation informally. In making these decisions, policemen rely on such visible attributes of status and attitude as color, age, dress, and demeanor as well as the nature of the offense itself and the reputation of the boy and his family.[29] This awesome discretionary authority of the police, their power to impose *Justice Without Trial,* as Jerome Skolnick entitled his important book on the police, has always been present, but never before has it seemed so questionable and indeed illegitimate to so many citizens. Many ghetto residents view arrests as a technique of control and repression, not as a valid exercise of law-enforcement powers.[30]

As a result of the increased isolation of policemen from civilians because of the spread of the radio car and the demographic changes in cities, policemen may be more contemptuous than ever of civilians, "assholes," who are animals at worst and at best do not have the officer's capacity for quick decisions and effective action. The policeman sees people as victims of drink and drugs, or acting out the impulses to greed, lust, and perversion, or trying to bluster or wheedle their way out from the consequences of their actions. Many policemen come to believe that no matter how respectable the facade, most men and women are still animals underneath and that it does not take much for the veneer to be stripped away and the reality underneath to show through. The patrolman's view of the world and the people in it, his tendency to socialize with his fellow officers, and the instinctive resentment that many civilians have toward policemen, on or off duty, sets him dangerously apart from the rest of urban society.[31]

The process of separation is even more pronounced as a result of the white migration, including policemen, to the periphery of metropolitan areas. Few officers actually live in the ghetto or the inner city; their incomes and their color enable most of them to escape its congestion, filth, and crime. The man who commutes from a suburb to an inner-city neighborhood may not always be sensitive to the nuances of the community, its complexities, its decent people who are forced to live side by side with pimps and muggers, and its frustrations. He sees himself as a man doing an important, a dangerous, and an unappreciated job, putting life and limb on the line every time he goes on the street, and for people who hate him.

The Negro writer James Baldwin noted the cop's dilemma in the ghetto. No matter what his original intentions, the man in blue found that "the only way to police a ghetto is to be oppressive." Policemen represent "the force of the white world, and that world's real intentions are, simply, for that world's criminal profit and ease, to keep the black man corralled up here, in his place." Clubs and guns remind the residents of the costs of resistance. The citizens of Harlem retaliate by unremitting hatred of the policeman. "He moves through Harlem, therefore, like an occupying soldier in a bitterly hostile country; which is precisely what, and where he is, and is the reason he walks in twos and threes." No matter how unimaginative a man on a ghetto post might be, he has to realize the inhuman conditions under which most of its residents must live, and to be uneasy.[32]

> He can retreat from his uneasiness only in one direction: into a callousness which very shortly becomes second nature. He becomes more callous, the population becomes more hostile, and the situation becomes more tense, and the police force is increased. One day, to everyone's astonishment, someone drops a match in the powder keg and everything blows up. Before the dust has settled or the blood congealed, editorials, speeches, and civil-rights commissions are loud in the land, demanding to know what happened. What happened is that Negroes want to be treated like men.

Baldwin's eloquent words, published in 1961, foreshadowed the actions of Harlem in 1964, of Watts in 1965, of Detroit and Newark in 1967, and of a number of cities, especially Washington, D.C. in 1968. Many of the ghetto upheavals of these years were precipitated by a police-civilian incident. In Harlem it was the fatal shooting of a black teen-ager by an off-duty white police lieutenant, and in Newark allegations of brutal police treatment of a black cab driver and of police charging a group of civilians who had gathered outside the station house.[33] The riots provide the most spectacular manifestation of the breakdown of police-minority groups relations; there are also substantial problems involved in day-to-day contacts.

The motto on New Orleans patrol cars reads "to protect and to serve"; that on Cleveland's emphasizes the department's commitment to all citizens. But, as Baldwin points out, many ghetto residents do not agree with this conception of the police role. To them the police are oppressors, hired Hessians of the dominant whites whose function it is to keep the lid on, to remind the minority poor of their powerlessness, to milk the community with their demands for payoffs from the numbers' operators and prostitutes, and to keep established white areas safe from contamination.

The police, recruited from those social groups most hostile and fearful of blacks, the white working and lower-middle classes, may have their prejudices intensified by the nature of their work, although attitude studies show policemen in all-white precincts just as hostile to blacks as their colleagues who patrol the ghetto. The police subculture perceives and transmits to its white members images of strong antipathy between policemen and blacks no matter what conditions are in a particular city. Black policemen are more influenced in their views of these matters by the climate of the community in which they work.[34] As sociologist William Westley pointed out many years ago, policemen are trained to demand respect and deference from lower-class civilians. They cannot count on the moral authority of their uniforms—indeed as Baldwin indicates the reverse is true—so they must impress on the civilians they deal with that they are ready to use force to achieve this goal. In the department Westley studied, the most important reason advanced by policemen for the use of force was to induce respect. The policeman must "take charge"; if he backs down to a civilian, he makes the work of his fellow officers that much more difficult and dangerous.[35]

The results have been counterproductive; police hostility and belligerency breed increased community resentment and violent resistance to police action. This in turn heightens the policeman's sense of fear and danger and makes him more likely either to avoid a troublesome situation, and thus not provide protection for a potential or actual victim in a criminal or disorderly incident, or to take aggressive action at the first sign of disrespect or potential resistance.

The state of police-community relations assumes such vital importance not only because of the legal monopoly the police have on the use of force and their ability to deprive a person of liberty and mark him for life by making an arrest, but also because lower-class people often use the police as a general social service agency. The police are one of the few agencies available on a round-the-clock basis, seven days a week. The only other services similarly available are the emergency agencies, such as the fire department, the emergency rooms of hospitals, and the crisis maintenance crews of the utilities. These agencies have highly specialized functions; they come into play with the occurrence of specific situations, a fire, a bad automobile accident, or a breakdown of a gas or water line. But the police have a very broad mandate; preserving the peace and keeping order may involve them in a wide variety of situations, often highly emotional and personal in nature. Moreover, lower-class people call on the police in circumstances where middle-class people consult some other agency. A middle-class marriage going on the rocks leads to the services of a clergyman, a marriage counselor, or divorce attorney; a lower-class family dispute can get physical and have the neighbors calling the cops. People in trouble or disturbed at two o'clock in the morning know that the police will have someone on the other end of the line. If it is impossible to sleep because of a noisy party next door, or the possibly paranoid fear of prowlers, the police are the one agency that might reasonably be expected to do something about it.[36]

Since the police are so often called upon for peace-keeping and general-service functions, their attitude toward this aspect of their work is critically important. If the police conceive of their role primarily as law enforcement, they will terminate noncriminally related contacts abruptly as a waste of time and manpower, as not real police work. If they are hostile toward the people they serve, they will render any service grudgingly and condescendingly and in such manner as to remind ghetto dwellers of their powerlessness and oppressed condition. The combination of indifference toward peace-keeping functions and hostility to minority members often breeds animosity between the police and civilians even in noncriminal situations. Policemen who realize the importance of their non-law-enforcement functions do a great service both to the people they serve, who often have no other recourse than to call them, and to the state of police-community relations. Policemen who provide support for people in trouble and who do so in a civil manner make a significant contribution to urban life.[37]

According to George Berkley, police in western Europe do emphasize their general service functions, all of the varied things police do that are not really law enforcement. In many instances European officers think of themselves as akin to social workers.[38] Most American policemen would sneer at such a job description. Despite the fact that more calls to the police relate to disputes and disturbances than crimes per se, and even though most policemen spend most of their time on matters other than law enforcement, the popular image of the police is that of crime-fighters. As previously noted, the more professional the department, the more likely this is to be the case. Even in departments lacking the professional orientation of a William Parker, the "good collar" or the "good pinch" paves the way for recognition and advancement.[39]

The dream of almost every rookie patrolman is to get out of "the bag" (the uniform) and into the detective bureau. (Police slang differs widely from one city to another, an indication of the isolation of individual departments and the absence of lateral movement within police work. "Bag" is a New York expression.) The detective by definition is involved in the discovery and apprehension of criminals; the patrolman deals with the whole range of police activities, most of which deal with noncriminal matters. Yet surprisingly, most criminal arrests are made by the patrol force, not the detectives. To move from patrol to the detective bureau usually requires either a good connection or a good pinch. If the good pinch involves a gun battle, so much the better. The good pinch not only brings individual recognition and prestige, it also justifies the department to the public and takes the pressure off. The public demands action on major crimes, especially homicide where children or respectable adults are the victims. A speedy arrest in such a case reassures the citizens that the police department is doing its job.[40]

Police-training manuals and programs reinforce the law-enforcement conception of "real police work" as opposed to the service and peace-keeping tasks which occupy the majority of police time and manpower. College programs refer to "law-enforcement technology," while police academies spend considerable time upon evidence in criminal cases, from its gathering and collecting to the legal and judicial determinations of its admissibility in court. In many training programs, handling the domestic dispute—one of the most frequent police calls and one of the trickiest to handle—receives less than one hour of classroom time.[41]

The importance of specialized training in this area has recently been demonstrated. In 1967 New York established a pilot program, a Family Crisis Intervention Unit which began in a single precinct. Men with specialized training in psychology handle these calls, with an eye to restoring domestic tranquility without making an arrest or escalating actual or potential violence by their presence.

The value of the project can be seen in comparing the experience of the experimental precinct with a matched control precinct where domestic disputes were handled in the traditional manner. In twenty-two months the experimental precinct where the Family Crisis Intervention Unit was established had three times as many interventions as the control precinct; many of these were repeated interventions in the same family. People in trouble obviously came to be more willing to call on the police for help when they learned that the men involved were sympathetic and skilled. In the control precinct there was a higher rate of assault and homicide generally and specifically within families. The Family Crisis Intervention Unit lowered the level of violence by aiding people before their tensions and disputes reached the violent state. There were no homicides in any family where the unit had intervened. And since a significant proportion of all assaults and homicides occur within family groups, the possibilities for a general reduction in violence are substantial. Traditionally the domestic dispute has accounted for a high proportion of police injuries; men and women enraged at each other frequently turn on the policeman when he arrives. But no officer in the Family Crisis Intervention Unit was injured while on the job during these twenty-two months.[42]

Men assigned to this unit must believe that this is "real police work" and that their status is not compromised among their fellows and the public as a whole. For this to happen, the department as a whole and the public at large must come to see that keeping the peace and easing tensions is not only legitimate police activity, but perhaps the most important and most realizable occupational goal the police can establish.

It might be impossible to get the newspapers and television to deemphasize their coverage of the sensational, whether it be exposés of police corruption, medals for police heroics, or concentrated attention on major crimes involving respectable people. Police departments themselves, however, in their training programs and their reward systems, should give more emphasis to their peace-keeping and general-service roles. Humane and effective handling of domestic disputes should not be limited to a few men in experimental precincts. If a man does an effective job in restoring order in troublesome situations without making an arrest or using force, he should be recognized and rewarded just as much as the man who makes a good pinch. In practice patrolmen deal with disputes and disturbances by "cooling out" the participants and without making any arrests.[43] But that fact is not emphasized in the popular media. Both superior officers and civilian commentators should encourage policemen to be conciliators rather than to seek confrontations in "field interrogations" and the like. Textbooks and curricula for college and in-service training programs for future and existing policemen should recognize the nature and the importance of their general place in urban society. Achieving a reorientation of the police role both among civilians and within departments will not be easy at a time of public and political concern about crime in the streets.[44]

Moreover, as James Baldwin suggests, as long as blacks are systematically excluded and deprived, the police will be hated as the most visible symbol of that oppression no matter how they perform. The police suffer from the sins of society as a whole; almost as much as the residents of the ghetto, they are "niggers" who bear the brunt of social hypocrisy. Society has created the ghetto and then condemned the residents for the negative results and charged the police with picking up the pieces. As long as this pattern continues, it may be impossible for departments to improve community relations no matter what they do. Remaking the police image of their social role may bring only marginal or incidental gains, but that is at least better than nothing.[45] And who knows, it might be just possible to reverse the negative vicious circle now prevailing in which hostility feeds upon hostility by a more positive one in which police attention and concentration upon their general-service role might increase public respect and cooperation with the police in their law-enforcement role.

Civilian cooperation is vital to effective police work, no matter how defined. Citizen initiative was taken for granted in the days before the establishment of organized police. A police officer in the eighteenth or early nineteenth century acted only after being hired by a citizen. An organized police, designed as "preventive," had the legal authority to intervene in private affairs without being called upon to do so. But the legal power and the workaday reality are not the same thing. The vast majority of police intervention is "reactive," entering a situation after being called upon to do so by citizens, rather than "proactive," in which the policeman enters on his own initiative. This formulation is well developed by Albert J. Reiss, Jr. in his book, *The Police and the Public.*[46]

Reiss and his research associates rode in the back of patrol cars observing police-citizen encounters. Only rarely did cars on patrol come upon a crime or disturbance in progress. In almost all cases, someone had to call the communications center, which then dispatched a car to deal with the situation. If no one decides to call, the police will not find out about it. For the most part, civilians will call only when they see some personal advantage; they are not likely to ask the police to intervene out of a sense of public obligation. If citizens are assured of police civility and a willingness to provide whatever service is required, it seems probable that they will call more frequently and cooperate more fully when the police arrive.

Civilians are much more likely to resent "proactive" interventions such as stopping a motorist for speeding or those other cases when a policeman decides to intervene in a citizen's affairs on his own initiative. Policemen know this and so avoid such encounters whenever possible. A departmental emphasis on "aggressive preventive patrol" thus runs counter to citizen beliefs about when policemen may validly intervene in people's lives and the desires of patrolmen themselves. The police receive the most cooperation from civilians, and are therefore most effective, when there is a climate of civility between police and their constituency that encourages people to ask them to intervene and to accept that intervention as legitimate.[47]

Paradoxically, better police performance will probably make an individual department look bad. If police efficiency is judged by the clearance rate, the ratio between the number of crimes cleared by arrest compared to the number of crimes known to the police, the more people are encouraged to call and report the worse the clearance rate, and therefore the department's image, will be. Perhaps departments should be judged more by the willingness of people to call on them. The President's Commission found in a study of high-crime precincts that at least four times as many crimes occurred as were reported to the police because civilians would not call if they did not see any advantage for themselves or if they were likely to be treated uncivilly.[48] If a department responds effectively and civilly to calls for service, whether in criminal or noncriminal matters, there will be a much greater number of crimes known to the police. Such a rise should be considered as a hopeful rather than a distressing statistic, provided that departments have enough resources to handle the complaints.

The general-service, peace-keeping, and law-enforcement functions of the police may be conceptually separable, but in practice there is considerable overlap. How well the police perform in one area may determine whether citizens decide to mobilize them in another. If policemen do a good job "cooling" disputes, they will probably get more criminal calls. Secondly, when a policeman is dispatched, he is never sure of the kind of situation he is entering. A tenant at odds with his landlord may think himself the victim of a crime, when there is only a civil dispute in law. How does anyone know when a peace-keeping problem may become a criminal situation? Is an argument in danger of becoming an assault? Will the parties in a domestic dispute turn on the policeman? One of the hazards of police work is that a man is likely to get hurt when he least expects it. A seemingly ordinary situation may explode into violence with little or no warning. Joseph Wambaugh's novel *The New Centurions* makes this point very effectively. Wambaugh is a veteran Los Angeles police officer. When the policeman intervenes, he is never sure whether it will be as service officer, peace-keeper, or law-enforcer, and sometimes he will have to change roles during an encounter. Albert Reiss has demonstrated that the prospects for injury to a police officer are much greater when he intervenes on his own authority than when he is asked to by a citizen. Probably there is also greater danger when he intervenes at the behest of a third party, as in the case of many domestic disputes.[49]

For these reasons there is justification for some skepticism about proposals to remove general-service functions from the police. Those observers who are concerned about the crime rate often propose that all non-law-enforcement functions be given to some other agency to free the police to concentrate on criminal matters. Why should patrolmen give out dog licenses or provide ambulance service, as they do in a number of cities? Almost everyone would agree, I think, that there are some functions which could easily be transferred to other departments. The men who have a soft berth in passing out dog licenses would disagree as would those who have developed an amazing amount of interior work to be done to escape the rigors of the streets. But if the police did not provide round-the-clock availability for noncriminal matters, some other agency would have to be established which did. It would need the same sort of automobile and communications equipment that the police now have. On balance, then, it makes sense to continue to maintain police departments as general-service agencies with the emphasis on peace-keeping and law-enforcement.

Another possibility would be to separate policemen into those who would concentrate on law enforcement and those who would perform various other functions. This separation already exists with the division between the detective and the patrol branches, but some observers wish to go further. The President's Commission on Law Enforcement and the Administration of Justice recommended three levels of entry into police departments. The first level would be that of community-service officer, a position open to young men between the ages of 17 and 21 who would perform many of the general-service functions of the police. Their law-enforcement powers would be limited and they would not carry arms. The second level would be that of police officer, open to community-service officers or men who joined the department after some further education. The police officer would direct traffic, deal with disturbances, and handle other routine patrol matters. The highest entry level, also open to men from the other units who had proven themselves, would be that of police agent. Agents would require at least two years of college before appointment, with the ultimate goal of a bachelor's degree for all agents. The agent would perform the most sensitive and demanding departmental tasks, whether working with juveniles or investigating major crimes.

The proposal would serve to encourage both men with higher

education and slum youth to enter police work. Varying entry levels would mean that not all police officers had to begin as patrolmen, thus making the initial stages of a police career more attractive to ambitious and well-educated men. On the other hand, recruitment of minority youth, not necessarily high school graduates and even those with minor arrest records, would help bridge the gap between police and community in inner-city neighborhoods. This proposed organizational change is intended to broaden the range of police recruiting above working- and lower-middle-class men to college grads and below to street youth. The commission further recommended that blacks and Spanish-speaking men be recruited at all levels and not simply as community-service officers. Furthermore, movement from one level to another should be encouraged with age and further education.

Police agents, police officers, and community-service officers could be organized into neighborhood teams to provide police service within a limited area, thus decentralizing police operations to some extent and, hopefully, overcoming some of the separation between police and community so common in many cities. The police agent, the most highly educated and skilled member of the team, would replace existing detectives as well as supervise the work of officers and community-service officers.[50]

On the negative side there exists the possibility that this proposal will slight peace-keeping and general service in favor of crime deterrence and detection. The commission did recognize that police service functions are important, even to the point of recommending that officers participate in general community planning because of their knowledge of conditions which hamper human development. For example, policemen would know about substandard housing and street conditions or other hazards to the people of an area. But for the most part, the commission, in keeping with its charge to concentrate on crime and law enforcement and its membership of professionals in the field, gave top priority to crime-fighting in its hierarchy of police duties. There may also be some danger that officers and community-service officers would be treated as, and have the self-image of, second-class citizens. Departments would have to be careful to avoid the same kind of fragmentation and jealousy among the different classifications proposed that now prevails between patrol and detective forces. Sociologist Rodney Stark proposes that all men and women doing investigative work be separated from the police department entirely and put under the district attorney's control.

In the final analysis, the most important step departments can take to reverse the current trend of escalating hostility between themselves and minority groups is to end the double standard of police performance which cuts across class and ethnic lines. Middle-class whites usually perceive the police as protectors, except in their role as speed-limit enforcers, whereas members of lower-class groups, especially black and Spanish-speaking, see officers as corrupt, disrespectful, and brutal. In a poll taken for the President's Commission by the National Opinion Research Center, 63 percent of whites felt the police are "almost all honest"; only 30 percent of the nonwhites answered yes to this. Even more startling is that 10 percent of the nonwhites thought the police to be "almost all corrupt.' While 15 percent of' the nonwhites thought the police did an "excellent" job, 16 percent believed they did a "poor" job. The comparable figures for whites were 23 percent for "excellent" and 7 percent for "poor." In the years since this poll was taken, the image of the police among minority groups deteriorated even further.[51]

To decrease minority distrust and open more lines of contact between police and people will not be easy, as is demonstrated by the history of community-relations programs and proposals for civilian review boards to investigate citizen complaints against policemen. Most departments either do not have community-relations units at all or use them as public-relations gimmicks. In 1964 only 37 of 165 cities had community-relations units within their police departments. In too many instances these units were separated from the rest of police operations, staffed by light-duty men, or regarded as a dead end from which ambitious officers wished to escape. According to the Vorenburg Commission, an effective program required a large number of men, perhaps 1 percent of all sworn officers, with a full-time member in each precinct under the command of a senior officer who reported directly to the chief administrator. The unit had to be open to community feelings and to have a voice in appointments, assignments, and promotions. Under no circumstances should it be used to gather intelligence.[52]

Line officers of various ranks simply do not believe in community relations. As cops become increasingly defensive, any criticism stemming from citizens' groups, politicians, or speakers at community-relations meetings is bitterly resented. Policemen want to avoid or prevent situations where criticisms might be made. To some line officers, community relations means Commie relations, providing a forum for radicals and loudmouths and in general consorting with the enemy. San Francisco had one of the nation's most effective programs until 1967, when the district captains, backed by extensive rank-and-file support, succeeded in stripping it of any power. Its commander, Lieutenant Dante Andreotti, who had organized the unit in 1962, left the San Francisco Police Department for more congenial employment in the Department of Justice. Subsequent to the demise of the community-relations program, the San Francisco force has shown increased evidence of police militance and hostility to any external control.[53]

Civilian review boards, actual and potential, have had an even more difficult time. Existing review boards lack disciplinary authority; in most cases they can make recommendations to the commissioner or chief, who can either support or reject the recommendations. They do provide an avenue of complaint outside the department itself, so that civilians who feel that they have been abused or otherwise been the victim of malpractice can have the assurance that their complaints will receive a careful hearing. However, most boards lack independent investigative capabilities. People who might be intimidated by other officers would not hesitate to bring their complaints before a civilian body which would be free from the group pressure of the police to protect each other if at all possible.

It is for these reasons that policemen fiercely resist the establishment of such boards and work toward their abolition where they do exist. They certainly do not want civilians second-guessing them. To department members civilians can never judge complex matters of police judgment. Insulated, fearful, and hostile, the police would like to eliminate all civilian influence in their work. They resent intellectuals, labor leaders, and minority group members who might staff such boards and argue that the existence of such review handcuffs them and makes them afraid to take proper action. In their view only men with police experience can judge the validity of a given action.[54] Policemen feel secure only if they are being judged by their own. As men of action who are called upon to make rapid decisions which may have vital consequences, policemen do not want to admit the possibility that they might have made a mistake. This would impair their self-confidence and make decisions more difficult in the future.[55]

Philadelphia provides an interesting case study of the various forces for and against independent review. The Philadelphia civilian review board was established in 1958 after a particularly outrageous case of police mistreatment of a black civilian. The board functioned effectively for a number of years, following procedures designed to give maximum fairness both to complainant and officer. The police, however, never accepted the moral authority of the board and fought constantly against its continued existence. When a sympathetic mayor, James Tate, came into office, the department succeeded in eliminating the board.[56] In New York City in 1966, the Patrolmen's Benevolent Association forced the civilian review board, established under Mayor John Lindsay, to a referendum, in which the board was abolished by a vote of two to one.[57] Many middle- and stable working-class residents obviously saw no reason for the board. To them it looked like a plot hatched by blacks, radicals, and upper-class do-gooders to destroy police effectiveness and endanger law and order. They were more concerned about criminals than about police misconduct because the police usually treated them civilly, if not respectfully; and they had increased reason for concern about being victimized by criminals. People in such circumstances could not see why others hated the men in uniform; many of them were probably not aware of the extent to which police behavior varied toward different social and racial groups.

William A. Westley has offered the most convincing explanation for the differences in police behavior toward various social groups in his book *Violence and the Police,* published in 1970 but based on a 1951 doctoral dissertation. Westley studied the department in Gary, Indiana, an industrial city of about 140,000 people, with a large black and recent immigrant population and a substantial number of transient, unattached males. Policemen in Gary were recruited from large working-class families where there was little aspiration for higher mobility. The most important motive for becoming an officer was the security and good pension that the job offered. When a young man became a patrolman he found that he had done more than just take a job; he entered into a new social milieu, almost a way of life. The irregular hours, the separation from the community, the pattern of discipline, and the lure of the pension kept men highly conscious of their occupational and social role.[58]

As an occupational and social group, the police came to define their goals primarily as the maintenance of their position and their self-respect, not the enforcement of the law or keeping the peace. The men Westley studied felt themselves to be a small and isolated group in the midst of a hostile public. Most civilians either patronized or despised them and posed constant threats to their security and self-esteem. To counter these threats, the police adopted the norms of secrecy and violence. Anyone who violated the norm of secrecy was a "stoolie" and suffered the silent treatment. This was a powerful sanction as it deprived the man of necessary information. Secrecy demanded that a man never inform on a brother officer, even if it meant committing perjury. Outsiders were not to be told department business; anything that might bring discredit upon an individual or the department had to be suppressed. In a later study of Philadelphia policemen, Leonard Savitz found that older patrolmen who had little prospect for promotion most strongly supported this norm of secrecy, whereas detectives were most ready to inform on fellow officers. Detectives also placed a higher premium on making a good pinch than in aiding an officer in distress. In general, detectives were most prone to place their individual interests ahead of police solidarity.[59]

The second major norm sanctioned the use of violence where it was not permitted by law. For example, policemen justified the use of force against sex offenders. The public put great pressure on the department to deal with such offenders, often in situations where the victims refused to testify or where women brought charges against men to further other ends. The police found these cases to be confusing and troublesome, and one accepted way to deal with a peeping tom or exposer was to administer a good beating. The man involved was hardly likely to protest because public knowledge of his actions would bring worse injury than the beating.[60] Aggressive drunks caused numerous breaches of the peace and posed threats to the policeman's self-esteem, his person, or the cleanliness of his uniform. The club could settle these matters before they became serious. In Gary most of the drunks were black, and the prejudiced white policemen thought blacks inherently inferior anyway and criminal to boot, thereby strengthening the norm of the use of force in such cases.[61]

The most common reason given for the use of force was to induce respect for the police. The maxim "You gotta make them respect you" was drilled into the rookies and became, along with the maintenance of secrecy, their most important occupational guideline.[62] In dealing with some elements of the population, children and higher-class men and women, policemen believed that the best way to induce respect was to be respectful themselves. They often resented the patronizing attitude of the "better elements," but they respected their political power and their access to communications media.[63]

With slum dwellers, and especially black slum dwellers, the pattern was far different. Here officers felt themselves to be in an alien and hostile world, as indicated previously in the quotation from James Baldwin. The police did not question the social patterns that created the ghetto; indeed departments have always functioned to protect and advance the interests of the dominant groups in the community. What they did insist on was respect from the slum dwellers who they knew despised them. The use of rough treatment, up to and including force, was an accepted way to achieve this respect. In Gary, policemen did not talk to blacks; they shouted at them in the hope that this would curb lying. Policemen considered blacks to be inherently inferior and prone toward crime. Verbal or physical attacks upon the policemen's self-esteem could easily trigger violent responses. The maintenance of respect and self-esteem took precedence over the enforcement of the law.[64]

So twenty years ago, policemen and civilians faced each other in hostile confrontation; in the intervening time the polarization has obviously become much more pronounced as a result of the social changes outlined earlier in this chapter.[65] The situation became even more serious with the emergence of large-scale rioting among ghetto residents and dissident students and hangers-on around universities in the second half of the 1960s.

Chapter 11

Riots and the Police

The decade of the 1960s will go down in American history as the period of Vietnam in foreign affairs and the "long, hot summers" domestically. In addition the nation saw a new kind of student riot, one that led to the police bust. The police not only acted as controllers and suppressors of riots, but as rioters themselves.

The United States has a long, ugly history of racial violence, including use of the whip to control slaves, the Draft Riots of 1863 in New York, the disgrace of lynching, and the race riots of the early twentieth century.[1]

There were serious riots in August 1900, in cities as diverse as Akron and New York City. In Akron on August 22, a black man was accused of sexually assaulting a white child. A mob threatened to storm the city building, which contained the police office and jail, to take the prisoner. The authorities had already removed him as a precautionary measure and actually let a delegation from the streets go through the building to assure the crowd that he was no longer present. In a subsequent exchange of gunfire between policemen in the building and civilians outside, two children were fatally shot. The mob then secured some dynamite and blew up the city building. The chief of police had left his post and already made his way to Cleveland some thirty-five miles away. The police patrol wagon wound up in the Ohio Canal and further violence threatened. Troops were summoned to the city and restored order. Two days later, the prisoner, Louis Peck, was indicted, pleaded guilty, and was sentenced to life imprisonment. He was on the train to Columbus to begin serving his sentence just eight minutes after he entered the courtroom. Apparently the authorities indicated strongly that they could not or would not protect him against lynching if he did not confess.[2]

Exactly one week before, a primarily Irish mob roamed New York's Tenderloin beating Negroes. The police did nothing to restrain the mob and in fact joined in the assaults. The riot began when a white policeman in civilian clothes accosted a black couple and was stabbed in the ensuing melee. Policemen and civilians joined in extensive attacks upon Negroes in the area over the next several days. Frank Moss—an attorney who had served as assistant counsel of the Lexow Committee which had so embarrassed the department in 1894 and who later replaced Theodore Roosevelt as a police commissioner—compiled a convincing case of totally unwarranted police aggression. A Tammany-dominated board of commissioners ignored the evidence Moss had collected and refused to put any credence in the blacks who testified before them about the brutality. The commissioners simply whitewashed the affair.[3]

The period during and immediately after World War I was marked by especially serious racial clashes in Houston, East St. Louis, Washington, D.C., Chicago, and more than twenty other places. The typical pattern in these riots involved an initial act of white aggression against blacks followed by black retaliatory violence. The white community then marshaled overwhelming force to beat back this challenge to the racial status quo.[4]

In Chicago, the riot had its origins in the long record of racial conflict over gut issues of housing and jobs. Unions excluded blacks and then complained bitterly when blacks acted as strikebreakers. From 1915 on, the black population grew very rapidly, and any attempt on the part of newcomers to seek housing outside the constricted black belt brought threats of force and in many cases actual bombing. The summer of 1919 was one of extraordinary bitterness in the city as strike after strike erupted, and Irish and Polish youths beat up blacks who were found outside the black belt. A mayoralty election intensified all of these hostilities as one candidate, the notorious Big Bill Thompson, relied heavily upon a black bloc vote. During the week-long rioting, the police not only arrested blacks much more frequently than whites but also participated in some of the rioting themselves. Thirty-eight people died, twenty-three of them black, and hundreds were made homeless in the violence.[5]

In recent years the riots have followed a different pattern of black assault on white-owned businesses and other institutions. One of the first of the new-style upheavals came in Detroit in 1943, when the army had to be called in. This proved to be a forerunner of the riots of the 1960s in that the primary targets were buildings and goods, not people, although thirty-eight people did die in that 1943 riot, most as a result of police activity. There were few racially inspired incidents of mass violence in the 1950s, although the army had to be sent in to Little Rock, Arkansas, in 1957 because of Governor Orval Faubus' defiance of a desegregation order for the city's Central High School.

The 1960s saw a marked increase in mass confrontations from the sit-ins and freedom rides of the early years of the decade in the South to the mass eruptions of the black areas of New York, Los Angeles, Cleveland, Washington, Newark, Detroit, and a host of smaller cities from 1964 on. Housed in overcrowded, rat-infested slums, with limited job opportunities and having to buy inferior merchandise at inflated prices and ruinous credit rates, the people of these areas obviously had a much wider range of grievances than simply police performance. It is significant, however, that in all of the major riots before the assassination of Martin Luther King, the precipitating incident involved a hostile contact between a policeman and a civilian. As the most visible symbol of the white power structure, the uniform could easily form the target for all the accumulating frustrations of the ghetto.[6]

In the years immediately preceding the Detroit riot in 1967, researchers found growing white support of the police and growing black distrust. Increasingly, whites perceived the police as a buffer protecting the white community from the black; conversely blacks looked at the police as controllers rather than protectors. In a polarized community, especially, the ideal that the police served all groups in the city equally broke down. The practice of preventive patrolling aroused great hostility among those most affected by the practice, the unemployed, black youth, teen-agers, and black-power advocates. The riot itself began when police raided an after-hours drinking spot in the Twelfth Street ghetto area. About 75 percent of the black residents of the neighborhood surveyed after the riots believed that the police had moved too slowly to control the disorders in the beginning. Paradoxically, more than half also believed that police efforts overall were excessively repressive. These responses throw light on the police dilemma: people of the ghetto want police protection, but they are likely to object strongly to particular police actions.[7]

Partly, of course, the dilemma is of the police's own making. Previous behavior in the ghetto raises tensions, and unless the initial response to disorder is precisely calculated to control incipient rioting without fueling further disorder, the situation can easily get out of hand. This is what happened in Detroit in 1967. In Newark in the same year unverified reports of sniper fire led to indiscriminate shooting and needless deaths.[8]

The Report of the National Advisory Commission on Civil Disorders, the Kerner Commission, emphasized the importance of initial response in riot situations generally. In the summer on evenings and weekends, the streets of ghetto areas are normally filled as people seek to escape the stifling heat of the crowded dwellings. Furthermore, because of the age patterns of the black community, there are many youths on the street. In such an atmosphere, any police action, even the most routine, can quickly draw a crowd and precipitate a serious disorder. The commission noted that most policemen do not understand the people of the area and are likely to engage in actions which to them seem unexceptionable but which are highly inflammatory. Taking an arrested man by the arm might be normal police procedure but could appear demeaning and contemptuous to the people of the area. If a crowd gathers and is hostile, then the police action at this stage can be decisive as to whether the incident reaches serious proportions or not. Unfortunately for the police, no one tactic has proven effective in all situations. The police have to mount enough force to control an incipient disorder, but if they overreact and send in too many cars and men with too much riot equipment, they can increase tensions to the danger point.

The commission found that few if any departments met all the requirements for effective control of disorder. The police must have an experienced senior officer on the scene to make an accurate determination of the number of men needed. Furthermore, they have to be able to marshal that manpower quickly and efficiently. This is no easy task. The commission found that the average department had only 13 percent of its patrol force available between the hours of 4:00 P.M. and midnight, when most riots began. Most departments had no effective contingency plans for the control of disorders and were likely to be short of essential equipment. The biggest drawback the commission discovered lay in the field of training. Policemen were trained to work as individuals or in pairs with small groups of civilians. To control a disorder they had to reorient themselves to become an effective team operating in large units over a considerable extent of territory. But no department conducted exercises of this nature; what riot training did exist came in recruit school and emphasized the role of the individual policeman.[9]

Standard riot-control manuals draw heavily upon the experience of the British Army in colonial situations. The riot-control force is expected to act as a disciplined unit in facing, controlling, and dispersing an impersonal mob. But policemen are neither trained nor conditioned to act as part of a disciplined collectivity; in their normal work they act with a good bit of autonomy either individually or in two-man teams.

More importantly, they are trained and conditioned to look for the *individuals* responsible for crime and disorder; they are not predisposed to look upon crowds as impersonal entities. Rather, cops look for agitators or leaders to bust. This encourages them to break ranks and charge into crowds in pursuit of particular people who distinguish themselves in any way. In a number of instances, such as at Los Angeles in June 1967, and Berkeley, California in June 1968, the police became rioters themselves. These incidents were not ghetto upheavals; the Los Angeles riot grew out of an antiwar demonstration and the Berkeley events developed out of the hostility between the police and the youth culture of Telegraph Avenue. They do indicate, however, some of the general obstacles to effective riot control on the part of police. As in Chicago during the Democratic convention, the police encouraged and indulged in violence rather than controlling it. Their lack of discipline and restraint created riots.[10]

Although police forces wear uniforms and use military titles, they do not exhibit military discipline and control. All too often commanders do not control their men. The traditions of solidarity and the collective strength of the rank and file overbalance the rhetoric of discipline and command. Commanders can make life miserable for an individual patrolman who defies them; they can do little when their subordinates take concerted action. Senior officers who will privately admit that excessive use of force by their men is one of their more serious problems will publicly deny any allegations, even when the evidence is overwhelming. Unfortunately, many white middle-class people support police violence directed against ghetto blacks and demonstrating radicals of various stripes. The police know this and feel free to act out their frustrations by clubbing individuals rather than controlling crowds as impersonal entities.[11]

Other deficiencies involved communications and equipment. Commanders could not coordinate the activities of their men once they had left the range of their car radios. Only a minority of cities provided patrolmen with individual radios during the riot years of the 1960s. In the last few years the number of such radios has risen rapidly. The New York City policemen who faced the draft rioters of 1863 did so with a wooden stick and a gun; the policemen who faced the urban disorders a century later were equipped with a wooden stick and a gun. For a number of reasons, police forces had not developed a battery of nonlethal weapons or instruments to control rioters without maiming or killing them. Gas, although effective, repelled civilians in more ways than one, and few cities had an adequate number of gas masks. In the aftermath of the riots some departments have been tempted to buy weapons of mass destruction which have no place in urban communities.[12]

Space precludes a more extended treatment of the police problem in controlling civil disorders; suffice it to say that urban departments must work to minimize the possibility of disorder by improving their performance in inner-city areas. At the same time they must develop the doctrine, the techniques, the training, and the equipment to bring disorders under control as quickly and humanely as possible. The police cannot end the pathology that is the lot of the ghetto dwellers; only society as a whole can do that. Until the majority makes the decision that the ghetto walls must come tumbling down, policemen have the unenviable task of preserving order and protecting property in an explosive social situation. Perhaps their anger should be directed not at the disorderly and criminal in the ghetto, but at those who permit the continued existence of such conditions.

Furthermore, the search for solutions to the problems created by disorder should not divert police departments and other government officials from the basic tasks of providing services to people in trouble and reducing the frictions of urban life.

Yet the control, and far better the prevention, of urban riots must remain in the hands of local government. In the late 1960s there was a tendency to rely more and more heavily upon the army. The army proved much more effective than the National Guard in Detroit in 1967, and since that time local officials as well as the Pentagon have looked more quickly to army intervention as the answer to their problems. Unlike the police or the guard, the army is trained and disciplined for collective action. Commanders can control the amount of force used and, unlike policemen, soldiers are not out to distinguish themselves by making a "good pinch" of conspicuous agitators or leaders. The former Attorney General Ramsey Clark eloquently points out the dangers of this trend. The army cannot be mobilized and shipped that quickly for riot duty unless garrisons are posted in cities. Any money spent in this fashion limits the amount available for local police, money which could be spent on their entire range of duties; and further reliance on the army would increase the dangers of militarism and denial of civil liberties in American society.[13]

While racially related violence is an old story in American cities, the student riots of the 1960s were a new phenomenon. Student protests occurred in the nineteenth century—one historian referred to student discipline in the old-time college as "autocracy tempered by rebellion"—but they did not include the massive confrontations between students, other disaffected young people, and the police such as scarred Columbia University in New York City in the spring of 1968, the Democratic convention in Chicago that same summer, and numerous campus communities.

In a sad sequence of fractured communications and gross miscalculation among administrators and various student groups, Columbia reached a crisis stage which administrative heads thought could be resolved only by calling in the police. The university officials hoped that the police could remove demonstrators from buildings and restore tranquility to the campus in a peaceful manner. The expectation was that, with sufficient numbers of men and a department commitment to minimum force, students would leave the buildings they were occupying rather than oppose the police. The university could then resume normal functioning.[14]

Almost all of these calculations proved false. There were many more demonstrators in buildings and outside than the authorities anticipated; the department did not send as many men as originally planned; the students resisted; and the police reacted with extremes of clubbing. These events took place on the night of April 29-30, 1968. During the next several weeks the campus seethed with unrest, bringing about another and more serious police "bust" in the early morning of May 22, when the university president called them in to clear the campus after renewed building takeovers.

What seemed to enrage the police were the epithets, the abuse, the "foul" language hurled at them by middle-class young people who had the advantages of family position and opportunities for education denied the men in uniform. Here were people who had everything the nation had to offer scorning and mocking the American dream. To the patrolman who moonlighted to pay his bills and provide a decent environment for his family, the sight of young men and women who "had it made" by his standards cursing, jeering, and destroying and rejecting must have been overwhelming. The student protestors in their dress, demeanor, language, and behavior violated all of the moral principles of lower-middle-class respectability. Many ambitious policemen earn college and advanced degrees through long years of off-duty study, which means considerable time spent away from their families. Such men could hardly understand and sympathize with middle- and upper-class youth who had their educations paid for by their parents. The economically secure could scorn materialism; advantaged youth with no responsibilities other than their own maturation could curse and mock the men trying to make a living in a blue suit.

The violent confrontations between police and youthful dissidents highlighted some of the less savory aspects of American social life in the 1960s. Some upper-middle-class members condemned lower-middle- and working-class people as bigots because of their indifference or hostility toward the aspirations of blacks and other minority groups. Yet the advantaged are often bigoted themselves; however, their targets are not blacks so much as white workers, policemen included. Each class seems to single out the one just below it in the social scale to be the object of its prejudice and contempt. So working-class whites fearfully watch their neighborhoods for any sign of racial change, while the upper-middle class berates the lower-middle class for its conventionality and its insensitivity to the needs of the poor, forgetting that it's easier to be charitable on $15,000 a year than $9,000.

Alienated youth from middle- and upper-class families, those who reject American capitalism with its pursuit of status through the acquisition of money and position, may not be so free from class prejudice as they suppose. They may be able to identify, in theory at any rate, with the outcasts and the losers of the society; they do not have any sympathy with those who support and are responsible for enforcing the official morality. It may well be that the protestors' contempt for policemen is not all ideological, that at least to some extent the cops are derided because they are Irish or Italian, speak with working-class accents, and live in heavily mortgaged houses in "ticky-tacky" suburban developments.[15]

Unlike other occupational groups, policemen do not have to suffer this contempt in silence. As noted previously, they have a very strong occupational concern for respect and deference from the civilian population. In addition, working-class culture in general and the police in particular put heavy emphasis on masculinity, on not "taking any crap," and the police bust at Columbia and later at Chicago may be understood in part as a reaction to the class as well as ideological put-down of the police by the alienated affluent.

Society has given policemen the legal power to use force and provided them with guns and clubs for this purpose. However, there is no guarantee that this force and violence will always be used in legally sanctioned ways, especially when large numbers of officers collide with civilians they despise. The Columbia University authorities hoped for a limited use of force to achieve certain goals; when the police came on campus their occupational and social grievances led to a much greater use of force than anyone in the university had contemplated. The police may be an instrument in the hands of the dominant groups in society, but Columbia seems to indicate that the instrument has a mind and will of its own and is not always willing to operate within the framework of law and established social policy.

It is easy to say that policemen, like civilians, must be under the rule of law; achieving that end at the present seems difficult, if not impossible. As cities decay and social tensions become more acute, and as the conflict of life-styles between the "straights" and the "liberated" continues, the job of the police as order-keepers becomes more difficult and infinitely more important. But the police are anything but neutral in these conflicts; their sympathies are against the blacks and the hippies. The very factors that heighten tension and weaken the sense of civility and comity in the society as a whole make police adherence to a rule of law unlikely.[16]

Police morale has declined drastically in many cities in recent years as inflation has eaten away at their buying power, as the threat of riot and assassination has raised the prospect of injury and death, as crime rates have risen, and as all the accumulated grievances and gripes against government become focused on its most visible symbol, the uniformed patrolman. In an age whose watchwords are freedom and liberation, police officers resent the control their job exercises over their personal lives. They can be called on twenty-four hours a day; they work on an around-the-clock, seven-day-a-week basis; superiors who want to curb corruption keep close watch on their on-the-job activities and off-the-job spending; and they must lead conventional personal lives to avoid official disfavor. Outsiders often demand that departments more vigorously recruit minority group members, even if this means dropping physical and mental requirements or ignoring minor arrest records. Many police officers are bitter that these moves will lower the status of their occupation and threaten their position in the public eye. In Portland, Oregon, in 1968 the chief of police proposed to add six more blacks to the 800 member police force (none of the existing five black members served on uniform patrol). The plan called for thorough physical and psychological exams before appointment, but the written exam would be deferred until after the men had spent some time on the job and undergone preparatory training for the test. Counsel for the Police Association challenged this procedure on the basis that it would impair efficiency and morale, and rank-and-file feelings ran high on the issue.[17]

In recent years, the nation's big-city departments seem to have become more isolated, more hostile, and more fearful of any civilian involvement in their work and more intent than ever upon achieving autonomy. Mayors like John Lindsay of New York and Carl Stokes of Cleveland who wanted to remold the police of their cities faced implacable departmental opposition. Policemen have reacted to what they perceive as their deteriorating position by insisting more firmly than ever on group solidarity and cohesion. With some exceptions, such as West Coast cities and Washington, departments have not tried to encourage bright young college graduates, interested in doing something to improve the quality of urban life, to become police officers. Most of the nation's forces remain bastions of white working- and lower-middle-class conservatism, buffeted by the winds of social change and the acids of inflation and increasingly angry about the direction in which their society is moving and their own position within it.[18]

Cities must raise the status, pay, and quality of policemen and recruit more minority group members at the same time. Neither task will be easy. Able and socially minded young people will have to be convinced that policemen perform valuable services, and departments will have to modify their self-image to be attractive. Cities, already in financial despair, will have to get money from state and federal sources to raise salaries. Municipal authorities and police departments will have to take whatever steps are necessary to increase the number of Spanish-speaking and black recruits.

The position of the black policeman has never been an easy one. In the South virtually no Negro policemen were hired until after World War II, and they were restricted to patrolling black areas. In only one-third of Southern communities studied in 1959 and 1961 could black policemen arrest offenders equally regardless of race. Despite the fact that black policemen were more carefully recruited and trained than white and often had greater educational qualifications, their prospects for promotion have been very limited.[19]

Northern cities also restricted black policemen to black areas and limited their promotion possibilities. In New York black policemen were paired with white, so that if a black civilian had to be arrested the black policemen could do it and protect the department against charges of racial discrimination.

His white colleagues often force the black policeman to take extraordinary risks in order to prove himself. Moreover, he is forced to be especially hard on black offenders to show that he's not "soft" or "chicken." Black youth taunt the black policeman even more than they do the white. The black patrolman has to arrest people for actions which are not considered particularly criminal or immoral in the black community, such as gambling or intoxication. If he does not take action, he can be charged with misconduct by his white counterparts and superiors.

The referendum battle over the civilian review board in New York in 1966 exposed the marginality of the black policemen. The organized police establishment mobilized their forces to defeat the board, but the organization of black policemen, the Guardians, supported the black community's demands for civilian review. This led the Patrolmen's Benevolent Association to accuse members of the Guardians of putting their race above their occupation. In the eyes of the majority of members of the department, they had committed the unpardonable sin of breaking police solidarity in the face of outside attack.

Black policemen can take some comfort in the view that if their white colleagues were any good, they would not be policemen. This conception provides some psychological solace, but at the cost of belittling the prestige of their own occupation. Blacks do not become policemen because of the intrinsic charm of the job, but because of the civil service opportunities. In fact there are proportionately far more blacks in the police of New York's Housing Authority and Transit Authority than in the police department itself. The reason is that appointment and promotion opportunities in these forces are freer and less restricted by the traditions of Irish and now Italian solidarity.[20]

Mayor John Lindsay tried to break the power of the Irish Mafia at police headquarters by installing such men as Sanford Garelik, a Jew, and Lloyd Sealy, a black, in key positions. It will take sustained external pressure of this kind to make police forces more receptive to black applicants and to make possible the promotion of those new members. There will also have to be considerable work by people both within and without police departments to convince black youth of the personal and social value of a police career. Black young men, who look upon the police as their enemies, will have to be persuaded that becoming a policeman is not a betrayal, a literal cop-out.

Ultimately American cities can be safe only if they become true communities where all of the people see themselves as engaged in a common enterprise and sharing a common fate. While we can never achieve utopia in human affairs, if we do not make the attempt we may be doomed to ever-increasing hostility, violence, and despair. The police cannot make up for the failures of the society, and any attempt to make repression serve as an antidote for social decay will only exacerbate our present difficulties. As so many have said, the primary question is whether we have the will to make our cities fit communities to live and grow in. A good test is how we treat our police. Do we supply them with more weapons and greater firepower or do we give them the leadership, the training, and the resources so that they may keep the peace peacefully?

Notes

Bibliographical references may be abbreviated in the Notes; for full citations see the Bibliography.

CHAPTER 1

1. For a detailed history of the colonial towns, see Carl Bridenbaugh, *Cities in the Wilderness* and *Cities in Revolt*. The first volume carries the seaboard towns from their founding until 1742, and the second from 1742 until 1775. Material on constables and watchmen appears on pp. 63-68, 215-216, 374-375 of *Cities in the Wilderness* and 107-108, 297-299 of *Cities in Revolt*.

2. On the London watch, see Radzinowicz, Vol. II, p. 181. On New York, see Richardson, pp. 3-11.

3. Radzinowicz, Vol. IV, pp. 116-118; Woodham-Smith, pp. 22-23.

4. Bailyn, pp. 38-59.

5. Radzinowicz, Vol. II, pp. 263-269.

6. *Ibid.,* p. 239.

7. *Ibid.,* p. 262.

8. *Ibid.,* pp. 297-306. Quotation on p. 306.

9. Rudé.

10. Radzinowicz, Vol. II, pp. 217-224.

11. Radzinowicz, Vol. III, pp. 97-98; Radzinowicz, Vol. IV, pp. 110-111.

12. Radzinowicz, Vol. IV, pp. 112-114.

13. Woodham-Smith, pp. 22-23.

14. Radzinowicz, Vol. IV, pp. 153-157.

15. Quotations from Thompson, p. 82.

16. Radzinowicz, Vol. III, pp. 141-193. Quotation from p. 157.

17. Radzinowicz, Vol. IV, p. 163.

18. Radzinowicz, Vol. III, pp. 246-266.

19. *Ibid.,* pp. 432-437.

20. *Ibid.,* pp. 448-474. Quotation from p. 454.

21. Radzinowicz, Vol. IV, pp. 252-296.

22. *Ibid.,* pp. 184-188.

23. *Ibid.,* pp. 189-190. See also Lee, pp. 245-261.

24. Radzinowicz, Vol. IV, pp. 164-166.
25. Wilbur R. Miller, Jr.
26. Gorer, cited in Niederhoffer, pp. 8-9.
27. Allan Silver, "The Demand for Order in Civil Society: A Review of Some Themes in the History of Urban Crime, Police and Riot," in Bordua, pp. 1-24. The quotation from p. 8. See also Critchley.
28. Wilbur R. Miller; President's Commission, *Task Force Report,* pp. 25-34.

CHAPTER 2

1. Pintard, pp. 254-255; Lane, *Policing the City,* p. 29.
2. Wade, pp. 98-100.
3. Sam B. Warner, "If All the World," pp. 26-43, and *The Private City,* pp. 67-69.
4. Beaumont, pp. 245-249; Richards.
5. Richardson, pp. 28-29.
6. Lane, *Policing the City,* pp. 29-33.
7. Warner, *Private City,* pp. 125-151.
8. Richardson, pp. 29-49.
9. Warner, *Private City,* pp. 125-132.
10. Fosdick, *American Police Systems,* pp. 63-65.
11. Warner, *Private City,* pp. 147-156, 94-97.
12. Lane, *Policing the City,* pp. 3-38; Fosdick, *American Police Systems,* pp. 66-67.
13. Still, p. 232.
14. Richardson, p. 60.
15. *Ibid.,* p. 55.
16. Fosdick, *American Police Systems,* pp. 68-76.
17. Lane, *Policing the City,* p. 39.
18. Richardson, p. 92.
19. Wilbur R. Miller. The arrest figures are from Miller; the possible interpretations are mine.
20. Lane, *Policing the City,* pp. 48-51.
21. *Ibid.,* pp. 47-48, 169-170; Richardson, pp. 57, 110.
22. Dykstra, pp. 123-133.
23. *Ibid.,* pp. 239-264.
24. Richardson, pp. 62-63.
25. *Ibid.,* pp. 207-212.

CHAPTER 3

1. Richardson, pp. 51-53.
2. Woolsey, pp. 97-114. Quotation from p. 113.
3. Fosdick, *American Police Systems,* pp. 76-80.
4. Richardson, pp. 77-81. Fosdick, *American Police Systems,* pp. 79-80.
5. Richardson, pp. 82-108.

6. *Ibid.,* pp. 109-164.
7. Fosdick, *American Police Systems,* pp. 90-95.
8. Lane, *Policing the City,* pp. 191-198.
9. *Ibid.,* pp. 216-219, 289.
10. Richardson, pp. 160-163.
11. *Ibid.,* pp. 214-216.
12. *Ibid.,* pp. 228-233, 244-245, 268-269.
13. *Ibid.,* pp. 273-275, 280-281.
14. Orth.
15. Sikes.
16. Tom L. Johnson; H. L. Warner.
17. May.
18. H. L. Warner, pp. 330-332.
19. Fairlie; McKelvey, *Urbanization,* pp. 111-113, 254-255, on home rule generally.

CHAPTER 4

1. Richardson, pp. 175-179.
2. *Ibid.,* p. 259.
3. Fosdick, *European Police Systems,* pp. 200-204.
4. Walling, p. 600; Policeman's Wife, pp. 84-88; Banton, pp. 119, 156.
5. *Evening Post,* quoted by Andrews, pp. 209-210; Willemse, *A Cop Remembers,* pp. 82-85, 101.
6. Richardson, pp. 195-201.
7. Lane, "Crime."
8. Richardson, pp. 130-148.
9. McLean, pp. 120-137, has an excellent discussion on changing fashions in popular humor.
10. Sam Warner, *The Private City,* pp. 156-157, 165-169.
11. Richardson, p. 70; Lane, *Policing,* p. 197; Bocock.
12. National Commission, *Report on Crime,* pp. 185-187; Niederhoffer, pp. 142-144; James Q. Wilson, "Generational and Ethnic Differences."
13. Howard, p. 13.
14. Moley, "Politics and Crime."
15. Walling, pp. 178-180, 577-578.
16. Richardson, pp. 180-181. On Boston in the 1930s see Whyte, pp. 123-139. Whyte describes the patterned social relationships between policemen and bookmakers and the importance of the transfer.
17. Richardson, p. 188.
18. *Ibid.,* pp. 271, 279-280.
19. Howard, pp. 13-14.
20. Richardson, p. 180.
21. Lawrence.
22. Richardson, pp. 204-207.
23. *Ibid.,* pp. 201-204.
24. Gans.
25. Richardson, pp. 260-261.
26. Woods, pp. 96-109.

CHAPTER 5

1. Hoogenboom's book is the best history of the national civil service reform movement.

2. For the general outlook of patrician "reformers," see Sproat. For their views on police, see Foord.

3. Richardson, pp. 178-179; see Garrett, p. 134 for evidence on continued political influence on appointments in the twentieth century.

4. This section on the structural transformation of municipal government is based upon Hays and upon Weinstein, pp. 92-116.

5. For a good general discussion of the continuing importance of this dichotomy, see James Q. Wilson and Edward C. Banfield, *City Politics* (New York: Vintage Books, 1966).

6. McKelvey, *Urbanization,* pp. 241-242; McKelvey, *Metropolitan America,* pp. 9-10; Kenneth T. Jackson, "Metropolitan Government," pp. 442-462.

7. Bruce Smith, Jr., *Police Systems,* second revised edition, pp. 316-317, is critical of civil service practices, as is Stone, yet both condemn the influence of "politics" upon police performance. For a treatment of the New York Police Department as a closed bureaucracy in the 1950s, see Sayre and Kaufman, pp. 222, 431.

B. Bruce Smith, "Municipal Police Administration"; Smith, *Police Systems,* 1960 ed., pp. 318-320; Merriam.

9. Fosdick, *American Police Systems,* pp. 107-110; Richardson, pp. 216, 228, 243, 275, 280-281.

10. Fosdick, *American Police Systems,* pp. 108-109.

11. Fuld, *Police Administration,* pp. 30-48; Fosdick, *European Police Systems,* pp. 149-180. Fosdick has interesting comments on the circumstances under which his two volumes on the police were written and their contrasting findings in his autobiography *Chronicle of a Generation,* pp. 124-135.

12. National Commission, *Report on the Police,* pp. 26-35. This section was written by August Vollmer, long-time chief of the Berkeley, California, department.

13. On the alternating cycle of scandal followed by reform, see Lowi; Swett; and Moley, "Charles Francis Murphy."

14. Two readable, journalistic accounts of this famous case are in Root and Logan.

15. Schweppe, pp. 87-88.

16. Garrett, pp. 43-44; Reminiscences of Henry Bruere, p. 88.

17. Woods. The next several paragraphs are based on this book.

18. Schweppe, pp. 49, 77-82, 101-106.

19. *Ibid.,* pp. 84-91.

20. *Ibid.,* pp. 107-108; Garrett, pp. 68-82, 138.

21. Sayre and Kaufman, pp. 287-289.

22. This account of Kohler's career is based upon Howard.

23. Howe, pp. 100-145.

24. Bremner; Baker.

25. Kohler supplied these figures in a letter to the City Council dated January 2, 1909. *Cleveland City Council Proceedings*, 42 (January 4, 1909), p. 1.
26. Norton.
27. Howard.
28. National Commission, *Report on the Police*, pp. 26-35.
29. Bruce Smith, *Police Systems*, 1949 edition, pp. 7-9.
30. Riordon, pp. 22-27.
31. Haller, "Urban Crime and Criminal Justice"; Ahern, pp. 21-22.

CHAPTER 6

1. This section draws heavily upon James Timberlake, *Prohibition and the Progressive Movement, 1900-1920* (Cambridge: Harvard University Press, 1963).
2. Gusfield, p. 107.
3. Timberlake, *Prohibition*, pp. 117-119.
4. Timothy Smith, esp. p. 536.
5. See Prpic, pp. 120, 153, 158-159, on the importance of saloons for Croatian immigrants.
6. Sinclair, pp. 119-127.
7. Gusfield, pp. 126-139; Cowley, pp. 57-73.
8. Haller, "Civic Reformers," p. 45; Haller, "Urban Crime and Criminal Justice."
9. Landesco, pp. 815-1100.
10. Haller, "Civic Reformers," pp. 43-45.
11. Haller, "Urban Crime," pp. 626-627; Haller, "Urban Vice," pp. 292-305.
12. Haller, "Urban Crime."
13. Haller, "Civic Reformers," pp. 48-52.
14. Citizens' Police Committee.
15. Cleveland Foundation, pp. 6-9.
16. *Ibid.*, pp. 13-21.
17. *Ibid.*, pp. 36-41, 23.
18. *Ibid.*, pp. 24-35.
19. *Ibid.*, pp. 45-54, 64-74.
20. This section is based upon the clipping files of the Cleveland *Plain Dealer* for the period December 1935-February 1942.
21. Cleveland *News*, January 13, 1937.
22. President's Commission, *The Challenge of Crime*.
23. *Roe et al. v. Wade, District Attorney of Dallas County*, U.S. Reports, Vol. 410, pp. 113-178.
24. John Gardiner, *Politics of Corruption*, April 24-29, 1970.
25. *Challenge of Crime*, pp. 188-189, 197-200.
26. *Ibid.*, p. 189.
27. *Ibid.*; Skolnick, *Justice Without Trial*, pp. 96-110.
28. *New York Times*, August 13, 1972, Sec. II, p. 3, c. 8.
29. Kaplan. The discussion of the enforcement and constitutional problems surrounding marijuana control are based on this thoughtful book.

30. *Ibid.,* pp. 5, 11.
31. *Ibid.,* pp. 40-42.
32. *Ibid.,* pp. 42-44.
33. *Ibid.,* pp. 40, 363-364, 370-371.

CHAPTER 7

1. Taylor is a thorough treatment of urban public transit before the Civil War.
2. Richardson, pp. 122-123, 168.
3. Holt.
4. Sam B. Warner, *Streetcar Suburbs.*
5. Zane L. Miller, *Boss Cox's Cincinnati,* pp. 9-56.
6. Zorbaugh is a classic study of one such area in Chicago.
7. Haller, "Civic Reformers and Police," pp. 40-41; Spear, pp. 24-26.
8. Ware, pp. 122-123.
9. For a good discussion of residential change in a major city, see Mayer and Wade.
10. For a general discussion of the political forces for and against annexation, see Jackson, "Metropolitan Government."
11. President's Commission, *Task Force Report,* pp. 68-95.
12. Fogelson, "Institutional Change"; Skolnick, "The Berkeley Scheme."
13. Cleveland *Plain Dealer,* October 7, 1922.
14. Westley, *Violence and the Police,* p. 107.
15. Bruce Smith, *Police Systems in the United States,* 1960 ed., p. 65.
16. Gardiner, "Enforcement of Traffic," p. 158.
17. *Ibid.,* p. 153.
18. *Ibid.,* pp. 155-170; Westley, *Violence and the Police,* p. 59.
19. Mayer and Wade, *Chicago,* p. 331.
20. Vollmer, p. 132.
21. Vollmer noted the sharp rise (500% increase between 1913 and 1932) in automobile related deaths at a time when other accidental causes of death dropped. See *ibid.,* p. 119.
22. Gardiner, "Enforcement," p. 171. Bergman makes the case for enforcement cutting accident rates.
23. *Ibid.,* pp. 171-172; Kaplan, p. 43.
24. Richardson, pp. 170, 263: Speir, pp. 276-280.
25. President's Commission, *Task Force Report,* p. 58.
26. Cleveland *Plain Dealer,* February 18, 1973.
27. Skolnick, *Justice Without Trial,* pp. 170-173.
28. Serrin.
29. President's Commission, *Task Force Report,* pp. 52, 54-55.
30. Smith, *Police Systems* (1949 ed.), p. 14.

CHAPTER 8

1. *New York Times,* March 25, 1973, p. 33; June 8, 1970, p. 28.
2. Richardson, pp. 176-180; Logan.

3. James Q. Wilson refers to this pattern of police performance as the "watchman style." See his *Varieties of Police Behavior,* pp. 140-171.
4. Schweppe, pp. 87-88.
5. Sayre and Kaufman, p. 292.
6. *Ibid.,* p. 695; *Missouri Crime Survey,* pp. 35-39.
7. Stone; Smith, *Police Systems,* 1960 ed., pp. 316-317; Westley, pp. xiii-xviii.
8. Sayre and Kaufman, pp. 428-431.
9. Smith, *Police Systems,* 1949 ed., pp. 4-10.
10. Sayre and Kaufman, pp. 287-289.
11. Walling, pp. 178-180; Roosevelt, p. 167; *New York Times,* June 8, 1970, pp. 1, 28.
12. Sayre and Kaufman, pp. 287-289.
13. *New York Times,* September 6, 1970, p. 52.
14. *Ibid.,* April 13, 1973, p. 1.
15. Cleveland *Plain Dealer,* August 28, 1971, pp. A 1, 6; Masotti and Corsi.
16. Westley, "The Police," p. 309.
17. Two sociologists reflect upon the problems of police command in Bordua and Reiss; Sayre and Kaufman, pp. 287-289.
18. Smith, *Police Systems,* 1960 ed., pp. 318-319; Niederhoffer, pp. 58, 83; Radano, p. 135.
19. Glazer; Sayre and Kaufman, pp. 428-430.
20. Robinson.
21. On the general development of "professionalism" in American society, see Gilb. Mrs. Gilb notes the common elements of various definitions of professionalism on p. 27. On the conflict between bureaucratization and professionalization, see Kelling and Kliesmet.

CHAPTER 9

1. Gilb, pp. 64-81.
2. Woods.
3. Niederhoffer, pp. 55-57; Westley, *Violence and the Police,* pp. 156-180.
4. A Policeman's Wife, p. 79; H. L. Mencken, pp. 32-33.
5. In addition to Fosdick's *European Police Systems* and *American Police Systems,* see his *Chronicle of a Generation,* pp. 124-35. For a comparison of American and British police, see Banton.
6. The essays in Sellin provide a useful summary of academic thinking on crime and police in the late 1920s. Also see the National Commission publications.
7. National Commission, *Report on Police,* pp. 58-61.
8. Cahalane.
9. Vollmer, pp. 155-156.
10. Niederhoffer, pp. 17-18.
11. Wilson, O(rlando) W(infield), in Moritz. See also O. W. Wilson, "How the Police Chief Sees It," *Harper's Magazine,* 28 (April 1964), pp. 140-145.

12. *New York Times,* July 7, 1966, p. 68.
13. O. W. Wilson, ed., *Parker on Police,* pp. 11-13.
14. *Ibid.,* p. 14.
15. *Ibid.,* pp. 99-101.
16. President's Commission, *Challenge of Crime,* pp. 35-37.
17. Wilson, *Parker on Police,* p. 12.
18. *Ibid.,* p. 145.
19. *Ibid.,* p. 38.
20. Westley, *Violence and the Police,* pp. 70-72.
21. Wilson, *Parker On Police,* p. 102.
22. *Ibid.,* pp. 102-112.
23. Ramsey Clark, pp. 265-276.
24. Wilson, *Parker On Police,* pp. 127-129.
25. Niederhoffer, pp. 38-39, 114-117.
26. Two important books emphasizing these themes are Westley, *Violence and the Police,* and Skolnick, *Justice Without Trial.*
27. This discussion draws upon Lipset.
28. Kinzer; Pratt.
29. Jackson, *Ku Klux Klan,* pp. 235-249.
30. O'Dea.
31. Turner, p. 207.
32. Lipset; Jacobs, pp. 13-60.
33. Sayre and Kaufman, pp. 428-430; Chevigny, pp. 161-179.
34. Skolnick, ed., *The Politics of Protest.* Chapter VII, "The Police in Protest," pp. 241-292, details police rage and hostility toward the protestors and their increasing militancy in advancing their own aims.
35. Jacobs, pp. 13-60, is an unsympathetic portrait of the Los Angeles Police Department's "professionalism" under Chief Parker. See also the forthcoming Ph.D. dissertation by Joseph G. Woods.
36. James Q. Wilson, *Varieties of Police Behavior,* pp. 172-199; Piliavin and Briar.
37. James Q. Wilson, "Dilemmas of Police Administration."
38. Skolnick, *Justice Without Trial,* pp. 1-22; Niederhoffer, p. 173n.
39. Reiss, pp. 114-120.
40. Ramsey Clark's *Crime in America* is an eloquent exposition of these principles by a former attorney general. For the distinct deterioration of the United States Department of Justice under Clark's successor, John Mitchell, see Harris.
41. Kamisar indicates that such claims are of long standing.
42. Wilson, *Varieties of Police Behavior.* The "watchman style" is described on pp. 140-171.
43. President's Commission, *Task Force Report: The Police,* pp. 209-212.
44. National Commission, *Lawless Law Enforcement,* pp. 38-192.
45. Westley, *Violence and the Police,* pp. xiii-xviii. This material comes from a preface written in 1970 to a text written some twenty years previously but published in its entirety for the first time. Westley's 1951 Ph.D. dissertation has long been cited for its insight into police; its publication, including paperback, now makes it readily available.
46. This is the persuasively argued conclusion in Reiss.

47. *Ibid.,* pp. 156-172. The quotations are from pp. 169 and 170 respectively.
48. *Ibid.,* pp. 193-195, 202.

CHAPTER 10

1. This theme is fully developed in Richardson.
2. Whyte, pp. 123-139.
3. Richardson, pp. 195-201.
4. Dubofsky, pp. 63, 92-97.
5. Bernstein, pp. 485-490.
6. Brody, pp. 250-253.
7. For a review of recent literature, see Johnson and Gregory.
8. For a good journalistic survey of the plight of cities, see Lowe.
9. Ward is excellent on the inner-city concentration of employment before 1900.
10. On recent employment patterns, see Kain, pp. 1-43.
11. Jackson, "Metropolitan Government," pp. 452-457.
12. Piven and Cloward, pp. 200-217.
13. Weber, pp. 66-81.
14. Rainwater.
15. Downs, pp. 75-96; Kozol.
16. Powdermaker.
17. See Malcolm X and A. Haley for a brillian account of one sensitive young man's odyssey to black nationalism.
18. *New York Times,* Jan. 2, 1972, p. 27, Jan. 29, 1972, p. 33.
19. Spear, *Black Chicago,* pp. 24-26; Posten, pp. 920-933.
20. Willemse, *Behind the Green Lights,* pp. 84-86.
21. Kerner Commission, p. 309.
22. Niederhoffer, pp. 138-139.
23. Levy; Reiss, pp. 147-151.
24. President's Commission, *Challenge of Crime,* pp. 96-97.
25. *Ibid.,* pp. 212-224.
26. President's Commission, *Task Force Report,* pp. 181, 190.
27. Piliavin and Briar.
28. Chevigny, pp. 137-144.
29. Piliavin and Briar.
30. Skolnick, *Justice Without Trial;* Bayley and Mendelsohn, pp. 109-119.
31. Wambaugh, *The New Centurions.* This best-selling novel by a Los Angeles detective sergeant presents a vivid picture of the cop's view of the world.
32. Baldwin, pp. 65-67.
33. Kerner Commission, p. 206.
34. Grove and Rossi.
35. Westley, *Violence and Police,* pp. 121-128.
36. Cumming *et al.*
37. Goldstein.
38. Berkley.

39. Westley, *Violence and Police,* pp. 139-140.
40. *Ibid.,* Niederhoffer, pp. 82-84. Newspaper coverage of such crimes in every city shows the intense pressure on the police.
41. Parnas, pp. 916-920.
42. Bard and Berkowitz; see also Bard's "Family Intervention Police Teams" and "Iatrogenic Violence."
43. Reiss, p. 76.
44. The University of Akron's Associate Degree program in Law Enforcement Technology puts greater emphasis on law enforcement than peace-keeping, although the program does include a substantial amount of "human relations" material.
45. James Q. Wilson, "Dilemmas of Police Administration."
46. Reiss, pp. 88-105, 115-116.
47. *Ibid.,* pp. 57-65.
48. President's Commission, *Challenge of Crime,* pp. 97-100.
49. Wambaugh, especially pp. 118-120, 235-237, 374-375. On danger and the police personality, see Skolnick, *Justice Without Trial,* pp. 42-48, 63-65; Reiss, pp. 58-62; Westley, *Violence and Police,* pp. 60-61.
50. President's Commission, *Task Force Report,* pp. 122-124.
51. President's Commission, *Challenge of Crime,* pp. 255-257; Stark, pp. 237-238. The commission had field studies conducted in San Diego and Philadelphia which showed the variations in class and racial perceptions of the police. See Joseph D. Lohman and Gordon E. Misner, *The Police and the Community,* 2 vols. (Washington, D.C.: G.P.O., 1966).
52. President's Commission, *Task Force Report: The Police,* pp. 150-151.
53. Stark, pp. 204-205.
54. Turner, pp. 209-210. After a review of the problem of policing the police, the President's Commission recommended against the establishment of civilian review boards. See its *Challenge of Crime,* pp. 262-265.
55. Westley, *Violence and Police,* p. 81.
56. Turner, pp. 207-208.
57. Chevigny, pp. 105-106.
58. Westley, *Violence and Police,* pp. 27-28, 44-45, 205-210.
59. *Ibid.,* pp. 110-118; Savitz.
60. Westley, *Violence and Police,* pp. 61-64.
61. *Ibid.,* pp. 72-73.
62. *Ibid.,* pp. 121-122.
63. *Ibid.,* pp. 96-99.
64. *Ibid.,* pp. 99, 121-152.
65. *Ibid.,* pp. xii-xvii. In these pages, written in 1970, Westley provides a useful summary of some of the major changes in police-community relations in the twenty years since his study was done.

CHAPTER 11

1. Grimshaw is a useful anthology.
2. This account is based upon the reports in the Akron *Beacon Journal,* August 23-30, 1900.

3. Scheiner, pp. 121-127.
4. Rudwick and Meier.
5. Tuttle is a superb study of the background and progress of the riot. See also Spear.
6. Kerner Commission, p. 206.
7. Hahn.
8. Hersey; Kerner Commission, pp. 56-69, 84-108.
9. Kerner Commission, pp. 484-493.
10. Stark, pp. 125-131, 189-201.
11. *Ibid.,* pp. 178-189.
12. Kerner Commission, pp. 491-492.
13. Clark, pp. 257-261.
14. *Crisis at Columbia.* The next several paragraphs are based upon the report of this commission, headed by Archibald Cox.
15. Lerner.
16. Stark sees the conflict between police and ghetto residents as a conflict of subcultures. *Police Riots,* pp. 97-98.
17. *Ibid.,* pp. 204-205.
18. Lipset; Reichley.
19. Rudwick.
20. Alex, pp. 199-210.

Bibliography

Books and articles preceded by an asterisk are particularly useful.

*Ahern, James. *Police in Trouble: Our Frightening Crisis in Law Enforcement.* New York: Hawthorn Books, 1972.

*Alex, Nicholas. *Black in Blue: A Study of the Negro Policeman.* New York: Appleton-Century-Crofts, 1969.

Andrews, Avery. "Citizen in Action: The Story of Theodore Roosevelt as Police Commissioner." Typescript.

Bailyn, Bernard. "The Transforming Radicalism of the American Revolution." General Introduction to *Pamphlets of the American Revolution.* Vol. I. Cambridge: Harvard University Press, 1965.

Baker, Newton D. "Law, Police, and Social Problems," *Atlantic Monthly.* 116 (July 1915), 12-20.

Baldwin, James. *Nobody Knows My Name: More Notes of a Native Son.* New York: Dial Press, 1961.

Banfield, Edward C., and James Q. Wilson. *City Politics.* New York: Vintage Books, 1966.

*Banton, Michael. *The Policeman in the Community.* London: Tavistock, 1964.

*Bard, Morton. "Family Intervention Police Teams as a Community Mental Health Resource." *The Journal of Criminal Law, Criminology and Police Science.* 60 (June 1969), 247-250.

Bard, Morton. "Iatrogenic Violence." *The Police Chief.* 38 (January 1971), 16-17.

Bard, Morton, and Bernard Berkowitz. "Training Police as Specialists in Family Crisis Intervention: A Community Psychology Action Program." *Community Mental Health Journal.* III (Winter 1967), 315-317.

*Bayley, David H., and Harold Mendelsohn. *Minorities and the Police.* New York: Free Press, 1968.

Beaumont, Gustave de. *Marie, or Slavery in the United States,* translated by Barbara Chapman. Stanford: Stanford University Press, 1958.

Bergman, Roy J. "A Case for Traffic Law Enforcement," in Samuel G. Chapman, ed., *Police Patrol Readings.* Springfield, Ill.: Charles C. Thomas, 1964, 374-376.

212

Berkley, George E. *The Democratic Policemen.* Boston: Beacon Press, 1969.

Bernstein, Irving. *Turbulent Years: A History of the American Worker, 1933-1941.* Boston: Houghton Mifflin, 1970.

Bocock, John Paul. "The Irish Conquest of Our Cities," *Forum,* 17 (April 1894), 186-195.

*Bordua, David J., ed. *The Police: Six Sociological Essays.* New York: John Wiley, 1967.

Bordua, David J., and Albert J. Reiss, Jr. "Command, Control, and Charisma: Reflections on Police Bureaucracy," *American Journal of Sociology.* 72 (July 1966), 68-76.

Bremner, Robert. "Police, Penal and Parole Policies in Cleveland and Toledo: The Civic Revival in Ohio," *American Journal of Economics and Sociology.* 14 (July 1955), 387-398.

Bridenbaugh, Carl. *Cities in Revolt.* New York: Alfred Knopf, 1955.

Bridenbaugh, Carl. *Cities in the Wilderness.* New York: Alfred Knopf, 1955.

Brody, David. *Steelworkers in America: The Nonunion Era.* New York: Harper Torchbooks, 1969.

Cahalane, Cornelius F. *The Policeman.* New York: E. P. Dutton, 1923.

*Chevigny, Paul. *Police Power: Police Abuses in New York City.* New York: Pantheon Books, 1969.

Citizens' Police Committee. *Chicago Police Problems.* Chicago: University of Chicago Press, 1931.

Clark, Ramsey. *Crime in America.* New York: Pockets Books, 1971.

*Cleveland Foundation. *Criminal Justice in Cleveland.* Reprint ed. Montclair, New Jersey: Patterson Smith, 1968.

Cowley, Malcolm. *Exile's Return.* New York: Viking Press, 1956.

Crisis at Columbia: Report of the Fact-Finding Commission Appointed to Investigate the Disturbances at Columbia University in April and May 1968. New York: Vintage Books, 1968.

Critchley, T. A. *The Conquest of Violence: Order and Liberty in Britain.* London: Constable, 1970.

Cumming, Elaine, Ian Cumming, and Laura Edell. "Policeman as Philosopher, Guide and Friend," *Social Problems.* 12 (Winter 1965), 278-286.

*Doig, Jameson, ed., "The Police in a Democratic Society: A Symposium," *Public Administration Review.* 28 (September-October 1968), 393-430.

Downs, Anthony. *Urban Problems and Prospects.* Chicago: Markham, 1970.

Dubofsky, Melvyn. *When Workers Organize: New York City in the Progressive Era.* Amherst: University of Massachusetts Press, 1968.

Dykstra, Robert. *The Cattle Towns.* New York: Atheneum, 1970.

Fairlie, John A. "Police Administration," *Political Science Quarterly.* 16 (March 1901), 1-23.

Fogelson, Robert M. "Institutional Change in Urban America, 1890-1970: Problems and Questions." Paper read to Organization of American Historians, April 16, 1970.

*Fogelson, Robert M. *Violence as Protest: A Study of Riots and Ghettos.* Garden City, N.Y.: Doubleday, 1971.

Foord, John. "The Selection of Policemen," *The City Vigilant.* 1 (December 1894), 329-332.

*Fosdick, Raymond. *American Police Systems.* New York: Century Book Co., 1920.

Fosdick, Raymond. *Chronicle of a Generation.* New York: Harper & Row, 1958.

*Fosdick, Raymond. *European Police Systems.* New York: Century, 1915.

*Fuld, Leonhard. *Police Administration.* New York: G. P. Putnam, 1909.

Gans, Howard S. "In the Matter of the Lawlessness of the Police— A Reply to Mr. Justice Gaynor," *North American Review.* 177 (February 1903), 287-296.

Gardiner, John A. "Police Enforcement of Traffic Laws: A Comparative Analysis," in James Q. Wilson, ed., *City Politics and Public Policy.* New York: John Wiley, 1968.

*Gardiner, John A. *The Politics of Corruption: Organized Crime in an American City.* New York: Russell Sage Foundation, 1970.

Garrett, Charles. *The La Guardia Years.* New Brunswick: Rutgers University Press, 1961.

Gilb, Corinne Lathrop. *Hidden Hierarchies: The Professions and Government.* New York: Harper & Row, 1966.

Glazer, Nathan. "Is New York City Ungovernable?" *Commentary.* 32 (September 1961), 185-193.

Goldstein, Herman. "Police Response to Urban Crisis," in Doig, ed., "Police in a Democratic Society," 417-423.

Grimshaw, Allen D., ed., *Racial Violence in the United States.* Chicago: Aldine, 1969.

Grove, W. Eugene, and Peter H. Rossi. "Police Perceptions of a Hostile Ghetto: Realism or Projection," in Harlan Hahn, ed., *Police in Urban Society.* Beverly Hills: Sage, 1971.

Gusfield, Joseph R. *Symbolic Crusade: Status Politics and the American Temperance Movement.* Urbana: University of Illinois Press, 1963.

Hahn, Harlan. "Cops and Rioters: Ghetto Perceptions of Social Conflict and Control," in Harlan Hahn, ed. *Police in Urban Society.* Beverly Hills: Sage, 1971.

*Haller, Mark H. "Civic Reformers and Police Leadership: Chicago, 1905-1935," in Harlan Hahn, ed., *Police in Urban Society.* Beverly Hills: Sage, 1971.

*Haller, Mark H. "Urban Crime and Criminal Justice: The Chicago Case," *Journal of American History.* 57 (December 1970), 619-635.

*Haller, Mark H. "Urban Vice and Civic Reform: Chicago in the Early Twentieth Century," in Kenneth T. Jackson and Stanley K. Schultz, eds., *Cities in American History.* New York: Alfred Knopf, 1972.

Harris, Richard. *Justice, the Crisis of Law and Freedom in America.* New York: Avon Books, 1970.

Hays, Samuel P. "The Politics of Municipal Reform in the Progressive Era," *Pacific Northwest Quarterly.* 55 (October 1964), 157-159.

Hersey, John. *The Algiers Motel Incident.* New York: Alfred Knopf, 1968.

Holt, Glen E. "The Changing Perception of Urban Pathology: An Essay on the Development of Mass Transit in the United States," in Kenneth T. Jackson and Stanley K. Schultz, eds., *Cities In American History*. New York: Alfred Knopf, 1972.

Hoogenboom, Ari. *Outlawing the Spoils*. Urbana: University of Illinois Press, 1961.

*Howard, N. R. "I, Fred Kohler: Forty Years of Cleveland Politics." (Bound scrapbook of photocopied newspaper articles, Cleveland Public Library.)

Howe, Frederic C. *The Confessions of a Reformer*. Chicago: Quadrangle, 1967.

Jackson, Kenneth T. *The Ku Klux Klan in the City, 1915-1930*. New York: Oxford University Press, 1967.

Jackson, Kenneth T. "Metropolitan Government Versus Political Autonomy: Politics on the Crabgrass Frontier," in Kenneth T. Jackson and Stanley K. Schultz, eds., *Cities in American History*. New York: Alfred Knopf, 1972.

Jacobs, Paul. *Prelude to Riot: A View of Urban America from the Bottom*. New York: Vintage Books, 1968.

Johnson, Deborah, and Robert J. Gregory. "Police-Community Relations in the United States: A Review of Recent Literature and Projects," *The Journal of Criminal Law, Criminology and Police Science*. 62 (March 1971), 94-103.

Johnson, Tom L. *My Story*. New York: B. W. Huebsch, 1913.

Kain, John F. "The Distribution and Movement of Jobs and Industry," in James Q. Wilson, ed., *The Metropolitan Enigma*. Garden City, New York: Anchor Books, 1970.

Kamisar, Yale. "When the Cops Were Not Handcuffed," *New York Times Magazine*. November 7, 1965, 34, 35, 102, 107, 109.

*Kaplan, John. *Marijuana—The New Prohibition*. Cleveland and New York: World Publishing Co., 1970.

Kelling, George L., and Robert B. Kliesmet. "Resistance to the Professionalization of the Police," *The Police Chief*. 38 (May 1971), 30-39.

Kerner Commission. See National Advisory Commission on Civil Disorders.

Kinzer, Donald. *An Episode in Anti-Catholicism: The American Protective Association*. Seattle: University of Washington Press, 1964.

Kozol, Jonathan. *Death at an Early Age*. Boston: Houghton Mifflin, 1967.

*Landesco, John. "Organized Crime in Chicago," in *Illinois Crime Survey*. Montclair, New Jersey: Patterson Smith, 1968.

*Lane, Roger. "Crime and Criminal Statistics in Nineteenth Century Massachusetts," *Journal of Social History*. 2 (Winter 1968), 156-163.

*Lane, Roger. *Policing the City: Boston, 1822-1885*. Cambridge: Harvard University Press, 1967.

Lawrence, Clay. "Police Removals and the Courts," *Political Science Quarterly*. 20 (March 1905), 68-90.

Lee, W. L. M. *A History of Police in England*. London: Methuen & Co., 1901.

Lerner, Michael. "Respectable Bigotry," *The American Scholar*. 38 (Autumn 1969), 606-617.

Levy, Burton. "Cops in the Ghetto: A Problem of the Police System," *American Behavioral Scientist*. 11 (March-April 1968), 31-34.

Lipset, Martin. "Why Cops Hate Liberals and Vice Versa," *The Atlantic*. 223 (March, 1969), 76-83.

Logan, Andy. *Against the Evidence: The Becker-Rosenthal Affair*. New York: McCall, 1970.

Lowe, Jeanne. *Cities in a Race With Time*. New York: Random House, 1967.

Lowi, Theodore. *At the Pleasure of the Mayor*. New York: Free Press, 1964.

McKelvey, Blake. *The Emergence of Metropolitan America, 1915-1966*. New Brunswick: Rutgers University Press, 1968.

McKelvey, Blake. *The Urbanization of America, 1860-1915*. New Brunswick: Rutgers University Press, 1963.

McLean, Albert, Jr. *American Vaudeville as Ritual*. Lexington: University of Kentucky Press, 1965.

Malcolm X and A. Haley. *The Autobiography of Malcolm X*. New York: Grove Press, 1965.

*Masotti, Louis H., and Jerome R. Corsi. *Shoot-Out in Cleveland: Black Militants and the Police*. New York: Praeger, 1969.

May, Max B. "The New Ohio Municipal Code," *Annals of The American Academy of Political and Social Science*. 21 (January 1903), 125-128.

Mayer, Harold M., and Richard C. Wade. *Chicago: Growth of a Metropolis*. Chicago: University of Chicago Press, 1969.

Mencken, H. L. "Recollections of Notable Cops," in Alistair Cooke, ed., *The Vintage Mencken*. New York: Vintage Books, 1955.

Merriam, Charles E. "The Police, Crime and Politics," *Annals of the American Academy of Political and Social Science*. 146 (November 1929), 115-120.

*Miller, Wilbur R., Jr. "Police and the Rule of Law: London and New York City, 1830-1870." Paper delivered at the American Historical Association meeting, December 28, 1971.

Miller, Zane L. *Boss Cox's Cincinnati: Urban Politics in the Progressive Era*. New York: Oxford University Press, 1968.

The Missouri Crime Survey. Montclair, New Jersey: Patterson Smith, 1968.

Moley, Raymond. "Charles Francis Murphy," *Dictionary of American Biography*. 13, 346-347.

Moley, Raymond. "Politics and Crime," *Annals of the American Academy of Political and Social Science*. 125 (May 1926), 78-84.

National Advisory Commission on Civil Disorders, *Report*. New York: E. P. Dutton, 1968. Cited in notes as Kerner Commission.

National Commission on Law Observance and Enforcement [Wickersham Commission]. *Lawless Law Enforcement*. Washington, D.C.: Government Printing Office, 1931.

National Commission on Law Observance and Enforcement [Wickersham Commission 1931]. *Report on Crime and the Foreign Born.* Montclair, New Jersey: Patterson Smith, 1968.

*National Commission on Law Observance and Enforcement [Wickersham Commission 1931]. *Report on Police.* Montclair, New Jersey: Patterson Smith, 1968.

*Niederhoffer, Arthur. *Behind the Shield: The Police in Urban Society.* Garden City: Anchor Books, 1969.

Norton, William J. "Chief Kohler of Cleveland and His Golden Rule Policy," *The Outlook.* 93 (November 6, 1909), 537-542.

O'Dea, Thomas. *American Catholic Dilemma: An Inquiry into the Intellectual Life.* New York: Sheed and Ward, 1958.

Orth, S. P. "The Municipal Situation in Ohio," *The Forum.* 33 (June 1902), 430-437.

*Parnas, Raymond I. "The Police Response to the Domestic Disturbance." *Wisconsin Law Review* 1967 (Fall 1967), 914-960.

*Piliavin, Irving, and Scott Briar. "Police Encounters with Juveniles," *American Journal of Sociology.* 70 (September 1964), 206-214.

Pintard, John. *Letters . . . to his Daughter . . ., 1816-1833.* Vol. I. New York: New York Historical Society, 1939-40.

Piven, Frances Fox, and Richard A. Cloward. *Regulating the Poor: The Functions of Public Welfare.* New York: Pantheon Books, 1971.

A Policeman's Wife [Andrea Kornmann]. *Our Police.* New York: The Author, 1887.

Posten, Ted. "The Numbers Racket," in Donald R. Cressey and David A. Ward, eds., *Delinquency, Crime, and Social Process.* New York: Harper & Row, 1969.

Powdermaker, Hortense. "The Channeling of Negro Aggression by the Cultural Process," *American Journal of Sociology.* 48 (May 1943), 750-758.

Pratt, John W. *Religion, Politics and Diversity: The Church-State Theme in New York History.* Ithaca: Cornell University Press, 1967.

*President's Commission on Law Enforcement and the Administration of Justice. *The Challenge of Crime in a Free Society.* New York: Avon Books, 1968.

*President's Commission on Law Enforcement and the Administration of Justice. *Task Force Report: The Police.* Washington, D.C.: Government Printing Office, 1967.

Prpic, George. *The Croatian Immigrants in America.* New York: Philosophical Library, 1971.

Radano, Gene. *Walking the Beat.* Cleveland: World Publishing Co., 1968.

*Radzinowicz, Leon. *A History of English Criminal Law and Its Administration from 1750.*
Vol. I: *The Movement for Reform.* London: Stevens & Sons, 1948.
Vol. II: *The Clash Between Private Initiative and Public Interest in the Enforcement of the Law.* London: Stevens & Sons, 1956.
Vol. III: *Cross-Currents in the Movement for the Reform of the Police.* London: Stevens & Sons, 1956.
Vol. IV: *Grappling for Control.* London: Stevens & Sons, 1968.

Rainwater, Lee. *Behind Ghetto Walls: Black Families in a Federal Slum.* Chicago: Aldine, 1970.

Reichley, A. James. "The Way to Cool the Police Rebellion," *Fortune Magazine.* 78 (December 1968), 109-113, 150-152.

*Reiss, Albert J., Jr. *The Police and the Public.* New Haven: Yale University Press, 1971.

Reminiscences of Henry Bruere, Columbia University Oral History Project.

Richards, Leonard L. *Gentlemen of Property and Standing: Anti-Abolition Mobs in Jacksonian America.* New York: Oxford University Press, 1971.

*Richardson, James F. *The New York Police: Colonial Times to 1901.* New York: Oxford University Press, 1970.

Riordon, William. *Plunkitt of Tammany Hall.* New York: Alfred Knopf, 1948.

Robinson, Cyril D. "The Mayor and the Police—A Look at the Political Role of the Police in Society." Unpublished paper.

Roosevelt, Theodore. "Administering the New York Police Force," *American Ideals and Other Essays.* New York: AMS Press, 1969.

Root, Jonathan. *One Night in July: The True Story of the Rosenthal-Becker Murder Case.* New York: Coward-McCann, 1961.

Rudé, George. *The Crowd in History: A History of Popular Disturbances in France and England, 1730-1848.* New York: John Wiley, 1964.

Rudwick, Elliott. "The Unequal Badge," in Samuel Chapman, ed., *Police Patrol Readings.* Springfield: C. C. Thomas, 1964, 46-54.

Rudwick, Elliott, and August Meier. "Negro Retaliatory Violence in the Twentieth Century," *New Politics.* 5 (Winter 1966), 41-51.

Savitz, Leonard. "The Dimensions of Police Loyalty," in Harlan Hahn, ed., *Police in Urban Society.* Beverly Hills: Sage, 1971.

*Sayre, Wallace, and Herbert Kaufman. *Governing New York City.* New York: Russell Sage Foundation, 1960.

Scheiner, Seth M. *Negro Mecca: A History of the Negro in New York City, 1865-1920.* New York: New York University Press, 1965.

*Schweppe, Emma. *The Firemen's and Patrolmen's Unions in the City of New York.* New York: King's Crown Press, 1948.

*Sellin, Thorsten, ed., "The Police and the Crime Problem," *Annals of the American Academy of Political and Social Science.* 146 (November 1929).

Serrin, William. "God Help Our City," *The Atlantic Monthly.* 223 (March 1969), 115-121.

Sikes, George C. "The City Government Question in Ohio," *The Outlook.* 71 (August 23, 1902), 1008-1010.

Sinclair, Andrew. *Era of Excess: A Social History of the Prohibition Movement.* New York: Harper Colophon Books, 1964.

Skolnick, Jerome. "The Berkeley Scheme: Neighborhood Police," *The Nation.* 212 (March 22, 1971), 372-373.

*Skolnick, Jerome. *Justice Without Trial.* New York: John Wiley, 1966.

*Skolnick, Jerome H., ed., *The Politics of Protest: A Task Force Report Submitted to the National Commission on the Causes and Prevention of Violence.* New York: Clarion Books, n.d.

Smith, Bruce. "Municipal Police Administration," *Annals of the American Academy of Political and Social Science.* 146 (November 1929), 1-27.

*Smith, Bruce. *Police Systems in the United States.* Revised edition. New York: Harper & Row, 1949.

*Smith, Bruce, Jr. *Police Systems in the United States.* Second revised edition. New York: Harper & Row, 1960.

Smith, Timothy. "Immigrant Social Aspirations and American Education, 1880-1930," *American Quarterly.* 21 (Fall 1969), 523-543.

Spear, Allen. *Black Chicago.* Chicago: University of Chicago Press, 1967.

Speir, F. Leslie. *Cleveland: Our Community and Its Government.* Cleveland: Cleveland Public Schools, 1941.

Sproat, John G. *"The Best Men": Liberal Reformers in the Gilded Age.* New York: Oxford University Press, 1968.

*Stark, Rodney. *Police Riots.* Belmont, Cal.: Wadsworth, 1972.

Still, Bayrd. *Milwaukee: The History of a City.* Madison: State Historical Society of Wisconsin, 1948.

Stone, Donald E. "The Control and Discipline of Police Forces," *Annals of the American Academy of Political and Social Science.* 146 (November 1929), 63-73.

Swett, Steven C. "The Test of a Reformer: A Study of Seth Low, New York City Mayor, 1902-1903," *New York Historical Society Quarterly.* 44 (January 1960), 3-41.

Taylor, George Rogers. "The Beginnings of Mass Transportation in Urban America," *The Smithsonian Journal of History.* 1 (Summer 1966), 35-50 and 1 (No. 3) (1966), 31-54.

Thompson, E. P. *The Making of the English Working Class.* London: V. Gollancz, 1964.

Timberlake, James. *Prohibition and the Progressive Movement. 1900-1920.* Cambridge: Harvard University Press, 1963.

Turner, William W. *The Police Establishment.* New York: Putnam, 1968.

*Tuttle, William M., Jr. *Race Riot: Chicago in the Red Summer of 1919.* New York: Atheneum, 1970.

*Vollmer, August. *The Police and Modern Society.* Berkeley: University of California Press, 1936.

Wade, Richard C. *Slavery in the Cities: The South 1820-1860.* New York: Oxford University Press, 1964.

Walling, George. *Recollections of a New York Chief of Police.* New York: Caxton Book Co., 1887.

*Wambaugh, Joseph. *The New Centurions.* Boston: Little, Brown and Co., 1970.

Ward, David. *Cities and Immigrants, A Geography of Change in Nineteenth Century America.* New York: Oxford University Press, 1971.

Ware, Caroline F. *Greenwich Village, 1920-1930.* New York: Harper Colophon Books, 1965.

Warner, H. L. *Progressivism in Ohio, 1897-1917.* Columbus: Ohio State University Press, 1964.

Warner, Sam B., Jr. "If all the World were Philadelphia: A Scaffolding for Urban History, 1774-1930," *American Historical Review.* 74 (October, 1968), 26-43.

*Warner, Sam B., Jr. *The Private City: Philadelphia in Three Periods of Its Growth.* Philadelphia: University of Pennsylvania Press, 1968.

Warner, Sam B. *Streetcar Suburbs: The Process of Growth in Boston, 1870-1900.* New York: Atheneum, 1968.

Weber, Arnold R. "Labor Market Perspectives of the New City," in Benjamin Chinitz, ed., *City and Suburb: The Economics of Metropolitan Growth.* Englewood Cliffs, New Jersey: Prentice-Hall, 1964.

Weinstein, James. *The Corporate Ideal in the Liberal State.* Boston: Beacon Press, 1968.

Westley, William A. "The Police: A Sociological Study of Law, Custom, and Morality," in Ernest W. Burgess and Donald J. Bogue, eds., *Contributions to Urban Sociology.* Chicago: University of Chicago Press, 1964.

*Westley, William A. *Violence and the Police: A Sociological Study of Law, Custom, and Morality.* Cambridge, Mass.: M.I.T. Press, 1970.

*Whyte, William F. *Street Corner Society.* Chicago: University of Chicago Press, 1955.

Willemse, Cornelius W. *Behind the Green Lights.* New York: Alfred Knopf, 1931.

Willemse, Cornelius W. *A Cop Remembers.* New York: E. P. Dutton, 1933.

Wilson, James Q. "Dilemmas of Police Administration," in Jameson Doig, ed., *q.v.,* pp. 407-417.

Wilson, James Q. "Generational and Ethnic Differences Among Career Police Officers," *American Journal of Sociology.* 69 (March 1964), 522-528.

*Wilson, James Q. *Varieties of Police Behavior: The Management of Law and Order in Eight Communities.* Cambridge: Harvard University Press, 1968.

"Wilson, O(rlando) W(infield)," in Charles Moritz, ed., *Current Biography Yearbook,* 1966. New York: H. W. Wilson Co., 1966.

*Wilson, O. W., ed., *Parker on Police.* Springfield: C. C. Thomas, 1957.

Woodham-Smith, Cecil. *The Reason Why.* New York: E. P. Dutton, 1960.

*Woods, Arthur. *Policeman and Public.* New Haven: Yale University Press, 1919.

Woolsey, T. D. "Nature and Sphere of Police Power." *Journal of Social Science.* 3 (1871), 97-114.

Zorbaugh, Harvey. *The Gold Coast and the Slum.* Chicago: University of Chicago Press, 1957.

Index